Body Image and Perceptual Dysfunction in Adults

Body Image
and
Perceptual Dysfunction
in
Adults

JULIA VAN DEUSEN, PhD

Professor
Department of Occupational Therapy
Health Sciences Center
University of Central Arkansas
Conway, Arkansas

W.B. SAUNDERS COMPANY
Harcourt Brace Jovanovich, Inc.

Philadelphia London Toronto
Montreal Sydney Tokyo

W. B. SAUNDERS COMPANY
Harcourt Brace Jovanovich, Inc.

The Curtis Center
Independence Square West
Philadelphia, Pennsylvania 19106

Library of Congress Cataloging-in-Publication Data

Van Deusen, Julia.

Body image and perceptual dysfunction in adults / Julia Van Deusen.

p. cm.

Includes index.

ISBN 0–7216–3172–X

1. Body image. 2. Perception, Disorders of. I. Title.
[DNLM: 1. Body Image. 2. Perceptual Disorders–rehabilitation. WM 204 V217b]

RC455.4.B64V36 1993

616.89–dc20

DNLM/DLC

for Library of Congress   92–49775
                                        CIP

Body Image and Perceptual Dysfunction in Adults   ISBN 0–7216–3172–X

Printed in Mexico

Last digit is the print number: 9   8   7   6   5   4   3   2   1

DEDICATION

To Van Fox and to Jeanelle Fox
For their acceptance.

CONTRIBUTORS

SUSAN FINE, MA, OTR, FAOTA
Director, Therapeutic Activities, Payne Whitney Clinic of New York Hospital–Cornell Medical Center; Senior Lecturer, Department of Psychiatry, Cornell Medical College; Assistant Clinical Professor, College of Health Related Professions, State University of New York Health Sciences Center at Brooklyn; Private Practioner in Psychosocial Rehabilitation

JOANNE JACKSON FOSS, MS, OTR
Lecturer, Department of Occupational Therapy, College of Health Related Professions, University of Florida, Gainesville

CAROLYN SCHMIDT HANSON, MA, OTR
Lecturer, Department of Occupational Therapy, College of Health Related Professions, University of Florida, Gainesville

DIANE HARLOWE, MS, OTR, FAOTA
Director of Occupational Therapy and Speech Services, St. Marys Hospital Medical Center, Madison, Wisconsin

PREFACE

An assumption basic to this book is that deficits in perceptual skills or body image disturbances will interfere with occupational performance areas. Occupational performance areas include activities of daily living (ADL) and work and leisure activities. Definitions of these terms may be found in the glossary. The clinical literature documents the extent that adults with diverse diagnoses have shown impaired perceptual skills and body image problems. However, there is but limited record of a tie between these disturbances and deficits in occupational performance.

This book was designed to stimulate experienced occupational therapists, physical therapists, and other health professionals to precisely observe, evaluate, and research perceptual and body image dysfunction relative to their patients' work, leisure, and daily living needs. This book assumes that readers will have an entry level knowledge about rehabilitation as well as a basic comprehension of research terminology. For those readers who need to review research concepts, books such as the handbook by Isaac and Michael (1981) may be helpful. Although I did not intend this book as a procedures manual, it may be useful for undergraduate students and beginning therapists as resource material.

I have taken the view that occupational function is of paramount concern for patient rehabilitation regardless of the professional's discipline or the patient's diagnosis. I envisioned an advanced textbook for rehabilitation specialists that focused on a specific category of dysfunction—deficits in perception and body image across diagnoses rather than addressing the gamut of rehabilitation procedures relevant to a specific diagnosis, as is more common. The content of this book has been limited to body image, visual-perceptual, and somesthetic discrimination deficits because I believe these are of major importance to the rehabilitation process but are not as emphasized in the literature as are some of the other aspects of rehabilitation.

In Part I, visual and somesthetic perceptual dysfunction is discussed. In Part II, the focus is on body image disturbances.

Somesthetic perceptual dysfunction refers to performance problems from deficient interpretation of tactile and proprioceptive input. Visual-perceptual dysfunction includes problems with visual discrimination of form, shape, colors, or positions of objects; problems with visuospatial orientation, and the inability to distinguish figures from the background stimuli. The more complex forms of perceptual dysfunction involve problems with deficient synthesis, speed, and timing of sensory input across modalities. Body image as used in this book is defined as a dynamic integration of the body schema with environmental inputs providing emotional and cognitive components. Body schema is a neurally derived synthesis of tactile, proprioceptive, and pressure sensory associations about the body and its parts. Disturbance of body image can involve any or all of its neural or psychosocial components.

Each chapter of this book concerns a specific diagnostic category. For ease of use by advanced students, clinicians, and researchers, I have organized the content of each chapter with the summary of background information first, followed by the assessment and treatment literature. Each topic is illustrated with case material related to the content on body image or perceptual dysfunction. Case reports have been based on actual patients described in the literature or observed in the clinic by the authors. All case descriptions have been modified to prevent any possibility of identification of actual patients.

ACKNOWLEDGMENTS

Any successful project requires the efforts of many individuals. I wish to express sincere thanks to all those people who have contributed to this text, especially

The late A. Jean Ayres, who introduced me to the excitement of research and stimulated my interest in body image and perception.

My contributors, for sharing their particular expertise.

Kay Walker, my chairperson at the University of Florida, who was an outstanding facilitator of productivity.

Vivian Moore, for secretarial assistance.

The editorial staff at W. B. Saunders Company, for their continuing professional help.

My graduate students, who forced me to recognize the need for this text.

Those occupational therapy colleagues at the University of Florida, who emphasized teaching and service, thereby freeing my time to write.

The many therapists who reviewed sections of the manuscript and contributed considerably to its quality.

CONTENTS

I

INTRODUCTION TO PERCEPTUAL DYSFUNCTION

ASSESSMENT CATEGORIES

Screening Tools

Specific Clinical Tools

Batteries

Functional Tools

TREATMENT

Environmental Change

Patient Change

The Principle of Gradation

The construct perceptual dysfunction presents problems in that the rehabilitation literature uses many different terms, some with slightly different meanings, to refer to this concept. In this book, perceptual dysfunction is defined as the inability to perform relative to the interpretation and use of sensory stimuli. The perceptual dysfunction of physically or psychologically challenged adults also has been referred to by the synonymous or more inclusive terms of sensorimotor integration disorders, neurobehavioral problems, sensory processing, and perceptual-motor deficits. I have chosen to use the term perceptual dysfunction because it best describes the construct presented in this book. Problems that are representative of perceptual dysfunction include the following

1. Patients' inability to dress themselves because of the inability to spatially relate body parts to clothing parts.
2. Patients' inability to distinguish objects such as vases from eating utensils because of form discrimination deficits.
3. Patients' inability to find their way around the hospital owing to spatial disorientation.

The content of Part I is limited to discussions of somesthetic and visual perceptual dysfunction. In this way, the discussion is

1

focused on central nervous system problems rather than peripheral nervous system ones. Thus, poor function due to conditions such as visual field or visual acuity deficits, which are essentially peripheral in origin, are not included. Nor are problems due to poor tactile sensation included. Again, by limiting this book to perceptual dysfunction, it covers only problems resulting essentially from afferent (or sensory) system lesions as opposed to those from motor system deficit. Thus, I have not dealt with the multitude of dysfunctions associated with lack of tone, spasticity, or other problems related to motor system disorders. Part I of this book generally is concerned with problems of interpretation of sensory input as opposed to those of attending to tactile or visual stimuli. Thus, in Part I, the major focus is not with such disorders as hemi-inattention but with those problems in which the cerebral cortex performs the major role. However, because of her approach to the treatment of perceptual dysfunction, the author of the chapter on schizophrenia has discussed the material in a comprehensive manner emphasizing attention and other neural aspects influencing perception.

ASSESSMENT CATEGORIES

There are many instruments available from commercial test companies and described in the professional literature that assess perceptual dysfunction in adult populations. Because of this array of potential tools for use by rehabilitation personnel, I have defined four categories for instrument organization in terms of use: 1) screening, 2) specific clinical, 3) batteries, and 4) functional. The reader may find it helpful to classify the various instruments described in the following chapters according to these categories.

Screening Tools

Screening tools are designed to enable identification of adults who may present problems in perception and will need more intense evaluation. Such tools do not provide confirmation of perceptual deficit, in general, or a valid assessment of a specific perceptual problem such as figure-ground dysfunction. An example of a screening tool is the Motor-Free Visual Perception Test (Colarusso and Hammill, 1972), a test designed for children and later normed for adults by Bouska and Kwatny (1983).

Specific Clinical Tools

These tools are designed to evaluate whether or not one specific kind of perceptual skill is within normal limits and to provide help in treatment planning, when indicated. Specific clinical tools may consist of standardized forms, objects, pictures, and the like. Software versions of these tools are available for computers. These instruments have been designed to assess the perceptual process or the end performance. Depending on the type of administration, confounding variables may be eliminated or their effects carefully observed to aid in treatment planning. Examples of specific clinical tools are the Tactile Form Perception Test (Benton et al, 1983) and Toglia's (1989) test for the visual perception of objects.

Batteries

A battery is a collection of tests standardized as a unit and designed to measure the construct of perceptual function (or sensory-motor integration). A battery differs from a set of specific clinical tools because reliability and validity data are available on the entire battery as a unit rather than for each individual tool. Patients scoring outside of normal limits on a battery can be assessed as having perceptual dysfunction, whereas those performing poorly on a set of specific tools can only be considered to have problems in specific deficit areas such as facial recognition or tactile form discrimination but not to have perceptual dysfunction as a unitary construct. However, the specific instruments of test batteries often have been validated as specific clinical tools, and the battery as a whole has been validated as a measure of the construct of perceptual dysfunction. Research results (Eriksson et al, 1988; Katz et al, 1989; Royce et al, 1976) suggest that batteries actually may be measuring two constructs: a lower and a higher level perceptual dysfunction. An example of an adult battery being used in rehabilitation is the Sensorimotor Integration Test Battery (Jongbloed et al, 1986).

Functional Tools

Instruments have been designed to detect perceptual dysfunction from the direct observation of patient performance of activities of daily living or to evaluate the degree to which such dysfunction interferes with activities of daily living. I consider these instruments as functional tools. They are relative newcomers to the field of rehabilitation but of obvious relevance. An example of a functional instrument is the Arnadottir OT-ADL Neurobehavioral Evaluation (A-ONE) instrument (Arnadottir, 1990).

TREATMENT

There are various ways in which interventions for adult perceptual dysfunction can be classified. Neistadt (1990) suggested two general categories: adaptive and remedial. She defines as adaptive those approaches that provide training in daily living skills through advantageous use of the patient's personal and environmental assets. Remedial approaches are those aimed toward recovery or reorganization of central nervous system functions.

An assumption common to these two categories of approaches is that functional activities are dependent on perceptual skills. Major differences in their basic assumptions center on whether the adult brain can repair itself after injury and generalize learning (remedial) or whether the brain is unlikely to repair itself after injury and cannot generalize learning (adaptive).

I have found a different categorization to meet my clinical and research needs (Van Deusen, 1988). The categories for intervention proposed below are conceptually the same as those I reported before, although with slightly altered names. I classify interventions to improve perceptual functions by their desired focus of change. Are procedures directed toward change in the environment or toward change of the patient? If the procedures are directed toward change in the patient, are they compensatory or restorative treatments?

Environmental Change

This approach to improving activities of daily living for adults with perceptual dysfunction involves changing the patient's home, work, and recreational environments. An assumption basic to this approach is that, at this point in time, the patient's performance cannot change; therefore, function can be improved only by altering the environment. My environmental change category is included in Neistadt's (1990) adaptive approach. An example of environmental change would be making all floors level by removing any recessed areas (eg, a shower or sunken living room) so that a person with visual perceptual problems could ambulate safely. Another illustration would be placement of a spouse's shirt in a favorable position for self-dressing.

Patient Change

If possible, the focus of rehabilitation is on change of the patient rather than his or her environment. Two approaches to change in adults with perceptual dysfunction are compensatory treatment and restorative treatment.

Compensatory Treatment

The rationale for this approach comes from learning theory. Its emphasis is on use of patient assets to compensate for deficits. The patient goal is to learn activities of daily living despite perceptual dysfunction. Shaping, positive reinforcement, repetition, and other procedures from learning theories are used in training. An example of this approach is having a person with deficient visual spatial perception memorize the directions to the store or bus stop. If memory is still intact, it can be used to compensate for the inability to visualize the routes. Thus, the functional problem is eliminated. My compensatory approach is similar to Neistadt's adaptive category, with similar basic assumptions.

Restorative Treatment

The restorative approach assumes that perceptual skills can be regained by effecting positive changes in the central nervous system. It is the same as the approach termed remedial by Neistadt (1990), with similar assumptions. My restorative approach (formerly referred to as the neurological approach) is based on concepts of the plasticity of the adult brain (Bach-y-Rita, 1981; Moore, 1986). An illustration would be use of gross motor activities (such as catching a basketball), which provide tactile and proprioceptive stimulation, before treatment progresses to exercises requiring complex visual discrimination.

The reader who finds it useful for his or her programming may wish to organize the treatment content in the chapters of Part I of this book according to my classifications. However, the various authors of the individual chapters have been allowed the freedom to organize treatment procedures (1) according to their own clinical experiences and (2) to be compatible with the literature in each specific area of perceptual dysfunction. Consequently, there are several organizational options available to meet the needs of readers.

The Principle of Gradation

Research literature supported one general principle for intervention with patients having visual or somesthetic dysfunction. This principle is that of therapeutic gradation. Therapeutic gradation was supported by three factor-analytic studies that consistently indicated a hierarchy of visual and somesthetic perceptual dysfunction for adult patients. Because the data are cross-cultural, the credibility of the hierarchy idea is enhanced. The accompanying Table 1 illustrates this hierarchy.

A Canadian Study

Royce and associates (1976) studied 176 subjects in Canada. These subjects were medically diagnosed as brain damaged from trauma, circulatory disease, or neoplasm. The correlation matrix from 54 variables was subjected to factor analysis. Ten interpretable factors were derived, of which six were perceptual, as Royce and associates (1976) and I define this construct (see accompanying Table 2). Factor one, perceptual organization, involved both tactile and visual stimuli. Its correlation with the right hemisphere perceptual areas corroborated a nonmodality specific perceptual integrative function as the essence of this factor. Factor three, perceptual-motor speed, included perceptual processing speed. The authors defined factor five, the pattern recognition factor, as a primitive (as opposed to complex) task of visual identification of shapes. Thus, it also was largely perceptual in nature. Factor seven, temporal

Table 1. PERCEPTUAL HIERARCHY

Levels	Constructs	References
One	Object identification Size estimation Shape identification Form recognition Object constancy Color recognition Body part identification	Eriksson et al (1988) Katz et al (1989)
Two	Perceptual organization Processing speed Integrated timing Spatial orientation Figure-ground	Eriksson et al (1988) Katz et al (1989) Royce et al (1976)
Three	Perceptual integration Visualization	Royce et al (1976)

Table 2. PERCEPTUAL FACTORS FROM STUDY BY ROYCE ET AL (1976)

Factor Number	Name of Perceptual Factor
One	Perceptual organization
Two	(Not a perceptual factor)
Three	Perceptual-motor speed
Four	(Not a perceptual factor)
Five	Pattern recognition
Six	(Not a perceptual factor)
Seven	Temporal resolution
Eight	Spatial orientation
Nine	Figure-ground
Ten	(Not a perceptual factor)

resolution, reflected the processing of convergent temporal input from the different senses. Royce and associates (1976) termed factor eight spatial orientation. This factor was characterized by the ability to maintain spatial relations among objects, including body parts as well as objects in extrapersonal space. Figure-ground identification defined factor nine, which involved the basic perceptual process of selecting a figure from a stimulus complex. Factor two (verbal comprehension), factor four (memory), and factors six and ten (abstraction factors) were factors defined by the authors as conceptual rather than as essentially perceptual in nature.

Royce and associates (1976) performed a second factor analysis resulting in three second-order factors defined by those first-order factors described above. One of these second-order factors was interpreted as verbal memory; the other two were perceptual in content: (1) perceptual integration and (2) visualization.

Perceptual integration is a general ability to process and synthesize sensory inputs including both visual and tactile stimuli. First-order factors having high loadings on perceptual integration were perceptual organization, perceptual-motor speed, and temporal resolution. Consequently, it was apparent that perceptual integration is a complex perceptual function dependent on adequate perceptual organization, processing speed, and integrated timing. Dysfunction of perceptual integration was associated with damage to frontal, temporal, and parietal areas of the right hemisphere.

The other perceptual second-order factor, visualization, is a general ability to imagine objects in space. The first-order factors, spatial orientation and figure-ground identification, had high loadings on visualization. Thus, visualization can be said to subsume these less complex perceptual skills. Poor visualization was associated with lesions of the right frontal and subcortical regions and of the left hemisphere occipital area.

A Swedish Study

Eriksson and associates (1988) studied 109 subjects on a stroke unit in Sweden. Their analysis showed that the visual perceptual variables separated into two groups: (1) a low-order group with relatively meaningless stimuli and (2) a high-order group with meaningful stimuli. The low-order perception was defined by variables such as form and color discrimination, whereas the high-order perception was defined by the ability to perform tasks such as drawing a clock or copying figures. Figure-ground and spatial relations were included with high-order perception in the study by Eriksson and associates. It will be recalled that these variables were the less complex ones in the Royce and associates study (1976). This evidence indicates a 3-level hierarchy grading from variables such as simple form discrimination to figure-ground to visualization.

An Israeli Study

Katz and colleagues (1989) studied the reliability and validity of a battery designed to measure orientation, perception, visuomotor organization, and thinking operations. The perception and visuomotor sections related to perceptual dysfunction as I have defined it. Perception items included object and shape identification, figure-ground, and spatial perception. Visuomotor items included copying and constructing three-dimensional and two-dimensional objects.

Katz and associates (1989) factor analyzed data from Israeli rehabilitation patients, 20 with craniocerebral injury and 28 with cerebral vascular accidents. Fifty-five adult, non–brain damaged controls were used. Their results were as hypothesized, with variables forming perception and visuomotor groupings. The data of the Katz and associates' study were consistent with those of Eriksson and associates (1988). Katz and colleagues' visuomotor organization factor was similar to that termed high-order by the Eriksson group, and their factor termed perception was similar to that termed low-order by Eriksson and associates. The major discrepancy was on spatial and figure-ground variables. Had there been a sufficient number of perceptual variables in the Katz and associates' study for a three-factor solution, based on the results of Royce and associates (1976) and Eriksson and associates, I suggest that figure-ground and spatial perception would have been at second level.

To summarize, because of the consistency of the research indicating a hierarchy of visual and somesthetic perceptual dysfunction, therapeutic gradation seems reasonable. Based on research, the following treatment hierarchy is worth trying and observing in a clinical setting:

1. The patient first must be able to perform tasks requiring visual and somesthetic discrimination of forms, shapes, colors, and positions of objects.

2. The treatment next should be focused on figure-ground identification and spatial orientation.

3. Complex perceptual skills involving synthesis of multisensory input, speed, and timing should be the final intervention goal.

This type of gradation is applicable to programming for the kinds of patient perceptual problems addressed in the following chapters.

References

Arnadottir G: The Brain & Behavior: Assessing cortical dysfunction through ADL. St. Louis, MO, CV Mosby Co, 1990.

Bach-y-Rita P: Brain plasticity as a basis of the development of rehabilitation procedures for hemiplegia. Scand J Rehabil Med 13:73–83, 1981.

Benton AL, deS Hamsher K, Varney NR, Spreen O: Contributions to Neuropsychological Assessment. New York, Oxford University Press, 1983.

Bouska MJ, Kwatny E: Manual for application of the Motor-free Visual Perception Test to the adult population. Philadelphia, Bouska and Kwatny (Box 12246), 1983.

Colarusso RP, Hammill DD: Motor-free Visual Perception Test Plates. Novato, CA, Academic Therapy Publications, 1972.

Eriksson S, Bernspang B, Fugl-Meyer AR: Perceptual and motor impairment within 2 weeks after a stroke: a multifactorial statistical approach. Occup Ther J Res 8:114–125, 1988.

Jongbloed LE, Collins JB, Jones W: A sensorimotor integration test battery for CVA clients: preliminary evidence of reliability and validity. Occup Ther J Res 6:131–150, 1986.

Katz N, Itzkovich M, Averbuch S, Elazar B: Loewenstein Occupational Therapy Cognitive Assessment (LOTCA) Battery for brain-injured patients: reliability and validity. Am J Occup Ther 43:184–192, 1989.

Moore J: Recovery potentials following CNS lesions: a brief historical perspective in relation to modern research data on neuroplasticity. Am J Occup Ther 40:459–463, 1986.

Neistadt ME: A critical analysis of occupational therapy approaches for perceptual deficits in adults with brain injury. Am J Occup Ther 44:299–304, 1990.

Royce JR, Yeudall LT, Bock C: Factor analytic studies of human brain damage: I. first and second-order factors and their brain correlates. Multivariate Behav Res 11:381–418, 1976.

Siev E, Freishtat B, Zoltan B: Perceptual and Cognitive Dysfunction in the Adult Stroke Patient. Rev ed. Thorofare, NJ, Slack, 1986.

Toglia JP: Visual perception of objects: an approach to assessment and intervention. Am J Occup Ther 43:587–595, 1989.

Van Deusen J: Unilateral neglect: suggestions for research by occupational therapists. Am J Occup Ther 42:441–448, 1988.

1

JOANNE JACKSON FOSS

CEREBRAL VASCULAR ACCIDENT: VISUAL PERCEPTUAL DYSFUNCTION

ASSESSMENT	TREATMENT
Variables Affecting Perceptual Assessment	**The Treatment Literature**
	Case Report
Assessment Batteries	
Specific Assessment	

Following a cerebral vascular accident (CVA), the more obvious motor and sensory deficits are compounded by conceptual and perceptual disabilities. The accumulation of sensory input, and the perceptual processing of that input, interact with the conceptual system in the normal nervous system. The significance of dysfunction anywhere in this process becomes obvious to the rehabilitation specialist owing to the added difficulties created in the ability of the patient to regain occupational functional type skills. Conceptual and perceptual deficits directly influence the length of hospital stay (Feigenson et al, 1977; Forer and Miller, 1980) as well as the degree of independence the stroke patient is able to ultimately achieve (Harlowe and Van Deusen, 1989; Kaplan and Hier, 1982; Lorenze and Cancro, 1962). There has been increasing interest among many health care professionals, including speech pathologists, psychologists, occupational and physical therapists, and others, concerning the evaluation and remediation of specific conceptual and perceptual disorders. This chapter is concerned with the evaluation and treatment of the visual-perceptual disorders experienced by stroke patients.

ASSESSMENT

Rehabilitation professionals often evaluate functional skills such as writing, reading, drawing, eating, dressing, ability to follow directions, ambulation, specific vocational skills, and a long list of other occupational performance areas. However, the influence of perceptual disorders on the performance of a patient often is not readily apparent. Subtle clues may alert the clinician to the need for screening in specific areas of perception. Any significantly abnormal scores on the screening items must receive a more thorough assessment in order to provide for a correct diagnosis of perceptual deficit.

Variables Affecting Perceptual Assessment

The complexity of and interaction between perceptual and sensory systems make it difficult to isolate one area of a system or even one system from another. Therefore, every effort possible must be made to separate influences that may interfere with the perception of sensation (Bouska et al, 1990). For example, examination of cranial nerve function may identify the origin of some problems observed in stroke patients; without this information, deficits may be misinterpreted. Primary sensory deficits such as decreased visual acuity, visual field deficits, decreased tactile and auditory awareness, and speech and language and conceptual deficits also will have to be accounted for before a diagnosis of perceptual deficit can be made.

Visual Deficits

A comprehensive visual screening enables the rehabilitation professional to make a decision to refer patients who have medical histories identifying them as at risk for primary visual deficits to a vision specialist. A qualified vision specialist may administer a complete visual assessment; however, a nonstandardized visual screening device used by a rehabilitation professional should include activities that provide information about visual attention, oculomotor movements (scanning and saccadic movements), visual fields, and visual neglect (Zoltan, 1990). Similar testing items also may be used by other professionals as part of a general neurological examination, but these screening procedures commonly are used clinically by rehabilitation professionals.

Zoltan and associates (1986) describe screening items that can be used to evaluate these areas. A suspended orange ball can be used to evaluate visual attention and ocular pursuits. When the ball is held static, the rehabilitation professional can record how long the patient is able to attend to the stimulus after being told to watch it. Observations of convergence and fixation also can be made. When the ball is moved horizontally, vertically, diagonally, clockwise, and counterclockwise, ocular pursuits are evaluated. The quality and range of eye movements, ability to cross the midline, and visual overshooting can be observed.

The King-Devick Test can be used when evaluating saccadic eye movements (Lieberman et al, 1983). This test consists of cards with randomly spaced lines of numbers connected by arrows. The patient calls out the numbers as fast as possible following the order indicated by the arrows. The fact that this test requires the patient's ability to call out numbers assumes a level of verbalization and conceptualization that may limit the usefulness of this task with the CVA population. Letter or symbol cancellation tasks often are used to identify visual scanning and visual field deficits. These tasks require the patient to find and cross out a targeted letter or symbol from among other letters or symbols on a page (Weinberg et al, 1977). Observations of other visual deficits such as visual neglect also may be observed during this task.

Evaluation of visual field deficits, such as homonymous hemianopsia, in the CVA patient often is accomplished by the use of confrontational testing (Bouska et al, 1990). As the patient fixates on a targeted area, such as the examiner's nose or forehead, a stimulus target is moved in an arc from the periphery. The patient then indicates the point at which the stimulus comes into view. Depth perception, another common visual deficit observed in stroke patients, also can be evaluated through the use of confrontational testing. The patient identifies the closest of two targets. These tests can be performed with or without an eye patch (Zoltan et al, 1986). The CVA patient may exhibit visual neglect with or without the presence of a visual field cut; therefore, it is important to test for both deficits.

The line bisection test is mentioned most often in the literature for the evaluation of visual neglect (Schenkenberg et al, 1980). The patient is instructed to draw a line through the center of each of the lines on a worksheet without adjusting the position or angle of the paper. Observations are made as to whether or not the cross lines are drawn accurately, if all areas of the page are covered, and in what order the patient approaches the items.

Tactile Deficits

Impaired or diminished sensation has been theorized to cause or complicate perceptual problems such as the agnosias, apraxia, and the ability to localize tactile input (Bobath, 1978). Screening for the presence, absence, or distortion of these sensations supplies information that is important for understanding both the patient's manipulation of testing items and the influence of tactile deficits on the results of perceptual evaluation. It is suggested that the rehabilitation professional consider using the evaluation tools discussed throughout this chapter, which are designed to minimize the influence of motor skill ability on actual test results (Table 1–1). The performance on the tactile screening items also is useful in formulating expectations for the treatment of functional skills requiring visual fine motor coordination as well as for considerations of patient safety.

The primary tactile, or protopathic, system is responsible for the awareness of pain, temperature, and light touch. Trombly and Scott (1989) recommend that all three areas mentioned earlier be tested in order to improve the accuracy of the results for the entire system. Similar testing items also may be used by other professions as a part of a basic neurological examination, but these screening procedures commonly are used clinically by rehabilitation professionals. Tactile awareness of pain, temperature, and light touch is evaluated by recording the responses of the patient to the specific stimulus applied to the dermatomal area of the skin most likely to be affected by the lesion.

Sensory deficits in the discriminative, or epicritic, system may be tested individually, with procedures that also are used commonly in rehabilitation clinic settings or through the use of functional testing items. After application of specific stimuli to test the localization of touch, 2-point discrimination, stereognosis, and kinesthesia, the patient's responses are observed and recorded (Anderson, 1971). The Moberg Picking-Up Test for Dexterity provides a more functional evaluation approach for the observation of the relationship of sensation to the function of the hand (Moberg, 1958; Trombly and Scott, 1989).

Speech and Language Deficits

Although speech and language disorders have been documented to occur in patients with right hemisphere damage, left hemispheric lesions are more likely to result in speech and language and communication problems. This chapter does not cover this topic, but the reader is urged to consider the effects of aphasia and dysphagia on the ability of the patient to understand and respond to testing items. Test items can be adapted to allow for nonverbal communicative responses, such as allowing the patient to point to the answer, draw responses, or answer by use of pantomime. It is suggested that the rehabilitation professional consider use of evaluation tools suggested throughout this chapter that do not require verbalization (see Table 1–1).

Conceptual Deficits

Conceptual deficits due to the neurological damage from a CVA also are not covered in this chapter. Conceptual processes have been identified to include those abilities that enable the person to understand, be attentive, make judgments, and take part in decision-making. The influences of deficits in this area impact the ability of the patient to perform on some of the evaluation items. Insight, memory, judgment, and attention span levels also have indications for treatment planning.

Effects of the Aging Process

Because of the older age of stroke victims who are referred for rehabilitation, the neurological changes due to the effects of the aging process also must be considered during the evaluation (Wolf, 1990). Research and clinical experience have shown that the normal aging process results in perceptual changes. These changes include a decline in performance in tasks requiring constructional skills, visual organization, and visual discrimination (Farver and Farver, 1982). Changes in visual, auditory, and tactile acuity and comprehension also result in functional losses in the aging normal population (Welford, 1962). Clinically, a reduction in the speed of sensory processing and of response times also are apparent in the older population. Chronic illnesses such as arthritis, heart conditions, diabetes, and cataracts are present in a higher percentage in this population. The functional abilities of the patient as well as his or her ability to perform specific tests may be affected by symptoms of these illnesses. Clinical experience has shown that chronic psychiatric illnesses such as schizophrenia often result in altered

Text continued on page 20

Table 1–1. OVERVIEW OF TESTS AVAILABLE FOR THE EVALUATION

Evaluation	Target Population	Skill Requirements
Arnadottir OT-ADL Neurobehavioral Evaluation (A-ONE)	Neurologically impaired adults	Fine motor Memory
Bender-Gestalt Test	Neurologically and psychiatrically impaired adults and children	Drawing ability
Color Perception Battery	Neurologically impaired adults	Memory Drawing ability Verbal
Draw-a-Person	Children	Drawing ability
Dvorine Color Plates	Neurologically impaired adults Color blindness and color agnosia	Motor or verbal communication
Embedded Figures Test (Hidden Figures)	Neurologically impaired subjects ages 10 and older	Fine motor Memory
Frostig Developmental Test of Visual Perception	Children ages 3 to 8 years	Fine motor
Graham-Kendall Memory for Designs Test	Adults with organic brain damage	Fine motor
Halstead-Reitan Battery	Neurologically impaired adults	Memory Fine motor Verbal or written language ability
Hooper Visual Organization Test	Neurologically impaired adults ages 13 to 69. Adults with organic brain damage	Verbal or written language ability
Ishihara Color Plates	Neurologically impaired adults Adults with color blindness and color agnosias	Verbal
Kohs Block Test	Neurologically impaired adults	Fine motor

OF PERCEPTUAL DYSFUNCTION IN BRAIN DAMAGED POPULATIONS

Comments	Reference
Evaluation uses functional ADL activities to test for deficits	Arnadottir, 1990
Must be administered and scored by a psychologist Also serves as a projective technique	Lezak, 1983
Includes 6 different color subtests including Ishihara Plates Aphasic and nonaphasic subjects may have color recognition anomic deficits	DeRenzi and Spinnler, 1967
Must be administered and scored by a psychologist Also serves as a projective tool	Harris, 1963
Aphasic and nonaphasic subjects may have color recognition anomic deficits	Lezak, 1983
Corrolates with figure ground subtest of SCSIPT	Witkin et al, 1971 Teuber and Weinstein, 1956
May be used as a nonstandardized screening device with adult populations	Frostig, 1966
Tests visual perception and memory skills	Graham and Kendall, 1951
Requires 6 to 8 hours to administer Must be administered by a psychologist	Lezak, 1983 Macciocchi, 1988
Designed as a screening device	Hooper, 1958
Aphasic and nonaphasic subjects may have color recognition anomic deficits	Lezak, 1983
Uses more complex designs to identify mild deficits	Lezak, 1983

Table continued on following page

Table 1-1. OVERVIEW OF TESTS AVAILABLE FOR THE EVALUATION OF

Evaluation	Target Population	Skill Requirements
Loewenstein OT Cognitive Assessment Battery	Neurologically impaired adults Children over six years	Fine motor and drawing ability Verbal
Luria-Nebraska Neuropsychological Battery	Neurologically impaired adults	Fine motor Verbal Cognitive and memory
McCarron-Dial System	Neurologically and psychologically impaired adults and children Learning-disabled children	Fine motor Verbal
Mooney's Closure Faces Test	Neurologically impaired adults	Fine motor
Motor-Free Visual Perceptual Test	Neurologically impaired adults and children	Motor or verbal communication
Michigan Neuropsychological Test Battery	Neurologically impaired adults	Memory Fine motor Cognitive
Ontario Society of OT Perceptual	Neurologically impaired adults	Verbal Fine motor
Rey's Complex Figures Test	Neurologically impaired adults (16 to 60-years-old) Children (4 to 14-years-old)	Drawing ability Cognitive organization
Sensorimotor Integration Test for Evaluation of CVA	Adults with diagnosis of CVA	Fine motor or verbal communication
Southern California Sensory Integration and Praxis Test	Learning disabled children Neurologically impaired adults (specific subtests)	Verbal or fine motor
Stick Test	Neurologically impaired adults	Fine motor
Test of Facial Recognition	Neurologically impaired adults	Verbal or motor communication
Test of Form Discrimination	Neurologically impaired adults	Verbal or motor communication
Test of Three-Dimension Constructional Praxis	Neurologically impaired adults	Fine motor
Wechsler Adult Intelligence Scales	Neurologically impaired adults	Fine motor

Developed for use with Cerebral Vascular Accident and Traumatic Brain Injury chapters by Joanne J. Foss and Carolyn S. Hanson.

PERCEPTUAL DYSFUNCTION IN BRAIN DAMAGED POPULATIONS *Continued*

Comments	Reference
Requires 30 to 45 minutes to administer Procedures to assess aphasic patients	Katz et al, 1989
Time limits penalize slow response Must be administered by psychologist	Lezak, 1983

Evaluator must be trained in use of this
    system before administration
Specific components validated for use as
    a neuropsychological assessment
	Dial et al, 1990

No time limits Little standardization data	Mooney, 1957
Time limits Designed as a screening tool	Colarusso and Hammill, 1972 Bouska and Kwatny, 1983
Three hours to administer by a psychologist	Smith, 1981
Identifies 6 areas of visual and tactile perception and praxis	Boys et al, 1988
Must be administered by a psychologist	Lezak, 1983
90-min administration time	Jongbloed et al, 1986

Easily administered
Certification in testing procedures and
    test interpretation required
Revised version titled Sensory Integration
    and Praxis Tests
	Ayres, 1972; 1984
	Petersen and Wikoff, 1983
	Petersen et al, 1985

No time limits Has a reversal component	Lezak, 1983
Short and long versions available Does not require memory skills	Benton and Van Allen, 1968
No time requirements	Benton et al, 1983
Contains 3 designs consisting of 6, 8, and 15 blocks	Benton and Fogel, 1962
Tests 2-dimensional skills Must be administered by a psychologist	Wechsler, 1981

perception. It is critical to have this information prior to assessing a patient, or valuable time and effort will be wasted. The possibility of misdiagnosis also is increased if the professional is not prepared with this information ahead of the scheduled evaluation time.

A complete medical history, including information about premorbid functioning, educational level, and cultural background, provides a knowledge base for formulating treatment expectations and objectives. This information also helps the rehabilitation specialist to adapt evaluation methods in order to obtain the most accurate picture of the strengths and weaknesses presented by each specific patient. Spouse, family, and patient interviews along with the chart review are sources for this information.

Patient State

The ability of the patient to participate in the testing procedures is a variable that the clinician has to control for as much as possible. Scores on all the tests and items discussed here are influenced by the capacity of the patient to understand the purpose and procedures of the evaluation. Active participation, attention to the tasks, and ability to communicate responses influence the validity of the resulting scores. The effects of fatigue on the above-mentioned requirements also must be appreciated by the specialist. When observing that such variables may have influenced the validity of the evaluation results, notations qualifying the scores should be made by the examiner if the effects cannot be controlled. Also, if adapted procedures are used to administer particular items, this should be noted as well.

It also has been observed clinically that the effects of the medications that the patient is using may cause variation in test results. Drugs commonly prescribed for the conditions found in the older populations may cause side effects that result in impaired perceptual functioning. Examples of these side effects include dizziness, decreased attention span, decreased alertness, and double vision.

A complete review of the medical history and, if possible, an interview with the patient and the family or caregiver provide valuable information that enables the specialist to adequately prepare for a comprehensive evaluation that is relevant to the specific needs of the patient.

Assessment Batteries

A difficulty for the clinician arises at this point owing to the lack of knowledge about the standardized comprehensive batteries available to evaluate the perceptual abilities in the brain-damaged adult population. When treatment is to be documented and recorded in measurable terms, standardization, reliability, validity, and clinical application of the chosen evaluations become important. Titus and colleagues (1991) suggest that because perceptual dysfunction can be assessed with evaluation tools that have a variety of emphasis and performance requirements, rehabilitation professionals should use a comprehensive range of tools for evaluation. Titus and colleagues further state that the chosen instruments should be standardized, reliable, valid, and practical for clinical use and that verbal, motor, endurance, and attention span requirements be limited to improve accuracy. Because of the lack of knowledge about the comprehensive batteries available for this population, clinicians often put together their own selection of subtests uniquely designed for a specific patient. Zoltan and associates (1986) found that perceptual tests developed for use with children commonly are used incorrectly by specialists not prepared to evaluate adult patients. Standardized scores for children cannot be extrapolated to adult age ranges because of the performance and learning differences in adults. Peterson and Wikoff (1983) and others have provided adult normative data that enable rehabilitation specialists to use evaluation devices with populations other than the ones for which the test was originally designed.

One screening tool that evaluates overall visual perceptual abilities is the Motor-Free Visual Perception Test (Colarusso and Hammill, 1972). Though used initially with children, this device was normed and revised by Bouska and Kwatny (1983) for use with adult brain-damaged patients.

A standardized battery for assessing sensorimotor integration in adult CVA patients was developed by Jongbloed and associates (1986). The Sensorimotor Integration Test Battery For CVA Clients provides information about the ability to integrate sensory input from several sensory modalities. It also helps the clinician delineate whether the problems identified are perceptual or visual, somatosensory, or motor deficits.

The Loewenstein Occupational Therapy Cognitive Assessment was developed to provide a profile of conceptual and perceptual problems in brain-damaged adults (Katz et al, 1989). Designed to aid the clinician in planning intervention, this battery is divided into 4 areas: (1) orientation, (2) visual and spatial perception, (3) visuomotor organization, and (4) thinking operations. In addition, it can be used as a screening device to initiate further testing and provide a means of measuring treatment progress.

Another battery, designed for identification of perceptual dysfunction in brain-damaged adults, is the Ontario Society of Occupational Therapists Perceptual Evaluation. This instrument, an objective, standardized evaluation, is a reliable test of perceptual dysfunction (Boys et al, 1988). It discriminates well between non-neurologically impaired patients and neurologically damaged individuals, thus providing diagnostic information. The authors also state that this evaluation may be able to provide a ranking system for the severity of the patient's perceptual dysfunction.

The McCarron-Dial System is a vocational evaluation battery developed for use with a range of patients with neurological disabilities, including CVA. The McCarron-Dial System measures 3 neuropsychological factors: (1) verbal-spatial-cognitive, (2) sensory-motor, and (3) emotional-coping abilities. The system uses 6 measures that include current and accepted batteries, such as The Haptic Visual Discrimination Test and the Wechsler Adult Intelligence Scale, along with functional and behavioral observations (McCarron and Dial, 1986). It has been reported that the McCarron-Dial System provides good prognostic information concerning the vocational placement and independent living skills of central nervous system–damaged individuals (Dial et al, 1990). While designating the specific areas of the brain that have been damaged, the computerized reports generated by the scoring of this battery also provide suggestions of specific treatment interventions and activities.

The Arnadottir OT-ADL Neurobehavioral Evaluation (A-ONE) is a recent addition to the list of evaluation tools available to rehabilitation specialists (Arnadottir, 1990). It was constructed to identify the functional performance in brain-damaged individuals with neurobehavioral deficits. The linkage between measuring functional performance and identifying the localization of the lesion makes this evaluation device promising for research as well as clinical use. The evaluation consists of two parts, the first of which contains items that identify activities of daily living skill performance and the specific functional components of the task. Also contained in the administration of part one is a subscale to identify specific neurobehavioral deficits such as apraxia and spatial disorders. Part two is available to the clinician who is interested in relating the results of part one of the evaluation to the location of the lesion and the neurobehavioral deficits and processing dysfunctions at that location.

Specific Assessment

As previously discussed, acquired brain damage, in this case CVA, may result in dysfunction anywhere in the visual-perceptual apparatus. After precipitating sensory deficits and premorbid conditions are noted, a visual-perceptual evaluation is in order.

This discussion of assessment of visual perceptual dysfunctions is structured into several categories, as shown in Table 1–2: visuospatial disorders; visual agnosias; visuoconstructive disorders; and the more complex visual discrimination skills, as indicated in visual analysis and synthesis (Bouska et al, 1990).

Visuospatial Disorders

Visuospatial disorders primarily are experienced by patients with lesions of the right posterior parietal and occipital regions of the brain (Bouska et al, 1990). Several sources have suggested that younger patients perform better on visuospatial tasks regardless of brain damage, because their visuospatial abilities are unaffected by age (Kaplan and Hier, 1982). This is a consideration when assessing these perceptual disorders and setting treatment expectations in the aging population. Functionally, a patient with visuospatial disorders may exhibit increased difficulties with activities requiring the use of objects and with the concept of space. In the Kaplan and Hier (1982) study, visuospatial abilities were found to be an important predictor of eventual independence level in functional skills in right brain–damaged patients. Another study identified visuospatial dysfunction as the most frequent skill problem in its subjects (Carter et al, 1983). In the literature, this type of disorder is discussed under various labels. Zoltan and colleagues (1986) describe spatial relations syndrome; others categorize the disorder as visual spatial disorientation. However, all categories involve disorders of the perception of spatial relationships of objects.

Benton (1979) and Zoltan and associates (1986) have identified

Table 1–2. VISUAL PERCEPTUAL DYSFUNCTION

Visuospatial disorders	**Visuoconstructive Apraxia**
Figure-ground	2-Dimensional construction
Form and space constancy	3-Dimensional construction
Visual memory	**Complex Visual Discrimination Skills**
Position in space	
Spatial relations	Analysis
Topographical disorientation	Synthesis
Visual Object Agnosias	Integration
Facial recognition	
Visual spatial agnosia	
Color agnosia	
Form and object recognition	
Metamorphopsia	

several specific disabilities that commonly occur as a result of visuospatial disorders. These problems include figure-ground deficits, form and space constancy, visual memory, position in space, spatial relations, and topographical disorientation.

Assessments that are geared toward evaluating these specific areas are presented. Figure-ground deficits, the inability to perceive the foreground separately from the background, can be evaluated using several individual test items from larger batteries of sensory integrative or perceptual assessments. The Southern California Sensory Integration Test was developed by A. Jean Ayres (1972) and has since been revised and republished under the title Sensory Integration and Praxis Tests (Ayres, 1984). This battery of 17 subtests was standardized and developed for use with learning-disabled children. However, there has been increasing interest among therapists and others for the application of these subtests to evaluating similar problems in brain-damaged populations. At the present time, there is some use of various subtests in adult populations and an increasing amount of research providing normative data for adult brain-damaged populations. Peterson and Wikoff (1983) have researched adult performance on the Figure-Ground Test, a subtest of the batteries developed by Ayres, and published normative data for adult males. They also have established a correlation of this test with the Embedded Figures Test. Normative data for female performance on the Figure-Ground Test was published by Petersen and associates (1985). The Figure-Ground Test consists of a series of cards that progressively increase in difficulty, with complex figures from which the subject identifies the specific stimuli figures. The subject identifies the stimuli presented that are recognized within the figures by pointing (Ayres, 1972).

The Embedded Figures Test is a standardized evaluation that also is cited for use in evaluating figure-ground problems (Witkin et al, 1971). The Embedded Figures Test was developed to measure the ability to visually comprehend a specific area from within a larger field. The items on this test include cards with simple designs and cards with more complex designs that contain the initial simple designs embedded within. The patient outlines the simple figures on the cards containing the more complex designs. The time recorded for the patient to correctly trace the figure determines that item's score. The motor skills needed for tracing the figures, as well as the memory skills required, should be a consideration when deciding to use this test with CVA patients. This test is recommended for ages 10 and older and has adequate reliability and normative sampling.

The Motor-Free Visual Perception Test is a general screening tool for the evaluation of visual-perceptual skills (Calarusso and Hammill, 1972). This device does not require the use of motor skills other than gross pointing abilities in the absence of verbalization. It measures figure-ground abilities as well as strengths and weaknesses in the visual-perceptual areas of discrimination, memory, spatial relationships, form constancy, sequential memory, and visual closure. Bouska and Kwatny (1983) published a manual of adult norms for the Motor-Free Visual Perception Test. They also have revised the original test to improve its application to brain-damaged adults.

Form and space constancy involves the ability of the patient to perceive variations in the form of objects and their arrangement in space. The Motor-Free Visual Perception Test subtest of visual form constancy is most often cited in the literature; however, as a part of a screening device, this subtest was not designed as a diagnostic tool. Clinicians also report using several subtests of the Southern California Sensory Integration Test as screening devices. Zoltan and associates (1986) suggest functional test items that include discrimination of like objects and the use of a formboard. The form constancy subtest of the Frostig Developmental Test of Visual Perception (Frostig, 1966) also is suggested in the literature; however, this test is normed for use with children between the ages of 3- and 8-years-old.

Visual memory, or the recall of spatial information for the location and relationships of objects and places, often is evaluated along with form and space constancy and topographical abilities. The Motor-Free Visual Perception Test also contains a Visual Sequential Memory subtest. These areas also can be evaluated functionally by asking the patient to describe the positions of objects or by requesting a map or a floor plan to be drawn.

Position in space, or the concept of spatial positioning of objects, is identified by the correct use of the descriptive words such as "in" and "out," "up" and "down," "beneath," and so forth. The Position in Space Test and Space Visualization Test are subtests of the Southern California Sensory Integration and Praxis Tests (Ayres, 1972) and can be used along with functional-type items such as positioning blocks or other objects as screening devices. The Frostig battery subtests of Spatial Relations and Position in Space often are used for evaluation of these disorders as well (Frostig, 1966). At the present time, there are no published data to validate the use of these subtests with this population.

Visual Agnosia

Visual agnosias, also referred to as visual object processing deficits, are manifested by the inability to recognize familiar and unfamiliar objects by sight despite the fact that recognition is possible through use of touch (Toglia, 1989). It is difficult to have a full understanding of this problem and make an accurate assessment of it without eliminating, as much as possible, the influences of other visual dysfunctions. It is stressed that test items identifying other disorders, such as a decline in visual acuity, visual field deficits, and visual inattention, should precede evaluation for agnosias. The literature discusses several types of visual agnosias (Zoltan, 1986). Among these are the visual object agnosias, which include difficulties with facial recognition (prosopagnosia), visual spatial agnosia, color agnosia, form constancy, and metamorphopsia. At the present time, there are no standardized assessments for most visual object agnosias.

Toglia (1989) has suggested an approach to evaluation and treatment of visual object perception that is not deficit specific and that places an emphasis on the influence of object processing as it is related to the overall abilities of visual information processing. The method of evaluation described in this approach is termed dynamic investigation. This investigation involves analyzing task parameters, task grading, the use of systematic cuing, and investigative questioning. The information gathered through the use of this type of evaluation provides a more individualized understanding of the reasons for a specific patient's performance and allows the clinician to predict how the patient will respond to the different types of treatments. Thus, the rehabilitation professional is able to design a treatment plan that is best suited to the needs of the patient.

Nonstandardized evaluation materials currently available for the assessment of specific visual agnosias involve recording and observing correct and incorrect responses for the visual recognition of objects, colors, and photographs (Quintana, 1989; Toglia, 1989; Zoltan et al, 1986). The patient also may respond with verbal descriptions or reproductions of objects. Because visual spatial agnosias are a form of visuospatial dysfunction, they can be evaluated by the methods previously discussed. Color agnosias are evaluated by use of the Ishihara Color Plates (Kanehura and Company, LTD, 1977) along with test items that require sorting by color hue. Facial agnosias may be evaluated through the use of the Test of Facial Recognition (Benton and Van Allen, 1968). This standardized test consists of photographs of unknown human faces from differing views that are matched by the subject (Lezak, 1983).

Visuoconstructive Dysfunction

The inability to construct or copy 2- or 3-dimensional designs is labeled visuoconstructive dysfunction, visuoconstructive apraxia, or constructional apraxia. Functionally, this problem often is manifested during performance activities that require the use of parts to form a whole. Examples of this type of activity are daily dressing routines, using a sewing pattern, and assembling a toy or woodworking project. It appears that the manner in which new tasks requiring constructional abilities are learned changes with age, and the types of items used to test this type of perceptual disorder must be evaluated with this in mind (Fall, 1987).

The relationship between dressing performance and visuoconstructive disorders has been discussed widely in the literature, and most clinicians have had the frustrating experience of trying to reteach dressing skills to a patient who appears to have all the motor, sensory, and cognitive abilities required. This relationship was detailed by Warren (1981) in her research concerning constructional apraxia, body scheme disorders, and dressing performance. Statistically significant correlations in the scores of CVA subjects revealed that their dressing performance was reflected in lower success rates on evaluations of constructional praxis as well as body scheme. These data suggests that body scheme and visuoconstructive functions contribute to overall dressing ability. Both of these findings are significant when assessing the functional manifestations of these visual-perceptual disorders.

There has been much debate in the literature as to the incidence and underlying cause of the symptoms of visuoconstructive disorders in the patient with specific unilateral damage. The variety of results yielded by the evaluations used to test visuoconstructive abilities may be understood by the rehabilitation professional when research into the roles of the brain hemispheres is reviewed. Although patients with either hemisphere damaged display symptoms that indicate constructive dysfunction, the performance of the two groups has different characteristics, and research appears to support different causes for the deficits depending on which hemisphere is affected (Arena and Gainotti, 1978; Benton, 1973; Quintana, 1989). A patient with right-sided hemispheric damage generally tends to approach drawing tasks in an unorganized manner and produce a complex, spatially disoriented drawing. These patients also tend to achieve less independence in functional self-care activities. The explanations for this suggest that in patients with right hemispheric damage, this is a function of visuospatial deficits. Meanwhile, the drawings of a left brain–damaged CVA patient usually are simple and lack detail. Arena and Gainotti's (1978) research supports an executive planning or conceptual disorder here. However, Titus and colleagues (1991) found that all the stroke subjects in their study, regardless of lesion side, performed significantly lower on tests of perceptual functioning than normal subjects; they therefore concluded that both groups need to be evaluated for perceptual dysfunction.

Tests standardized for use with adults and used to test visuo-constructive skills are Kohs' Blocks Test (Kohs, 1923) and the Block Design and Object Assembly subtests of the Wechsler Adult Intelligence Scale-Revised (Wechsler, 1981). Titus and associates (1991) found the Wechsler Adult Intelligence Scale-Revised, along with several other evaluation tools mentioned in this chapter, to be useful in understanding the perceptual performance of stroke patients. The Wechsler Adult Intelligence Scale-Revised requires supervision of a psychologist when used by other rehabilitation service modalities. These tests are designed to evaluate, through use of varying degrees of complex designs and puzzles, the ability of the subject to reproduce one- or two-dimensional figures. The results of the Lorenze and Cancro (1962) study suggested that those subjects who score in the lower ranges on these two subtests of the Wechsler Adult Intelligence Scale-Revised were not as successful in achieving improved dressing ability after treatment. They further suggest that the scores on these subtests have predictive value for the successful remediation of dressing and grooming skills.

Benton and Fogel (1962) developed the Three-Dimensional Constructional Praxis Test. Their research has shown that a patient who has performed adequately on two-dimensional tests of constructional abilities may not perform as well when evaluated using tests requiring three-dimensional construction abilities. This observation was originally articulated by Critchley (1953), who suggested that tests of three-dimensional constructional praxis might be of more diagnostic value than those tests that evaluate only two-dimensional abilities. Benton and Fogel's (1962) research further suggests that the two tasks be evaluated separately for a more accurate picture of constructional abilities. Also apparent in this study was the correlation between three-dimensional constructive disabilities and general mental impairment, as demonstrated by a decline in verbal intelligence scores. There was also a higher incidence of poor performance on the test in patients with right hemispheric lesions. This information helps rehabilitation specialists predict and interpret evaluation results.

The Three-Dimensional Constructional Praxis Test is a block design test for standardized use with adults. The test consists of three block assembly tasks that increase in complexity. The examiner initially demonstrates the assembly process; then the patient copies the models. The structures are built with one hand and are scored in terms of accuracy (Benton and Fogel, 1962). Titus and associates (1991) found that this test correlated well with some activities of daily living, had a high test-retest reliability, and therefore, might be a valuable tool for rehabilitation professionals for clinical research and treatment. Bradley (1982) also has found support for the use of three-dimensional tests of constructional praxia to predict upper extremity dressing abilities.

It is important to note when devising a screening device or choosing the appropriate evaluation method to assess the visuoconstructive abilities in a CVA patient whose score the method of test administration most likely will influence. Also, note that the performance of the patient is influenced by the testing method. Results of several studies conducted indicate that the type of test items used for the evaluation of constructional praxis in the healthy elderly influenced the performance of the subjects. Evaluations that were administered using models or demonstration of test item stimuli resulted in significantly higher scores than the other types of test stimuli used (Benton and Fogel, 1962; Fall, 1987).

Complex Visual Discrimination Skills

The process of analyzing, synthesizing, and integrating the information determined from one's perception of the environment is the final step in the process. Coordination of the spatial and constructive processes along with the emotional and conceptual connotations of the experience occur simultaneously. Therefore, attempts to consider this last step, the visual analysis, synthesis, and integration skills, in isolation is difficult (Bouska et al, 1990). Most tests designed to evaluate the more complex visual discrimination skills ask patients to discriminate very subtle differences in highly complex items. Generally, test items included fall into 3 categories: (1) figure-ground skills, (2) figure closure (a spatial task), and (3) constructive skills. Scores on the subtests that measure these abilities on the various test batteries already discussed often are considered together in order to make decisions about the patient's complex visual skill ability.

Commonly used tests that evaluate the complex visual skill abilities include the Hooper Visual Organization Test (1958). This test has been standardized for use with subjects 13 through 69 years old. It provides information on the ability of the patient to organize and integrate visual information. Test items ask the patient to determine what object can be made from the two or three pieces presented. The test requires the patient to be able to verbally name or write out the name of the object. The influence of communication skills on the final score must be considered. Also, Farver and Farver (1982) discovered a significant age-related decline in the scores of older, normal adults on this particular test. This test was intended for use as a screening device and to be part of a comprehensive battery of visual perceptual tests.

The Form Discrimination Test requires a subtle discrimination of the features of various visual configurations, thus, requiring visual analysis and synthesis (Benton et al, 1983). There are no time requirements, and the answers can be indicated by verbal response as well as pointing.

Functionally, tasks that require a higher level of discrimination and have a three- or four-step process reveal problems in the areas of visual analysis and synthesis. Tasks that might meet these requirements include food preparation, setting a table, and packing a suitcase.

TREATMENT

Current clinical treatment of visual perceptual dysfunction in adults generally can be categorized into two types, the first being those techniques that are designed to help the patient compensate or adapt to changes in functioning. Most of these techniques are aimed at changing the functional environment of the patient and maximizing the assets or strengths of the patient. The second category of treatment approaches includes the techniques aimed toward remediating or recovering perceptual function and those that have as their goal changing and reorganizing the central nervous system of the patient.

The Treatment Literature

Neistadt (1988) refers to these two treatment categories as the adaptive approaches and the remedial approaches, respectively. The adaptive approaches assume that the central nervous system damage in this population cannot be altered; therefore, a compensatory or adaptive approach should be taken. The assets or particular strengths of the patient are emphasized and used for functional adaptation. The functional training approaches, as described by Zoltan and associates (1986), rely on environmental adaptation and compensation techniques along with repetition and practice of each task. When specific tasks are selected, each task is broken down into component parts, and the patient repeats each component until it is mastered. Activity analysis is combined with prescribed technological adaptations that can range from fairly simple adaptive equipment and environmental modifications to the use of more complex computer-based compensations. The treatment goals using this approach focus directly on specific activities of daily living, and the patient often is limited to the practiced repertoire of situations.

On the other hand, the remedial approaches are based on the assumption that the adult brain retains its plasticity and that the central nervous system is capable of recovery. Treatment goals aim to retrain specific components of perceptual skills through the use of tabletop activities, such as the use of pegboards, pencil and paper tasks, block designs, and so forth. Some clinical facilities use a cognitive remediation programmed type approach using workbooks (Carter et al, 1982) or computerized programs for treatment. As more rehabilitation facilities have become computerized, this technology has become available for use in treatment. Software has been developed that provides efficient and motivating activities for the remediation of perceptual dysfunction. An assumption is made that treatment through use of these techniques automatically transfers, or generalizes, to functional and occupational tasks.

Sensorimotor categories of treatment such as Ayres' Sensory Integrative Treatment (Ayres, 1972) and Bobath neurodevelopmental treatment techniques (Bobath, 1978) are remedial or restorative in nature. Biomechanical techniques such as sensory retraining and the transfer of training approach are examples of approaches that have as their foundation a belief in the ability of the brain to repair itself. Sensorimotor integrative techniques also can be categorized as a remedial approach. Sensorimotor techniques combine the work of Bobath, Rood, and Ayres (Jongbloed et al, 1989). These theoretical beliefs combine to treat the sensory and motor systems as having a direct and interrelated effect on each other. The sensorimotor treatment methods emphasize the normalization of sensation and the facilitation of normal motor output.

Neistadt (1990) wrote that although the remedial approach assumes that generalization of skills takes place automatically, the adaptive approach decreases the requirement of generalization. Toglia (1989; 1991) and Abreu and Toglia (1987) propose a cognitive rehabilitative approach that combines elements of both approaches and expands on them by introducing systematic cognitive strategies that the patient can then generalize to various situations. This multicontextual treatment approach, described in detail by Toglia (1991), conceptualizes learning as having "a dynamic interaction between the learner's processing strategies, metacognitive skills, and experiences and the nature of the task, the environment, and learning criteria." In treatment, the 3 areas emphasized are: (1) the teaching and learning processes, (2) the environment, and (3) the positioning and movement patterns of the patient's body (Abreu and Toglia, 1987). Toglia (1989) emphasizes the need for research into the efficacy of this approach and comparisons of this model with other approaches.

Although rehabilitation professionals have understood clinically that independence in activities of daily living is essential for the achievement of self-worth and independence in patients, there has been a general inconsistency concerning the definition and treatment of perceptual dysfunction. Future research emphasis should consider the relationship between perception and functional or occupational abilities (Toglia, 1991).

Neistadt (1990) found in chart review studies that the remedial approaches are used predominantly in clinical practice. However, there are conflicting data about which approach is more successful. For example, a study Jongbloed and colleagues (1989) failed to find a significant difference in the effectiveness of the two groups of subjects, one group treated with a sensorimotor-based treatment program and the other treated with a functionally based approach. A review of other studies reveals conflicting results and a confusing array of study designs. No definitive decision can be made yet, because the studies performed have not taken into account the significant variables that may have influenced their results (Neistadt, 1988). Neistadt states that these variables directly influence the success of therapy and, therefore, need to be more carefully considered in future research before individual specialists can make decisions in their clinical practices.

Dutton (1989) wrote in her discussion of the controversy surrounding preparatory exercise and purposeful activity that the biomechanical and the sensorimotor treatment techniques can be carefully coordinated to provide the patient with the best of both approaches. Owing to the changes at the present time in our health care system and the lack of conclusive evidence to support either a strictly remedial or an adaptive approach, it appears that we can best meet the needs of our patients by combining both schools of thought. In order to provide the most effective and the most cost-efficient treatment for our CVA clients with visual-perceptual dysfunction, it appears that we need to combine our approaches and continue a systematic examination of the efficacy of our treatment practices.

CASE REPORT

Introduction

T.J. is a 66-year-old female with the diagnosis of hypertension, CVA, and lesion in the right hemisphere parietal lobe, with resulting left hemiplegia. She was hospitalized during the acute stages of this illness, then transferred to this program 4 weeks after onset. Discharge and referral reports indicate that this patient has made consistent progress during this initial recovery period, and a prognosis for a high level of independence was made.

Medical History

Client has had a long-standing history of hypertension, which was considered to be responsible for the CVA. There also is a history of two resolving transient ischemic attacks. On examination at the time of transfer, patient was alert and oriented, wore bifocal glasses with average visual correction, and displayed no apparent hearing loss. Speech was hesitant and slurred with fatigue but was easily understood. Patient ambulated independently, with some loss of balance and weakness in the left extremities. Patient reported difficulty with resuming self-care, homemaking, and leisure activities. No medications are prescribed that impact functioning level.

Social History

Client resides at home with husband, daughter, and grandchild. She graduated from high school and worked up until 4 years ago as an aide in a preschool program. She is active in church and child care activities.

Initial Evaluation

Patient was referred to this program by her physician for functional evaluation and treatment to increase level of independence. Patient displayed decreased strength and diminished active range of motion in left extremities, with an overall grade of fair. Right dominant extremity was within functional limits. Fine motor coordination in left hand was poor, with slightly decreased tactile discrimination for light touch and 2-point localization. Using the Klein-Bell Activities of Daily Living Scale, patient displayed minimal difficulties with lower extremity dressing and moderate problems with small fasteners (Klein and Bell, 1979). Though ambulation was independent, equilibrium and protective reactions were delayed.

Perceptual abilities were evaluated using the Loewenstein Occupational Therapy Cognitive Assessment. Four cognitive and perceptual areas were tested with normal performance in the areas of orientation and thinking operations. The subtest scores of visual and spatial perception and visuomotor organization indicated dysfunction and a need for further evaluation. Through the use of the Benton tests of Form Discrimination (Benton et al, 1983) and Three-Dimensional Praxis (Benton and Fogel, 1962) and the Embedded Figures Test (Witkin et al, 1971), dysfunction in several areas of visual perception were noted. Areas of difficulty were in those tasks that required complex visual organization and integration; 3-dimensional construction tasks, subtle shape and form discrimination, and complex spatial organization tasks.

Functionally, patient displayed difficulty organizing tasks such as set up for self-care activities, organizing work areas for homemaking tasks, and selecting appropriate tools for a specific task. While testing these areas, the influence of poor fine motor coordination and balance also is noted.

Treatment Goals

1. Increase gross and fine motor control in left upper extremity.
2. Increase standing and sitting balance and protective reactions.
3. Increase independence in self-care, homemaking, and leisure activities.
4. Increase visual perceptual functioning during activities of daily living.

Intervention for Visual-Perceptual Function

Intervention was planned to provide treatment through the use of functional as well as tabletop activities. To increase independence in occupational tasks, patient practiced strategies for task organization and tool selection through clinic activities. Patient and therapist identified specific self-care, home-care, and child-care tasks that the patient performed previous to hospitalization. These tasks then were broken down into component steps and practiced, with an emphasis on strategies for task arrangement. Treatment sessions also included practice in visual imagery of tools habitually used for familiar tasks and self-monitoring and adaptive strategies for unfamiliar situations. Self-monitoring devices used by this patient included periodic breaks during tasks to check the results of the previous steps, such as checking to see if all ingredients have been added and the oven preheated before mixing cake batter. Patient was reminded to take a break to check work initially with verbal cues by a therapist, then eventually, by use of a timer.

Tabletop activities used block, pegboard, and pencil and paper activities requiring complex form completion and discrimination, design copying, and block construction. Examples of such tasks include copying patterns with parquetry blocks, dot-to-dot picture completion, 1-inch block design copying, and hidden shape and object pictures.

Related computer tasks requiring figure-ground, form, and spatial discrimination and relationships and design completion also were used. After some initial hesitation about using a computer, the patient took part in arcade-type games requiring systematic strategies to reach a goal and used software designed to train basic visual, perceptual, and fine motor control. Adaptations were made in the seating system to provide support for decreased trunk balance and decreased strength in left upper extremity. Patient sat upright with a detachable keyboard on a lap tray for optimal positioning.

Toward the time of discharge, the patient was using word processing to type notes to friends and schedule her day.

References

Abreu BC, Toglia JP: Cognitive rehabilitation: a model for occupational therapy. Am J Occup Ther 41:439–448, 1987.

Anderson EK: Sensory impairment in hemiplegia. Archives Phys Med Rehabil 52(7):294–297, 1971.

Arena R, Gainotti G: Constructional apraxia and visuoperceptual disabilities in relation to laterality of cerebral lesions. Cortex 14,463–473, 1978.

Arnadottir G: The Brain and Behavior: Assessing Cortical Dysfunction through Activities of Daily Living (ADL). St Louis, CV Mosby Co, 1990.

Ayres AJ: Southern California Sensory Integration Tests Manual. Los Angeles, Western Psychological Services, 1972.

Ayres AJ: Sensory Integration and Praxis Test Manual. Los Angeles, Western Psychological Services, 1984.

Benton AL: Visuoconstructive disabilities in patients with cerebral disease: its relationship to side of lesion and aphasic disorders. Doc Ophthamol 34:67–76, 1973.

Benton AL: Visuospatial and Visuoconstructive Disorders. In Hulman K, Valenstein E (eds), Clinical Neuropsychology. New York: Oxford University Press, 1979.

Benton AL, Fogel ML: Three-Dimensional Constructional Praxis. Arch Neurol 7:347–354, 1962.

Benton AL, Hamsher K, Varney N, Spreen O: Contributions to Neuropsychological Assessment: A Clinical Manual. New York: Oxford University Press, 1983.

Benton AL, Van Allen MW: Impairment of facial recognition in patients with cerebral disease. Cortex 4:344–358, 1968.

Bobath B: Adult Hemiplegia: Evaluation and Treatment. London, William Hennemann Medical Books, 1978.

Bouska MJ, Kaufman NA, Marcus SE: Disorders of the Visual Perceptual System. *In* Umphred DA (ed): Neurological Rehabilitation (Vol 1) (2nd ed). St Louis, CV Mosby Co, 1990, pp 705–740.

Bouska MJ, Kwatny E: Manual for the Application of the Motor-Free Visual Perception Test to the Adult Population. Philadelphia, Temple University Rehabilitation Research and Training Center No 8, 1983.

Boys M, Fisher P, Holzberg C, Reid DW: The OSOT Perceptual Evaluation: A Research Perspective. Am J Occup Ther 42:92–98, 1988.

Bradley KP: Brief: the effectiveness of Constructional Praxis Tests in predicting upper extremity abilities. Occup Ther J Res 2:184–185, 1982.

Carter LT, Howard BE, O'Neil WA: Effectiveness of cognitive skill remediation in acute stroke patients. Am J Occup Ther 37:320–326, 1983.

Colarusso R, Hammill D: Motor-Free Visual Perception Test Manual. Novato, CA, Academic Therapy Publications, 1972.

Critchley M: The Parietal Lobes. London, Edward Arnold, 1953.

DeRenzi E, Spinnler H: Impaired performance on color tasks in patients with hemispheric damage. Cortex 3:194–216, 1967.

Dial JG, Chan F, Norton C: Neuropsychological assessment of brain damage: discriminative validity of the McCarron-Dial System. Brain Injury 4:230–246, 1990.

Dutton R: Guidelines for using both activity and exercise. Am J Occup Ther 43:573–580, 1989.

Fall CC: Comparing ways of measuring constructional praxis in the well elderly. Am J Occup Ther 41:500–504, 1987.

Farver PF, Farver TB: Performance of older adults on tests designed to measure parietal lobe functions. Am J Occup Ther 36:444–449, 1982.

Feigenson JS, Mc Dowell FH, Meese P, McCarthy ML, Greenberg SD: Factors influencing outcome and length of stay in stroke rehabilitation unit: part 1. Stroke 8:651–656, 1977.

Forer SK, Miller LS: Rehabilitation outcome comparative analysis of different patient types. Arch Phys Med Rehabil 61:359–365, 1980.

Frostig M: Developmental Test of Visual Perception (rev ed). Palo Alto, CA: Consulting Psychologists Press, 1966.

Grahman FK, Kendall BS: Memory for Design Test. Revised General Manual. Perception and Motor Skills. Monograph Supplement #2-VII. New York: Grune & Stratton, 1951.

Harlowe D, Van Deusen J: Construct validation of the St Mary's CVA evaluation: perceptual measures. Am J Occup Ther 38:184–186, 1984.

Harris DB: Children's Drawings as Measures of Intellectual Maturity. New York, Harcourt & Brace, 1963.

Hooper HE: The Hooper Visual Organization Test Manual. Los Angeles, Western Psychological, 1958.

Hung S, Fisher AG, Cermak S: The performance of learning disabled and normal young men on the test of visual perceptual skills. Am J Occup Ther 41:790–797, 1987.

Kanehara and Company, LTD. The Ishihara Color Plates. Tokyo, 1977.

Jongbloed LE, Collins JB, Jones W: A sensorimotor integration test battery for CVA clients: preliminary evidence of reliability and validity. Am J Occup Ther Res 6:131–150, 1986.

Jongbloed LE, Stacey S, Brighton C: Stroke rehabilitation: Sensorimotor Integrative Treatment versus Functional Treatment. Am J Occup Ther 43:391–397, 1989.

Kaplan J, Hier DB: Visuospatial deficits after right hemisphere stroke. Am J Occup Ther 36:314–321, 1982.

Katz N, Itzkovich M, Averbuch S, Elazar B: Loewenstein Occupational Therapy Cognitive Assessment (LOTCA) Battery for brain injured patients: reliability and validity. Am J Occup Ther 43:184–192, 1989.

Klein RM, Bell BJ: Klein-Bell Activities of Daily Living Scale: Manual. University of Washington, Division of Occupational Therapy, 1979.

Kohs SC: Intelligence Measurement: A Psychological and Statistical Study Based on the Block Design Test. New York, McMillan, 1923.

Lezak MD: Neuropsychological Assessment (2nd ed). New York, Oxford Press, 1983.

Lieberman S, Cohen AH, Rubin J: NYSOA King Devick Test. J Am Optom Assoc 54:631–637, 1983.

Lorenze E, Cancro R: Dysfunction in visual perception with hemiplegia: it's relationship to activities of daily living. Arch Phys Med 43:514–517, 1962.

Macciocchi SN: Neuropsychological assessment following head trauma using the Halstead-Reitan Neuropsychological Test Battery. J Head Trauma Rehabil 3(1):1–11, 1988.

McCarron L, Dial JG: McCarron-Dial Evaluation System: A Systematic Approach to Vocational, Educational and Neurophysiological Assessment. Dallas, McCarron-Dial, 1986.

Moberg E: Objective methods for determining the functional value of sensibility in the hand. J Bone Joint Surg 40b(3):454–459, 1958.

Mooney CM: Closure as affected by configural clarity and contextual consistancy. Can J Psych 11:1–11, 1957.

Neistadt ME: Occupational therapy for adults with perceptual deficits. Am J Occup Ther 42:434–440, 1988.

Neistadt ME: A critical analysis of the occupational therapy approaches for perceptual deficits in adults with brain injury. Am J Occup Ther 44:229–304, 1990.

Petersen P, Goar D, Van Deusen J: Performance of female adults on the Southern California Visual Figure-Ground Perception Test. Am J Occup Ther 39:525–530, 1985.

Petersen P, Wikoff RL: The performance of adult males on the Southern California Figure-Ground Visual Perceptual Test. Am J Occup Ther 37:554–560, 1983.

Quintana LA: Cognitive and Perceptual Evaluation and Treatment. In Trombly CA (eds): Occupational Therapy for Physical Dysfunction (3rd ed). Baltimore, Williams & Wilkins, 1989, pp 161–183.

Schenkenberg T, Bradford DC, Ajax ET: Line bisection and unilateral visual neglect in patients with neurologic impairment. Neurology 30:509–517, 1980.

Smith A: Principles Underlying Human Brain Functions in Neuropsychological Sequelae of Different Neuropathology. New York: Wiley-Interscience, 1981.

Teuber HC, Weinstein S: Ability to discover hidden figures after cerebral lesions. Arch Neurol Psych 76:369–379, 1956.

Titus MD, Gall NG, Yerxa EJ, Roberson TA, Mack W: Correlation of perceptual performance and activities of daily living in stroke patients. Am J Occup Ther 45:410–418, 1991.

Toglia JP: Visual perception of objects: an approach to assessment and intervention. Am J Occup Ther 43:587–595, 1989.

Toglia JP: Generalization of treatment: a multicontext approach to cognitive perceptual impairment in adults with brain injury. Am J Occup Ther 45:505–516, 1991.

Trombly CA, Scott AD: Evaluation and Treatment of Somatosensory Sensation. In Trombly CA (ed): Occupational Therapy for Physical Dysfunction (3rd ed). Baltimore, Williams & Wilkins, 1989, pp 41–55.

Warren M: Relationship of constructional apraxia and body scheme disorders to dressing performance in adult CVA. Am J Occup Ther 35:431–437, 1981.

Wechsler D: Wechsler Adult Intelligence Scale—Revised. New York, Psychological Corporation, 1981.

Weinberg J, Diller L, Gordon WA, et al: Visual scanning training effect on reading-related tasks in aquired right brain damage. Arch Phys Med Rehabil 58:479–486, 1977.

Welford HR: On changes of performance with age. Lancet 1:335–339, 1962.

Witkin HA, Oltman PK, Raskin E, Karp SA: A Manual for the Embedded Figures Test. Palo Alto, Consulting Psychologists Press, 1971.

Wolf PA: An overview of the epidemiology of stroke. Stroke 21 (suppl) II-4–II-6, 1990.

Zoltan B: Evaluation of Visual, Perceptual, and Perceptual Motor Deficits. *In* Pedretti LW, Zoltan B: Occupational Therapy Practice Skills for Physical Dysfunction (3rd ed). St Louis, CV Mosby Co, 1990, pp 194–201.

Zoltan B, Siev E, Freishtat B: Perceptual & Cognitive Dysfunction in the Adult Stroke Patient: A Manual for Evaluation and Treatment (2nd ed). Thorofare, NJ, Slack, 1986.

2

CAROLYN SCHMIDT HANSON

TRAUMATIC BRAIN INJURY

This chapter focuses on the perceptual deficits of the traumatically brain-injured individual. In addition, a brief overview of problems encountered by this population is presented. A variety of perceptual tests and batteries that commonly are used with the traumatically brain-injured individual are reviewed. The chapter concludes with a section on restorative strategies and computer application in the clinic.

Traumatic brain injury (TBI) occurs most frequently as a result of motor vehicle accidents, falls, and industrial accidents (Levin et al, 1982). Conservative estimates indicate that over 2 million people each year sustain brain injuries, with 500,000 requiring hospitalization. Approximately 70,000 to 90,000 people will suffer debilitating losses and require therapeutic intervention. Unfortunately, another 2000 people will live a vegetative existence (Goldstein, 1990). A large number of these TBI individuals will be treated by rehabilitation specialists.

Brain trauma sustained from an accident is due to the shearing and stretching of nerve fibers and blood vessels that transpire during the acceleration and deceleration of the brain within the skull at the time of impact (Gentilini et al, 1985). Jane and Rimel (1981) state that the basic pathology in all brain injury is attributed to axonal disruption and morphological alterations. A majority of brain injuries occur in the frontal lobe region (Arnadottir, 1990). Individuals with frontal lobe lesions typically demonstrate the following characteristics: motor deficits; neurobehavioral deficits, especially loss of memory, aggressiveness, and lack of insight and judgment; and personality changes (Arnadottir, 1990).

As a result of blunt or penetrating trauma sustained from a brain injury, cerebral edema may ensue and contribute to diffuse injury (Levin et al, 1982). Adults who sustain one brain injury are at risk for having another injury that can be even more severe (Rimel and Jane, 1983). In contrast to the diffuse effects of a traumatic brain injury, more localized effects result from a stroke. Thus, the individual with a TBI generally has more widespread deficits than the individual who has suffered a stroke (Jennett, 1983).

All head injuries are unique owing to the particular area affected in the brain coupled with the premorbid personality of the individual (Jennett, 1983). Some of the most frequent complaints of the TBI individual include headaches, fatigue, dizziness, memory loss, blurred vision, and depression (Hoff et al, 1989). Cognitive problems that commonly are exhibited by the TBI individual are poor judgment and initiative, impulsivity, distractiblity, short attention span, and decreased learning ability (Griffith, 1983). Perceptual dysfunction also may interfere in the recovery process and frequently is intertwined with cognitive and visual dysfunction. It is interesting to note that a number of TBI individuals, prior to their injury, have had documented perceptual and learning problems (Zoltan, 1990).

Compounding the fact of possible perceptual deficits, the TBI patient may lack insight and deny any physical or mental limitations, which makes evaluation and treatment more difficult. Prognosis for the patient depends on the extent of the brain damage as well as factors such as age, appropriate and timely medical intervention, premorbid personality, and behavior (Gummow et al, 1983). The individual who was motivated and strong-willed before the injury will have a more successful recovery than the emotionally unstable person who has a poor work and school history (Haas et al, 1985) combined with a possible alcohol or drug abuse problem (Adamovich et al, 1985). Jennett (1983) cogently states: "The victims of head injury are not a random sample of their age group; they include an undue proportion of people with some kind of social deviancy. They are risk takers in cars and on motorcycles, and they are drinkers and declared alcoholics."

OVERALL ASSESSMENTS USED WITH THE TBI POPULATION

There are many screening tools and batteries that can be used to evaluate the overall functioning of the TBI population. Several widely used scales measure the severity of a coma and its sequelae. For example, the Glasgow Coma Scale is based on motor, physical, and cognitive responses (Jennett et al, 1976) and frequently is cited in research studies. The Glasgow Outcome Scale consists of 5 levels related to work ability, ranging from good recovery (rated a "5") to death (rated a "1") (Jennett and Bond, 1975). The Disability Rating Scale has been compared with the Glasgow Outcome Scale and is a 30-point scale ranging from recovery without gross impairment (rated a "0") to death (rated a "30") (Gouvier et al, 1987; Hall et al, 1985). The Disability Rating Scale is applicable to the person who has sustained a severe head injury, has been comatose for at least 6 hours, and is between 15 and 60 years of age (Hall et al, 1985).

Another assessment that has not been researched as thoroughly as the aforementioned scales is the Rancho Los Amigos Scale of Cognitive Levels. This assessment is based on 8 distinct steps of awareness, ranging from a Level I, indicating no response, to a Level VIII, demonstrating purposeful and appropriate behavior (Hegen et al, 1972). The Developmental Assessment of Recovery from Serious Head Injury (DARSHI) method evaluates the patient according to observed chronological development. Tests from infant scales and items from the Stanford-Binet Intelligence Scale are used to determine the extent of recovery (Eson et al, 1978). In measuring concussion recovery, the Paced Auditory Serial Addition Task is used. The individual with TBI is requested to add numbers mentally that are presented in a particular sequence (Gronwall, 1977). Another commonly used tool is the Galveston Orientation and Amnesia Test (GOAT), which evaluates the major spheres of orientation in the form of a 10-item questionnaire (Adamovich et al, 1985). The GOAT has been standardized on young adults who have recovered from a mild closed head injury (Levin et al, 1982).

In reference to intellectual capacity, the Wechsler Adult Intelligence Scale (WAIS) is used frequently (Lezak, 1983; Mandleberg, 1976; Trombly, 1989). The WAIS was first published in the United States in 1955 and consists of 11 subtests, which are divided into verbal and performance components. The performance subtests can be used to test perceptual skills. These subtests are digit symbol, picture completion, block design, picture arrangement, and object assembly (Lezak, 1983). The WAIS takes from 75 minutes to 2 hours to administer by a neuropsychologist, although parts of this test sometimes are used by rehabilitation specialists (Trombly, 1989). Another general intelligence test is the Wide Range Achievement Test, which evaluates achievement in spelling, reading, and arithmetic.

A number of activities of daily living (ADL) assessments are used in the clinics, with several being mentioned in the literature. The Barthel Index evaluates functional status in 10 self-care categories (Mahoney and Barthel, 1965). A total of 100 points on this inventory would indicate a person independent in all ADL. The Klein-Bell ADL Scale, Katz Index, and Kenny Self-Care Evaluation commonly are used in the clinic (Donaldson et al, 1973). Donaldson and associates (1973) compared the Kenny Self-Care Evaluation, Barthel Index, and Katz Index with the Donaldson ADL Evaluation Form. The authors of this evaluation form maintain that this form is objective and a good source of data for communication among health professionals. The Arnadottir OT-ADL Neurobehavioral Evaluation (A-ONE) has been found to be a reliable and valid instrument for detecting perceptual disorders in individuals over 16 years of age with central nervous system dysfunction. This new evaluation enables the rehabilitation specialist to simultaneously detect multiple deficits while observing ADL performance (Arnadottir, 1990).

In predicting vocational and social adjustment, the Katz Adjustment Scale has been used. This particular scale is based on a questionnaire that is completed by the patient's friend or relative and provides ratings of personal and social functions (Katz and Lyerly, 1963). The McCarron-Dial System is used to describe the impact of disability on personal, social, and vocational outcomes. It consists of three neuropsychological factors: verbal-spatial-cognitive, sensory-motor, and emotional-coping (Dial et al, 1990). The components of this assessment have been validated separately as a neuropsychological assessment but not as a battery per se.

THE CONSTRUCT OF PERCEPTION

Adamovich and associates (1985) state that perception is the integration and interpretation of information received from the sense organs that is based on an internal representation (ie, classification abilities) of the stimulus. The integration of the senses with the mental processes is an ongoing experience (Zoltan, 1990). Abreu and Toglia (1987) suggest that perception is a subjective way in which a person judges the external environment.

In order to have a perceptual deficit, the primary senses must be intact or else other deficits (eg, motor and conceptual) are involved. For example, if a person has difficulty with visual acuity, diplopia, or oculomotor skills, this may indicate a visual, not a perceptual, deficit. Craniofacial trauma may affect visual acuity and, by itself, would not imply a perceptual deficit. Perceptual deficits rarely are observed in isolation, which makes identification of particular problems challenging (Zoltan, 1990). It is no wonder that research in this area has been relatively neglected.

Perceptual skills often are difficult to separate from conceptual skills, which typically include awareness, judgment, memory, attention, and problem-solving. Conceptual dysfunction ". . . is exemplified by difficulty in processing information regardless of the sensory modality" (Abreu and Toglia, 1987). For example, a person with unilateral neglect also may have a short attention span and memory loss, demonstrating combined perceptual and conceptual deficits. Many rehabilitation specialists use a cognitive rehabilitation approach when working with individuals with perceptual deficits. Cognitive rehabilitation is defined as ". . . the reattainment of the mental abilities required to successfully and accurately receive sensory input, process information and act in a manner as independently and appropriately as is possible, given physiological limitations, following insult to, and compromise of, the brain and its functions" (Bracy, 1986a).

Before visual-perceptual tests are conducted, it is suggested that an eye chart or observation be used to determine visual acuity and peripheral vision (Bouska and Kwatny, 1983; Zoltan et al, 1986). On an informal basis, the patient's posture and movements can be observed, such as crossing the midline and the ability to track a particular object in space (Wahlstrom, 1983). For an individual with severe deficits, a visual acuity chart may be so overwhelming that only one visual stimulus at a time should be presented. A checklist of symptoms of visual system dysfunction developed by Gianutsos and Ramsey (1988) is a helpful resource for the rehabilitation specialist. Hosale and Taguchi (1990) specify additional criteria to be satisfied before a perceptual evaluation is conducted. They suggest that the patient be able to clearly understand instructions, verbalize answers, or reliably use an upper extremity with which to communicate and attend to tasks for at least 1 minute.

SPECIFIC PERCEPTUAL ASSESSMENT

Visual-Perceptual Dysfunction

Perhaps the most widely researched area in perception is visual perception. Visual deficits are the most disabling and, therefore, it is essential to identify the particular problems involved. The classification that I use attempts to simplify and organize commonly available perceptual tests. The following tests were mentioned on several occasions in the literature on brain injury. It is important to note that several of these tests evaluate more than one perceptual area. There is also inconsistency in the literature regarding classification of these tests.

Visuospatial Disorders

Visuospatial disorders consist of impairment of the following: figure-ground, form constancy, position in space, spatial relationships, directionality, and topographical orientation. For example, individuals with these deficits have difficulty finding specific objects in a full dresser drawer and in maneuvering a wheelchair down the hall. Visuospatial disorders may affect an individual's judgment regarding safety.

Figure-ground impairment involves the inability to differentiate foreground from background. A widely used test for this impairment is the Ayres Figure-Ground Test (Ayres, 1963; Harlowe and Van Deusen, 1984; Lezak, 1983; Petersen and Wikoff, 1983; Zoltan et al, 1986). Though this test was originally standardized on children, it has been found to be challenging and appropriate for adults (Lezak, 1983). Other figure-ground evaluations include an Overlapping Figures Test by Poppelreuter (Lezak, 1983) and the Hidden Figures Test developed by Gottschaldt (Teuber and Weinstein, 1956).

Form constancy impairment is the inability to recognize subtle variations in form. One method used in the clinic is having the TBI patient match particular shapes on a formboard (Zoltan et al, 1986). The Frostig Form Constancy Test (Frostig, 1964) (which is standardized on children) has been used with TBI adults, but more research is needed on this test in order to justify its use with this particular population (Mitchan, 1982; Zoltan et al, 1986).

A position in space impairment refers to an inability to relate to concepts such as up, down, over, and under in conjunction with objects. It is informally tested by asking the individual to point to a dish on the top shelf, the chair behind the desk, and so forth or by using picture cards and requesting relationships between illustrated objects.

A spatial relationship impairment is the inability to differentiate self from objects in space as well as relate objects in space to each other. There are several standardized tests involving spatial relationships. The Hooper Visual Organization Test (Hooper, 1958) is a set of 30 pictures consisting of common objects that are illustrated in two or more pieces that are easily recognized by the normal individual. The patient is to identify what the object is by naming it out loud or writing it in a test booklet. Normative data are available for individuals from 13 to 69 years of age. A variation of this idea is Gollin figures, which are incomplete drawings that the patient is to complete by drawing in the missing parts (Gollin, 1960). The Motor-Free Visual Perceptual Test has been extensively used with children as well as brain-injured adults (Bouska and Kwatny 1983; Colarusso and Hammill, 1972). An object on top of the page is to be matched with one of four other options presented underneath. The Motor-Free Visual Perceptual Test has been used to detect evidence of unilateral neglect. It is timed with the adult population but not with children. The block design subtest of the WAIS evaluates the ability to manipulate blocks so that they duplicate those on a displayed card (Brooks et al, 1980; Lezak, 1983). The Kohs Block Design Test is similar to the WAIS subtest but should be used only with the very intelligent patient with mild deficits (Lezak, 1983).

Directionality and topographical orientation are evaluated on a more informal basis. A road map can be used to ascertain sense of direction by asking the patient to plan a driving trip from Miami, Florida to Dallas, Texas. For topographical orientation, request the patient to find the route from a hospital room to the cafeteria or the therapy department. Observe the patient while climbing stairs or encountering barriers by setting up an obstacle course in order to evaluate distance and depth perception as well (Zoltan et al, 1986).

Visual Agnosia Disorders

Agnosia is an impairment in recognition. Individuals with visual agnosia have normal visual acuity but cannot identify objects using their eyes. However, they can identify objects by touch when vision is occluded (Gregory and Aitkin, 1971). Color agnosia is the inability to identify colors on command. Perhaps the most frustrating agnosia is facial agnosia, for example, when a person with TBI cannot recognize a friend.

Object recognition is suggested by Zoltan and associates (1986) as a nonstandardized visual agnosia evaluation procedure. Several common objects named by the rehabilitation specialist are handed one at a time to the patient, and he or she is instructed to demonstrate or explain their function. Patients also can attempt to name common objects or point to the appropriate object that has been previously identified. The response is recorded as being intact or impaired (Toglia, 1989).

Color agnosia can be evaluated with the Ishihara (1964) or Dvorine (1953) color plates. These tests also identify individuals who have the two most common types of color blindness (Lezak, 1983). The Color Perception Battery developed by DeRenzi and Spinnler (1967) includes color naming and drawing, pointing to colors, color memory, and the Ishihara plates. In a study performed by DeRenzi and Spinnler (1967), individuals with right hemisphere lesions had a great deal of difficulty with purely perceptual tasks.

Facial agnosia is an impairment in recognizing familiar faces (also known as prosopagnosia) and discriminating differences in unfamiliar faces. The Test of Facial Recognition requires the matching of faces under different circumstances, such as when side views and different lighting conditions are employed (Benton and Van Allen, 1968). Mooney's Closure Faces Test is another test that evaluates one's ability to identify faces of both genders, young and old, and when obscured by exaggerated shadows (Mooney, 1957). In the area of facial discrimination, it has been demonstrated that individuals with right hemisphere lesions perform inferiorly to those with left hemisphere lesions (Levin et al, 1977).

Visuoconstructive Disorders

Visuoconstructive impairment refers to defective assembling and graphomotor performance. The tests included in this category are drawing and 2- and 3-dimension constructional tasks. In reference to constructional tasks, Lezak (1983) stated that individuals with right hemisphere damage typically show a fragmented response, whereas those with left brain damage are able to demonstrate correct overall construction skills but omit important details. Individuals with a visuoconstructive disorder often have difficulty dressing themselves.

The Graham-Kendall Memory for Designs Test consists of 15

geometric designs that are rated simple to complex (Graham and Kendall, 1951). The patient is shown a shape for 5 seconds and then requested to reproduce it on paper. Another test involving drawing of designs is the Rey Complex Figure Test, which requires immediate and delayed recall of complex asymmetrical designs (Brooks et al, 1980). The Bender-Gestalt Test involves copying 9 geometric patterns. Scoring depends on the quality of the figures reproduced and their relationship to one another (Lezak, 1983). Other graphomotor tasks include the Draw-A-Person test (Harris, 1963). Having the patient draw a house, a clock, and a flower commonly is used to test for visuoconstructive disorders, but different criteria are used to judge performance.

An example of a 2-dimensional test is the Stick Test (Lezak, 1983). While sitting next to the patient, the rehabilitation specialist creates a design with four standard-sized sticks and requests him or her to recreate the design as accurately as possible underneath. After the 10 designs are completed, the specialist moves across the table and requests the patient to copy the design from the specialist's point of view (a reversal effect). An example of a 3-dimensional test is block construction, which is the substance of Benton's Three-Dimension Constructional Praxis Test. Patients are instructed to stack blocks into certain patterns of specified groups of 6, 8, and then 15 blocks (Benton and Fogel, 1962). Additional nonstandardized constructional tasks used in the clinic include building structures with erector sets, Legos, and Tinker Toys (Cicerone and Wood, 1987; Lezak, 1983; Neistadt, 1988). Zoltan (1990) stated that there is a strong correlation between stick and block designs; therefore, performing these two types of tests may mean unnecessary duplication.

Somesthetic and Auditory Agnosias

Visual-perceptual dysfunction predominates in the literature, but there are other perceptual disorders as well. Somesthetic and auditory dysfunction may occur after TBI. These usually are expressed in the form of a perceptual agnosia.

Somesthetic dysfunction includes tactile agnosia and finger agnosia. Tactile agnosia (otherwise known as astereognosis) is the inability to recognize objects even though sensation is intact. Tactile agnosia can be evaluated with the Ayres Manual Form Perception subtest of the Southern California Sensory Integration Test (SCSIT) (Zoltan et al, 1986) and the Tactual Performance Test (part of the Halstead-Reitan Neuropsychological Battery). Nonstandardized tests for tactile agnosia include the identification of common objects, geometric forms, and different textures (Zoltan et al, 1986). Finger agnosia is evaluated by having the patient place his or her hands palms down on a table. A hand chart illustrating and naming all the fingers is placed in front of the individual so that all fingers are pointed in the same direction. The therapist touches the patient on one finger and then asks for identification of that finger on the chart. This can be performed with vision occluded or not. Additional tests include identifying the finger in question by name and imitating different finger movements performed by the specialist (Zoltan et al, 1986).

Auditory agnosia is the inability to identify differences in sounds even though hearing is intact. This type of agnosia can be evaluated with two tests of the Halstead-Reitan Neuropsychological Battery—the Seashore Rhythm and Speech Sounds Perception Test. Speech pathologists frequently are involved in the rehabilitation of individuals with auditory agnosia.

BATTERIES TO ASSESS THE TBI PATIENT

Test batteries are comprehensive evaluation tools that are used by the experienced evaluator. Two batteries that have been extensively used with the TBI population are the Halstead-Reitan and Luria-Nebraska Neuropsychological Batteries. Other batteries that test perceptual and cognitive dysfunction are the SCSIT, the Michigan Neuropsychological Test Battery, and the Loewenstein Occupational Therapy Cognitive Assessment Battery for Brain-Injured Patients.

The Halstead-Reitan Neuropsychological Battery is widely used with alert TBI patients and takes from 6 to 8 hours to fully administer (Macciocchi, 1988; Reitan and Wolfson, 1988). This battery was "designed to measure the full range of human neuropsychological abilities" (Reitan and Wolfson, 1988). Subtests of this battery include tactile, auditory and aphasia screening, visuospatial, grip strength, memory, and abstract thinking assessments. There are several versions of this test available. The Luria-Nebraska Neuropsychological Battery takes about 2½ hours to administer and was designed for subjects 15-years-old and older. According to Toglia and Golisz (1989), advantages of the Luria-Nebraska Neuropsychological Battery are that it is easily transportable and inexpensive. Its disadvantages are that it may not detect mild brain dysfunction and it does not evaluate ADL. The Michigan Neuropsychological Test Battery consists of several visual perception coordination tests (eg, Purdue Pegboard Test and Symbol

Digit Modalities subtest) and intelligence tests such as the WAIS (Smith, 1981). This test battery takes about 3 hours to administer.

The Loewenstein Occupational Therapy Cognitive Assessment for Brain-Injured Patients was designed for occupational therapists who work with the TBI population. This test evaluates 4 main areas: (1) orientation, (2) perception, (3) visuomotor organization, and (4) thinking operations (Katz et al, 1989).

The SCSIT originally was developed by Ayres (1976) to evaluate children, although it is mentioned frequently in the adult TBI literature. Subtests of this battery often are used for evaluation purposes. It is suggested in the Ayres (1976) manual that therapists have a good knowledge of statistics, science, and test measurement; an understanding of sensory integrative dysfunction; and a thorough acquaintance with the manual before administering any of the subtests of the SCSIT.

As with the WAIS, the Halstead-Reitan, Luria-Nebraska, and Michigan Neuropsychological Test Batteries predominantly are administered by neuropsychologists. The SCSIT should be administered only by specially trained therapists who have a great deal of experience with this particular type of testing. Lezak (1983) recommends that a battery be suitable (appropriate for the patient's needs), practicable (portable, inexpensive, easy to administer), and useful (allows the therapist to obtain the information that is desired). In her all-encompassing book on neuropsychological assessment, Lezak (1983) stated that it is indeed difficult for a test battery to satisfy all of the aforementioned criteria.

TREATMENT

Rehabilitation Programs Incorporating Perceptual Training

A variety of programs incorporating perceptual training were described in the literature. Programs offering perceptual training typically use ADL, computer activities, work tasks, academic remediation skills, and group exercises. The following examples represent typical programs located in different regions of the United States.

A specialized Head Injury Program in the eastern part of the United States uses computer tasks (Apple IIe) and Valpar work samples (vocational tasks such as mechanical and electronic assembly, clerical tasks, and so forth) with its inpatient population (Jacisin and VanKirk, 1989). An outpatient program in the western part of the United States emphasizes individual and small group instruction in basic academics, self-care, social skill development, and homemaking (Cole et al, 1985). A northeastern medical center has designed a program specifically for individuals with visuospatial deficits. Proponents of this program believe that providing high levels of cognitive stimulation will maintain and perhaps improve perception (Gordon et al, 1985). Three major components constitute this program: (1) cognitive remediation, which includes eye-hand and perceptual-cognitive integration tasks; (2) group approach exercises; and (3) community activities (Ben-Yishay and Diller, 1981).

A midwestern work-study program provides jobs for hospital inpatients so that they have the opportunity to perform work tasks in a safe clinical setting. A transitional living area for 6 TBI residents allows them to live on their own but have access to professional help 24 hours a day (Bonfiglio and Yosko, 1987). A comparable transitional living arrangement in the southwest uses 4 residential facilities to normalize the rehabilitation experience. The facilities are a camp, a ranch, a nursery, and a townhouse. After undergoing rehabilitation, some residents stay and work at a particular site, acting as role models for other patients (Seaton, 1985).

A large number of facilities use microcomputers in perceptual training. Games as well as educational and perceptual programs commonly are found in the clinics (Anderson and Parente, 1985; Ojakangas, 1984; Polkow and Volpe, 1985; Skinner and Trachtman, 1985; Voorhees, 1985). At one particular center in the midwest, the patient is required to have a computer at home before cognitive rehabilitation is initiated. Patients are expected to spend the day in a multidisciplinary program and then to work on computer lessons at home for approximately 3 hours (Bracy, 1986b).

Restorative Strategies

It has been documented that substantial savings per person can be obtained, because greater gains will result when an individual is admitted early to a head injury program (Adamovich et al, 1985; Cope and Hall, 1982; Vogenthaler, 1987). Early intervention is deemed essential in order to promote better recovery (Dougherty and Radomski, 1987; Gloag, 1985; Lezak, 1983; Trombly, 1989). A variety of techniques are used to assist TBI individuals in their recuperation. Some basic strategies are discussed in this section that pertain to improving perceptual abilities as well as other deficit areas.

During the early phases of recuperation, the patient should be evaluated and treated in a calm, structured environment where there is minimal background noise and visual stimulation (Conboy et al, 1986). The judicious use of positive reinforcement is important during every session, whether of a social (attention and praise) or tangible (cookies, tokens, privileges) nature (Gloag, 1985). Dougherty and Radomski (1987) emphasize repetition and overlearning (continuing to study and practice after demonstrating proficiency) as being important in working with the TBI population. They also believe in supportive confrontation, when necessary. Gummow and associates (1983) agree that treatment should be frequent, repetitive, and short in duration.

Signs of fatigue and stress need to be monitored for the patient to demonstrate the best possible effort (Hopkins and Smith, 1988). The patient's body alignment and positioning may influence the learning situation, because a change in positioning can cause a possible breakdown in processing. The brain-injured person often has difficulty in processing and organizing information, even when correctly positioned. Therefore, proper body alignment is another important factor to include when structuring a conducive atmosphere for learning (Abreu and Toglia, 1987).

While performing activities, a crucial part of treatment is teaching the patient to control and monitor performance. This involves learning how to detect and correct errors as well as use feedback effectively. The patient should be aware of deficit areas and understand the goals of the program (Gummow et al, 1983). In order for the patient to be successful, he or she must be motivated. Family members often are involved in motivating the TBI individual. However, motivation depends on premorbid personality as well as the general nature of the injury (Gummow et al, 1983). In a study conducted by Haas and associates (1985), 31% to 50% of TBI patients who were sampled had poor academic histories. This may alter the course of therapy, and these authors suggest that more emphasis should be placed on prevention programs while students are attending high school. Meaningful and familiar tasks also assist in motivating the patient during treatment (Burke et al, 1988; Lundgren and Persechino, 1986; Simon, 1988).

Panikoff (1983) proposes that recovery from a traumatic brain injury follow a sequence from basic survival skills to more complex, nonrepetitive tasks, and finally, to interactive skills. Treatment modalities such as computer activities, gross motor tasks, group activities, games, crafts, work simulation, and ADL are used at various stages in the patient's recovery. In teaching ADL to the TBI population, Giles (1989) has found success in using frequent repetition of a sequence of actions; verbal cuing, when necessary; and emphasizing the patient's achievement.

Various components of tasks can be modified and manipulated

by the specialist, such as the rate of speed at which an activity is performed, the amount of information presented, the duration of the activity, the particular sensory modality used, and the complexity of the task (Barth and Boll, 1981). Situational strategies also may be taught in order for patients to get the most out of their treatment. These strategies include: planning ahead, choosing a starting point, searching for more information before beginning an activity, and scanning from left to right.

Occupational trials and actual work situations have been used effectively with the TBI population. Ben-Yishay and associates (1987) recommend certain job tasks for the TBI patient only after intensive and systematic remedial intervention. These authors have found work to be beneficial in the rehabilitation of the brain-injured person. Gordon and associates (1985) have noted that the patients whose faculties of perception improve the most are the ones who engage in stimulating activities such as work tasks.

The individual with TBI views driving as an important activity. Driving often is beyond the scope of many patients, because it incorporates a high level of both perceptual and conceptual components. Sivak and colleagues (1984) designed a driving program for brain-injured people that focused on visual scanning, directed eye movements, spatial perception and discrimination, figure-ground, visual imagery, attentional capacity, and general problem-solving abilities. Paper and pencil activities such as trailmaking (sequentially connecting letters in the alphabet) and cancellation tasks (crossing out a particular letter in a series of letters) were used to improve perceptual skills as a part of this program. Sivak and colleagues (1984) made the following conclusions regarding their driving program: (1) Driving performance is affected by residual perceptual capabilities; (2) Perceptual skills can be improved by using paper and pencil activities; (3) Training results in improved driving; and (4) Driving performance following perceptual training is related to the degree of improvement of perceptual skills.

Rosamond Gianutsos, who has often been called a computer pioneer in rehabilitation (Frangicetto, 1988), has devised a computerized driving evaluation program entitled the Driving Advisement System. In addition, she has created COGREHAB, a series of computerized programming for the TBI patient. Gianutsos, a well-known author of articles on brain injury, stated that part of rehabilitation is "shifting the responsibility for recovery back to the individual, in part as a therapeutic strategy and also to show them a lot of respect for what they're contending with" (Frangicetto, 1988). Ruff and associates (1989) concur with Gianutsos regarding personal responsibility for improvement and add that TBI individuals should obtain feedback from others concerning their goals and progress. The ability to profit from this feedback is crucial to the rehabilitation process.

Use of the Computer with the TBI Patient

There are many advantages in working with computers. Besides perception, other cognitive functions, such as attention, memory, reaction time, judgment, problem-solving, and language, can be addressed with the variety of software and hardware that is on the market. Lynch (1989b) suggests that computers be leased as an option, because systems can be costly.

Computers are used to improve attention and concentration by providing interesting and motivating material. Lessons can be repeated until the individual feels confident of subject mastery. Owing to its unbiased presentation as well as its immediate and consistent feedback, the computer objectively confronts the patient's denial of his or her deficits (Namerow, 1987). Bracy and associates (1985) stated that there is high public acceptance of this technology, which is currently popular, flexible, and available. Johnson and Garvie (1985) believe that the computer is an "ideal therapist." They have witnessed restless patients working quietly on the computer for long periods of time. They suggest that a keyboard guard would assist the clumsy or tremulous patient and emphasize that the auto-repeat mechanism should be removed. Other simple modifications include obtaining a joystick, light pen, or touch screen for easier access to the computer.

There are also disadvantages with this particular type of treatment. The patient interacts with no one socially and engages in no verbal communication. Many programs are of an aggressive nature (eg, exploding spaceships, frogs run over by trucks) (Zoltan et al, 1986). There is limited generalization from computer programs to real life situations. Though the patient interacts with the computer, the therapist should be available to ensure that the program level is challenging. The computer is not a substitute for a friend, therapist, or family member (Reeder, 1984). Once these disadvantages are weighed and considered, it appears that when the computer is correctly used, it has a great deal to offer. Many rehabilitation specialists working in head injury programs testify to the computer's beneficial aspects (Bracy et al, 1985; Jacisin and VanKirk, 1989; Kerner and Acker, 1985; Kreutzer and Morrison, 1986; Lynch, 1983; Polkow and Volpe, 1985; Voorhees, 1985).

The therapeutic use of computers has been advocated since the late 1970s, when games such as Pong, Breakout, and Enduro were in vogue (Reeder, 1984). Several neuropsychologists have been extremely interested in promoting the computer and have developed specific software for the TBI population. Popular programs that are geared for improving perceptual skills such as figure-ground, directionality and spatial relationships are Captain's Log, First Mate, Foundations, MasterType, Visuospatial, Facemaker, and Ribbit (a slower version of Frogger). There are hundreds of programs available, and it is probably wise to review any program that you intend to purchase. The Apple IIe computer frequently is mentioned in the literature and is used in the clinic primarily because of the ample selection of Apple software (Bracy et al, 1985; Kerner and Acker, 1985; Kreutzer and Morrison, 1986).

Although the computer often is used in the rehabilitation of the TBI individual, evidence of the benefit of computer-assisted programming is inconclusive (Lynch, 1989a; Frangicetto, 1988). It is apparent that more research needs to be conducted. Lynch (1989a) stresses the need for more carefully controlled studies and lists the following as possible research topics: (1) the ideal time to initiate computer-assisted treatment, (2) the ideal length and distribution of sessions, (3) the method of determining when to terminate computer-assisted treatment, and (4) the types of software and hardware that are pertinent for various neurological conditions. Lynch (1989b) mentioned that when selecting computer-assisted technology, the specialist should carefully consider the amount of the deficit (should be rather large to warrant computer intervention), alternatives to computer treatment (eg, paper and pencil tasks, activities), and the effectiveness of visual-perceptual training (which is wholly dependent on the hardware and software used).

Although research on video games is limited, this type of programming has been found to be therapeutic when used 3 to 5 times per week with the brain-injured individual. Those who appear to benefit most from computer-assisted therapy are highly motivated and have good family involvement (Purdy and Neri, 1989). A study by Dorval and Pepin (1986) demonstrated that there were significant improvements in spatial relationships of normal adults after 8 sessions of playing Zaxxon (a video game that focuses on the visualization of spatial relationships and simulates 3-dimensionality). Before any definitive conclusions can be made about the proven effectiveness of video games, more controlled studies with the brain-injured population are in order.

Supplemental Materials on TBI

The American Occupational Therapy Association (AOTA, 1989) practice division has published material on treating TBI that recommends the following Apple software: The Brunswick Hospital Center Cognitive Assessment and Training Programs, rehabilitative software for young adults with head injuries, and visual perceptual diagnosis testing and training programs. For more information on computers, the AOTA (1985) practice division also has published material that can be easily obtained by AOTA members.

Kreutzer and Morrison (1986) have reviewed dozens of Apple programs and have summarized them individually in chart form. Perceptual components such as visual scanning, eye-hand coordination, and sensory discrimination are mentioned frequently in the charts. Cognitive components, such as reaction time, attention, and concentration, also are listed in the Apple program review article. This is an excellent resource for any rehabilitation specialist interested in computer application. For a selection of a variety of additional perceptual and cognitive programs, Lynch (1983, 1986) also has reviewed microcomputer games and commercial software.

Carter and associates (1980) have published a workbook that can assist individuals in focusing attention and improving memory, gross and fine visual discrimination, and verbal learning and time judgment. Pretests and posttests suggested in the book help the patient monitor progress.

New Medico, a chain of head-injury programs located primarily in the eastern and midwestern United States, has many informative brochures and case studies that can be easily obtained (phone number: 1-800-CARE-TBI).

The National Head Injury Foundation (508-485-9950) prints a *"Catalogue of Educational Material,"* which lists a host of pertinent articles on computer topics as well as other areas of interest. Videotapes and audio cassettes are also listed and are available for purchase. The Family Helpline number is 1-800-444-NHIF.

Some companies will send demonstration disks of computer software to promote their products (eg, Brain Train, 804-794-4841 or 1-800-633-1221, which offers both Apple and IBM programs).

CASE REPORT

F.R., a 17-year-old male, sustained a closed head injury with intracerebral hemorrhage as a result of a motorcycle accident. After being hospitalized for 6 weeks, he was transferred to a specialized head injury rehabilitation program, where he resided for 6 months. F.R. then was referred to an outpatient work-hardening program for 3-times-weekly sessions of occupational and physical therapy.

Medical History

F.R. had no medical problems prior to his motorcycle accident. He is now status postsubdural hematoma, status posttracheostomy, status postlaparotomy with repair, and status postgastrostomy. He has a leg-length difference resulting from a comminuted fracture of his right tibia and fibula and ambulates with a slow, antalgic gait (has a ¾-inch heel lift). F.R. demonstrates right-sided weakness with increased tone of the right dominant hand. According to his medical records, this young man has decreased short-term memory as well as perceptual deficits as a result of the motorcycle accident.

Social History

F.R. lived at home with his mother and two sisters prior to the accident. Reportedly, he dropped out of high school in ninth grade with below-average grades. Interests include listening to music, working on motorcycles, and engaging in a variety of outdoor team sports.

Work History

For the past year before the accident, F.R. was a foreman in a construction company and supervised six men. He had previously worked as a short-order cook in his hometown.

Occupational Therapy Evaluation

F.R. stated that he was able to feed, dress, and bathe himself with the use of adaptive equipment at the hospital and home (grab bars, shower stool). He does not balance a checking account, shop at a grocery store, or drive. These activities may be explored in time. Vision was tested with the Snellen Eye Chart and found to be 20/20, when using both eyes. However, peripheral vision was impaired. Hearing appeared normal and sensation was intact. In performing fine motor activities such as the Crawford Small Parts Dexterity Test, F.R. placed in the lowest percentile owing to incoordination. He also placed in the lowest percentile on the Bennett Hand Tool Dexterity Test, which measures one's ability to manipulate small hand tools. Grasp strength using the Jamar dynamometer revealed a 40# grasp on the right and 80# on the left.

When perceptual abilities were evaluated, it was found that F.R incorrectly matched 4 out of 8 shapes on a geometric form-board. F.R. performed well on the Hooper Visual Organization Test. A 3-dimension constructional task was attempted, but the patient needed a great deal of cuing in order to even start this task. F.R. was unable to construct a 6-piece wood block design, the simplest of three standard designs. He had no difficulty in identifying common objects. He demonstrated difficulty in differentiating his right side from his left. F.R. was able to follow instructions adequately but, at times, needed them repeated. Short-term memory deficits were apparent. During the testing session, F.R. requested to use the bathroom. He did not understand the directions to the facility and asked to be escorted.

The dominant right upper extremity was weak (generally, fair grade muscles) compared with the left. F.R. demonstrated hesitancy in fully extending the fingers of his right hand after sustaining a flexed position. He had to concentrate in order to use his hand. The right lower extremity had good strength but decreased range of motion of the ankle region. The left upper and lower extremities functioned well and showed normal range of motion and strength. F.R. was able to ambulate and stand for 20 minutes before complaining of fatigue.

Occupational Therapy Objectives

1. The patient will demonstrate increased motor control and strength of the right upper extremity.
2. The patient will demonstrate increased standing and walking tolerance.
3. The patient will develop and maintain good worker habits.
4. The patient will engage in simulated work tasks and explore vocational options.
5. The patient will be independent in all self-care activities.
6. The patient will improve in visual-perceptual areas.
7. The patient will improve his basic math and communication skills.

(Note: Objectives 1 through 4 are outside the scope of this text.)

Occupational Therapy Intervention

Before the beginning of every session, F.R. was requested to name all the staff members at the outpatient facility and tell of his experiences that morning. In order to help his memory, many times during the day, he was asked to recall different tasks he had previously performed. He had been instructed at the previous rehabilitation facility to carry a small notebook with him and write down important dates and events. He was to refer to this notebook daily. Initially, he was met at the front door and escorted to the therapy department or else his mother walked him to the door. After several weeks, he was able to find the department himself by taking the same route each time.

F.R. worked on the Baltimore Therapeutic Equipment (BTE) work simulator and was able, eventually, to start himself on the machine as well as record results. This involved a fixed sequence of events that F.R. mastered quickly. He engaged in a variety of activities to increase range of motion and strength. When engaging in unfamiliar activities, the patient would be asked to repeat the instructions to ensure his understanding of the activity.

Perceptual activities included the following: copying the pattern of a design card onto a pegboard, progressing from simple to complex designs; matching shapes onto a formboard; constructing 3-dimensional block designs; and working on a string art project that F.R. had been given during his lengthy hospitalization. Because F.R. was familiar with building tasks, he was asked to assemble a small wood project. Using scrap pieces of wood, F.R. designed a birdhouse. This project involved selecting similar sizes and types of wood and nailing the pieces together. After F.R. felt competent hammering nails, he enjoyed this activity. This also was good preparation for his string art project, which consisted of planning, multiple-step instructions, and then applying the string onto the form. A variety of computer games were used that the patient especially enjoyed. Apple software was used at least once a week to improve his reaction time, visual scanning, memory, discrimination, and ability to visualize spatial relationships. A percentage of correct answers for each test was recorded.

Other activities involving reading, writing, and math skills were performed. A daily log of activities or a letter to a relative was typed. The patient also worked on basic math skills and employed a calculator to check his work. When asked how he thought he performed on these tasks, he stated frequently that all his answers were correct. This was never the case, and it was pointed out to him that he did make errors, which he was asked to correct. He was able to correct his answers on most of his second attempts.

After 3 months of therapy, patient showed vast improvement in his ability to match shapes (8 out of 8 correct), construct 3-dimensional structures (6-, 8-, and 15-block designs as well as an original birdhouse), and master various perceptual programs presented on the computer. He was able to successfully complete a string art project, which he gave to his mother as a gift. He was hired by his uncle to perform clean-up tasks at construction sites several weeks after being discharged from outpatient therapy.

References

Abreu BC, Toglia JP: Cognitive rehabilitation: a model for occupational therapy. Am J Occup Ther 41(7):439–448, 1987.

Adamovich BB, Henderson JA, Auerbach S: Cognitive Rehabilitation of Closed Head Injured Patients. Boston, Little, Brown & Co, 1985.

Anderson J, Parente F: Training family members to work with the head injured patient. Cognitive Rehabil 3(4):12–15, 1985.

American Occupational Therapy Association Practice Division: Traumatic Brain Injury: Information Packet. Rockville, Maryland, 1989.

American Occupational Therapy Association Practice Division: Computers Information Packet. Rockville, Maryland, 1985.

Arnadottir G: The Brain and Behavior Assessing Cortical Dysfunction Through Activities of Daily Living (ADL). St Louis, CV Mosby Co, 1990.

Ayres AJ: The development of perceptual-motor abilities: a theoretical basis for treatment of dysfunction. Am J Occup Ther 17:221–225, 1963.

Ayres AJ: Interpreting The Southern California Sensory Integration Tests. Los Angeles, Western Psychological Services, 1976.

Barth J, Boll T: Rehabilitation and treatment of central nervous system dysfunction: A behavioral medicine perspective. In Prokop C, Bradley L (eds): Medical Psychology: Contributions to Behavioral Medicine. New York, Academic Press, 1981.

Benton AL, Fogel ML: Three-dimensional constructional praxis. A clinical test. Arch Neurol 7:347–354, 1962.

Benton AL, Van Allen MW: Impairment in facial recognition in patients with cerebral disease. Cortex 4:344–358, 1968.

Ben-Yishay Y, Diller L: Rehabilitation of cognitive and perceptual defects in people with traumatic brain damage. Int J Rehabil Res 4:208–210, 1981.

Ben-Yishay Y, Silver SM, Piasetsky E, Rattok J: Relationship between employability and vocational outcome after intensive holistic cognitive rehabilitation. J Head Trauma Rehabil 2(1):35–48, 1987.

Bonfiglio RP, Yosko K: The Schwab Head Trauma Phase III Unit: two years of independent living. Cognitive Rehabil 5(3):6–9, 1987.

Bouska MJ, Kwatny E: Manual for Application of the Motor-Free Visual Perception Test to the Adult Population. Philadelphia, Manual, PO Box 12246, 1983.

Bracy OL: Cognitive rehabilitation: a process approach. Cognitive Rehabil 3:10–17, 1986a.

Bracy OL: The NeuroScience Center of Indianapolis. Cognitive Rehabil 4(5):6–15, 1986b.

Bracy OL, Lynch W, Sbordone R, Berrol S: Cognitive retraining through computers: fact or fad? Cognitive Rehabil 3(2):10–23, 1985.

Brooks D, Aughton M, Bond M, Jones P, Rizvi S: Cognitive sequelae in relationship to early indices of severity of brain damage after severe blunt head injury. J Neurol Neurosurg Psychiatry 43:529–534, 1980.

Burke W, Wesolowski M, Zencius A: Long-term programs in head injury rehabilitation. Cognitive Rehabil 6(1):38–41, 1988.

Carter L, Caruso J, Languirand M, Berard MA: The Thinking Skills Workbook: A Cognitive Skills Remediation Manual for Adults. Springfield, Illinois, Charles C Thomas, 1980.

Cicerone KD, Wood JC: Planning disorder after closed head injury: a case study. Arch Phys Med Rehabil 68(2):111–115, 1987.

Colarusso R, Hammill D: Motor-Free Visual Perception Test Manual. Novato, California, Academic Therapy Publications, 1972.

Cole JR, Cope DN, Cervelli L: Rehabilitation of the severely brain-injured patient: a community-based, low-cost model program. Arch Phys Med Rehabil 66(1):38–40, 1985.

Conboy TJ, Barth J, Boll TJ: Treatment and rehabilitation of mild and moderate head trauma. Rehabil Psychology 31(4):203–215, 1986.

Cope DN, Hall K: Head injury rehabilitation: benefit of early intervention. Arch Phys Med Rehabil 63:433–437, 1982.

DeRenzi E, Spinnler H: Impaired performance on color tasks in patients with hemispheric damage. Cortex 3:194–216, 1967.

Dial JG, Chan F, Norton C: Neuropsychological assessment of brain damage: discriminative validity of the McCarron-Dial System. Brain Injury 4(3):239–246, 1990.

Donaldson SW, Wagner CC, Gresham GE: A unified ADL evaluation form. Arch Phys Med Rehabil 54:175–179, 1973.

Dorval M, Pepin M: Effect of playing a video game on a measure of spatial visualization. Percept Mot Skills 62:159–162, 1986.

Dougherty PM, Radomski MV: The Cognitive Rehabilitation Workbook. Maryland, Aspen, 1987.

Dvorine I: Dvorine Pseudo-Isochromatic Plates (2nd ed). Baltimore, Wavery Press, 1953.

Eson ME, Yen JK, Bourke RS: Assessment of recovery from serious head injury. J Neurol Neurosurg Psychiatry 41:1036, 1978.

Frangicetto T: Computer pioneer in rehabilitation: an interview with Dr Rosamond Gianutsos. J Rehabil 54(3):15–19, 1988.

Frostig N: Frostig Visual Perceptual Program. Chicago, Follett Publishing Co, 1964.

Gentilini M, Nichelli P, Schoenhuber R, et al: Neuropsychological evaluation of mild head injuries. J Neurol Neurosurg Psychiatry 48(2):137–140, 1985.

Gianutsos R, Ramsey G: Enabling rehabilitation optometrists to help survivors of acquired brain injury. Vision Rehabil 2(1):37, 1988.

Giles G: A rapid method for teaching severely brain injured adults how to wash and dress. Arch Phys Med Rehabil 70:156–158, 1989.

Gloag D: Rehabilitation after head injury—1: cognitive problems. BMJ 290:834–837, 1985.

Goldstein M: Traumatic brain injury: a silent epidemic. Ann Neurol 27(3):327, 1990.

Gollin ES: Developmental studies of visual recognition of incomplete objects. Percept Mot Skills 11:289–298, 1960.

Gordon WA, Hibbard MR, Egelko S, et al: Perceptual remediation in patients with right brain damage: a comprehensive program. Arch Phys Med Rehabil 66:353–359, 1985.

Gouvier W, Blanton P, LaPorte K, Nepomuceno C: Reliability and validity of the Disability Rating Scale and the Levels of Cognitive Functioning Scale in monitoring recovery from severe head injury. Arch Phys Med Rehabil 68(2):94–97, 1987.

Graham FK, Kendall BS: Memory for Design Test. Revised general manual. Percept Mot Skills. Monograph Supplement #2-VII. New York, Grune & Stratton, 1951.

Gregory ME, Aitkin JA: Assessment of parietal lobe function in hemiplegia. Occup Ther 34:9–17, 1971.

Griffith ER: Types of Disability. In Rosenthal M, Griffith ER, Bond MR, Miller JD (eds): Rehabilitation of the Head Injured Adult. Philadelphia, FA Davis Co, 1983.

Gronwall D: Paced auditory serial addition task: a measure of recovery from concussion. Percept Mot Skills 44:367–373, 1977.

Gummow L, Miller P, Dustman RE: Attention and brain injury: a case for cognitive rehabilitation of attentional disorders. Clinical Psychology Review 3(3):255–274, 1983.

Haas JF, Cope DN, Hall K: Premorbid prevalence of poor academic performance in severe head injury. Arch Phys Med Rehabil 66(8):539, 1985.

Hall K, Cope N, Rappaport M: Glasgow Outcome Scale and Disability Rating Scale: comparative usefulness in following recovery in traumatic head injury. Arch Phys Med Rehabil 66(1):35–37, 1985.

Harlowe D, Van Deusen J: Construct validation of the St Mary's CVA Evaluation: perceptual measures. Am J Occup Ther 38(3):184–186, 1984.

Harris DB: Childrens' Drawings as Measures of Intellectual Maturity. New York, Harcourt Brace, 1963.

Hegen C, Malkmus D, Durham P: Levels of cognitive functioning. Communication Disorders Service, Rancho Los Amigos Hospital, 1972.

Hoff JT, Anderson TE, Cole TM: Mild to Moderate Head Injury. Boston, Blackwell Scientific Publications Inc, 1989.

Hooper HE: The Hooper Visual Organization Test Manual. Los Angeles, Western Psychological Services, 1958.

Hopkins HL, Smith HD: Willard and Spackman's Occupational Therapy (7th ed). Philadelphia, JB Lippincott Co, 1988.

Hosale LD, Taguchi JF: Twenty-one steps to better perception: evaluation and treatment. Presented at AOTA conference in New Orleans, 1990.

Ishihara S: Tests for color blindness (11th ed). Tokyo, Kanehara Shuppan, 1964.

Jacisin RD, VanKirk DS: Head injury: innovations in day treatment. Cognitive Rehabil 7(2):12–14, 1989.

Jane JA, Rimel RW: Prognosis in head injury. Clin Neurosurg 29:346–352, 1981.

Jennett B: Scale and Scope of the Problem. In Rosenthal M, Griffith ER, Bond MR, Miller JD (eds): Rehabilitation of the Head Injured Adult. Philadelphia, FA Davis Co, 1983.

Jennett B, Bond M: Assessment of outcome after severe brain damage—A practical scale. Lancet 1:480–484, 1975.

Jennett B, Teasdale G, Braakman R, Minderhoud J, Knill-Jones R: Predicting outcome in individual patients after severe head injury. Lancet 1:1031–1034, 1976.

Johnson R, Garvie C: The BBC microcomputer for therapy of intellectual impairment following acquired brain damage. Br J Occup Ther 48(2): 46–48, 1985.

Katz MM, Lyerly SB: Methods for measuring adjustment and social behavior in the community: I. Rationale, description, discriminative validity and scale development. Psychol Rep 13:503–535, 1963.

Katz N, Itzkovich M, Averbuch S, Elazar B: Loewenstein Occupational Therapy Cognitive Assessment (LOTCA) Battery for brain-injured patients: reliability and validity. Am J Occup Ther 43(3):184–192, 1989.

Kerner M, Acker M: Computer delivery of memory retraining with head injured patients. Cognitive Rehabil 3(6):26–31, 1985.

Kreutzer J, Morrison C: A guide to cognitive rehabilitation software for the Apple IIe/IIc computer. Cognitive Rehabil 4(1):6–17, 1986.

Levin HS, Benton AL, Grossman RG: Neurobehavioral Consequences of Closed Head Injury. New York, Oxford Press, 1982.

Levin HS, Grossman RG, Kelly PJ: Impairment of facial recognition after closed head injuries of varying severity. Cortex 13:119–130, 1977.

Lezak MD: Neuropsychological Assessment. New York, Oxford Press, 1983.

Lundgren CC, Persechino EL: Cognitive group: a treatment program for head injured adults. Am J Occup Ther 40(6):397–401, 1986.

Lynch W: Cognitive retraining using microcomputer games and commercially available software. Cognitive Rehabil 1(1):19–22, 1983.

Lynch W: An update on software in cognitive rehabilitation. Cognitive Rehabil 4(3):14–18, 1986.

Lynch W: Ethics in computer-assisted cognitive retraining. J Head Trauma Rehabil 4(1):91–93, 1989a.

Lynch W: Computer-assisted visual-perceptual training. J Head Trauma Rehabil 4(2):75–77, 1989b.

Macciocchi SN: Neuropsychological assessment following head trauma using the Halstead-Reitan Neuropsychological Test Battery. J Head Trauma Rehabil 3(1):1–11, 1988.

Mahoney FI, Barthel DW: Functional evaluation: the Barthel Index. Md S Med J 44:61–65, 1965.

Mandleberg IA: Cognitive recovery after severe head injury: WAIS-A verbal and performance IQs as a function of post traumatic amnesia and time from injury. J Neurol Neurosurg Psychiatry 39:1001–1007, 1976.

Mitchan M: Visual perception and its relationship to an activity of daily living. Occup Ther J Res 2:245–246, 1982.

Mooney CM: Closure as affected by configural clarity and contextual consistency. Can J Psychol 11:80–88, 1957.

Namerow NS: Cognitive and behavioral aspects of brain-injury rehabilitation. Neurol Clin 5(4):569–583, 1987.

National Head Injury Foundation: Catalogue of Educational Material (2nd ed). Southboro, MA.

Neistadt ME: Occupational therapy for adults with perceptual deficits. Am J Occup Ther 42:434–440, 1988.

Ojakangas C: Courage residence: a unique transitional brain injury program. Cognitive Rehabil 2(6):4–10, 1984.

Panikoff L: Recovery trends of functional skills in the head-injured adult. Am J Occup Ther 37(11):735–743, 1983.

Petersen P, Wikoff RL: The performance of adult males on the Southern California Figure-Ground Visual Perception Test. Am J Occup Ther 37:554–560, 1983.

Polkow L, Volpe B: The next phase in head injury rehabilitation: reentry. Cognitive Rehabil 3(5):20–23, 1985.

Purdy M, Neri L: Computer-assisted cognitive rehabilitation in the home. Cognitive Rehabil 7(6):34–38, 1989.

Reeder CW: Computer use in cognitive retraining. Southboro, Massachusetts, National Head Injury Foundation, 1984.

Reitan RM, Wolfson D: The Halstead-Reitan Neuropsychological Test Battery and REHABIT: a model for integrating evaluation and remediation of cognitive impairment. Cognitive Rehabil 6(3):10–17, 1988.

Rimel RW, Jane JA: Characteristics of the Head-Injured Patient. *In* Rosenthal M, Griffith ER, Bond MR, Miller JD (eds): Rehabilitation of the Head Injured Adult. Philadelphia, FA Davis Co, 1983.

Ruff RM, Baser CA, Johnston JW, Marshall LF, Klauber MR, Minteer M: Neuropsychological rehabilitation: an experimental study with head-injured patients. J Head Trauma Rehabil 4(3):20–36, 1989.

Seaton D: Community reentry for the head injured adult. Cognitive Rehabil 3(5):4–8, 1985.

Simon KB: Outpatient treatment for an adult with traumatic brain injury. Am J Occup Ther 42(4):247–251, 1988.

Sivak M, Hill CS, Henson DL, Butler BP, Silber SM, Olson PL: Improved driving performance following perceptual training in persons with brain damage. Arch Phys Med Rehabil 65:163–167, 1984.

Skinner AD, Trachtman LH: Brief or new: use of a computer program in cognitive rehabilitation. Am J Occup Ther 39:470–472, 1985.

Smith A: Principles underlying human brain functions in neuropsychological sequelae of different neuropathological processes. *In* Filskov SB, Boll TJ (eds): Handbook of Clinical Neuropsychology. New York, Wiley-Interscience, 1981.

Teuber HC, Weinstein S: Ability to discover hidden figures after cerebral lesions. Arch Neurol Psychiatry 76:369–379, 1956.

Toglia JP: Visual perception of objects: an approach to assessment and intervention. Am J Occup Ther 43(9):587–595, 1989.

Toglia JP, Golisz K: Cognitive perceptual rehabilitation: principles and practices. Conference at New York Hospital, 1989.

Trombly CA: Occupational Therapy for Physical Dysfunction (3rd ed). Baltimore, Williams & Wilkins, 1989.

Vogenthaler DR: Rehabilitation after closed head injury: a primer. J Rehabil 53(4):15–21, 1987.

Voorhees SL: Cognitive rehabilitation: an important aspect of the rehabilitation approach. Cognitive Rehabil 3(4):4–7, 1985.

Wahlstrom PE: Remediation of Perceptual Dysfunction. *In* Rosenthal M, Griffith ER, Bond MR, Miller JD (eds): Rehabilitation of the Head Injured Adult. Philadelphia, FA Davis Co, 1983.

Zoltan B: Remediation of Visual-Perceptual and Perceptual-Motor Deficits. *In* Rosenthal M, Griffith ER, Bond MR, Miller JD (eds): Rehabilitation of the Adult and Child with Traumatic Brain Injury. Philadelphia, FA Davis Co, 1990.

Zoltan B, Siev E, Freishtat B: Perceptual and Cognitive Dysfunction in the Adult Stroke Patient (2nd ed). Thorofare, New Jersey, Slack, 1986.

CHAPTER

3

JULIA VAN DEUSEN

ALCOHOL ABUSE

The widespread abuse of alcohol has devastating effects on our nation's health. Some of the health problems associated with alcohol abuse are reversible in the abstaining alcoholic. One of the deficits least likely to be reversible is that of visuospatial-perceptual dysfunction. This dysfunction has been extensively documented for visual figure-ground tasks and in complex visuospatial performances. Tactile perception probably is not a deficit associated with alcohol abuse.

The etiology for the perceptual dysfunction observed in abstaining alcoholics is not clear. Various neuropsychological hypotheses

65

and developmental hypotheses have been posed. An array of tests have been used in research on alcoholism and perceptual dysfunction. Supervision by clinical psychologists is necessary for the use of most of these tests. Persons administering functional tests to patients in substance abuse centers should observe for perceptual deficits that may be interfering with patient performance.

Because there is evidence that training can improve perceptual function in the recovering alcoholic, intervention strategies deserve further research. Also, there is need for studies relating perceptual dysfunction of abstaining alcoholics to the various kinds of occupational performance.

Alcohol abuse is the term used throughout this chapter to describe the improper use of alcohol. Criteria for abuse in studies of adults varied from behavioral definitions to formal medical diagnoses. The definition of alcohol abuse used by the medical profession is given in the Diagnostic and Statistical Manual of Mental Disorders, Revised (American Psychiatric Association, 1987). In essence, it is a pattern of prolonged alcohol use despite knowledge that such use creates persistent social, occupational, psychological, and physical problems for the individual. A second criterion is that of consistent alcohol use when it is physically hazardous (eg, "driving under the influence").

There is widespread abuse of alcohol. Studies on incidence have provided varying estimates of the extent of abuse owing to differences in definition, geographical location, and other variables used by investigators. One group (Robins et al, 1984) defined abuse by medical diagnostic criteria and reported between 11.5% and 15.7% abusing subjects from 3 geographic sites. Up to 8.3% of persons over 65 years of age abused alcohol.

A national research survey of 5221 subjects showed that 4% were alcohol abusers (eg, drank in the morning) and that 5% had experienced severe consequences from drinking such as trouble with the police (Hilton, 1987). Ashley (1989) cited survey results that showed that 18.8% of males and 8.2% of females reported at least one of four behaviors associated with alcohol abuse: (1) skipped meals, (2) loss of memory, (3) cessation of drinking only when intoxicated, and (4) binge drinking. Also surveyed were nine other social and health problems related to alcohol abuse, such as harmed marriage, health, or work. Reports showed a less than 7% response for any of these problems.

According to Moore (1986), alcoholism is the third largest public health problem in the United States. Ashley (1989) listed the following as core health problems related to alcohol consumption: alcohol dependence and abuse, alcoholic psychosis, and liver cirrhosis. There are many other alcohol-related problems. Ashley

(1989) also cited research estimating that three million years of potential life are lost because of alcohol abuse with an economic impact of $117 billion. In 1986, Eckardt and Martin reported evidence of brain dysfunction in 50% to 70% of detoxified alcoholics who did *not* have organic brain syndrome. This chapter limits its discussion to the perceptual dysfunction of alcohol abusers who have *not* been diagnosed as having organic brain syndrome. Some of this chapter has, with permission, been drawn directly from my previous work (Van Deusen, 1989).

DOCUMENTATION

There is a large volume of literature reporting studies investigating the visual and tactile perceptual status of abstaining alcoholics.

Alcohol Abuse and Tactile Perception

The tactual performance test of the Halstead-Reitan Neuropsychological Battery involves placement of blocks in a formboard without the use of vision and the immediate drawing of the formboard from memory with the use of vision. One of the skills required for success is the efficient integration of kinesthetic and tactile feedback (Horton and Wedding, 1984). Kleinknecht and Goldstein (1972), after reviewing the early research in which this test was used, concluded that the Halstead-Reitan Neuropsychological Battery elicits poor performances in alcoholics. Goldstein and Shelly (1971), using one of the first factor analyses in this area, found tactual performance among those perceptual-motor variables associated with alcohol abuse. During the late 1970s and early 1980s, many researchers substantiated the earlier findings. It was well documented that alcoholic subjects performed worse than did nonalcoholic subjects in tactile perceptual function, as measured by the Halstead-Reitan Neuropsychological Battery (Claiborn and Greene, 1981; Hochla and Parsons, 1982; Loberg, 1980). In 1983, Fabian and Parsons replicated with alcoholic women the previous factor analytic findings obtained with alcoholic men (Goldstein and Shelly, 1971).

However, with the introduction of the Luria-Nebraska Neuropsychological Battery into alcoholism research, tactile dysfunction was no longer observed (Burger et al, 1987; Chmielewski and Golden, 1980). The discrepancy in findings can be explained by test differences. The tactual performance subtest of the Halstead-Reitan Neuropsychological Battery required motor skill, spatial memory, and new skill learning as well as tactile and kinesthetic perception (Horton and Wedding, 1984). The tactile component of the Luria-Nebraska Battery, however, specifically measured tactile and kinesthetic perception (such as stereognosis, two-point discrimination, and position sense), although the results of this test were confounded by the need for verbal responses (Chmielewski and Golden, 1980; Horton and Wedding, 1984).

Because of the extensive evidence described below regarding visuospatial deficits of alcoholics, it is reasonable to assume that poor tactual performance on the Halstead-Reitan Neuropsychological Battery may not be due to a tactile perceptual deficit per se but to the alcoholic's spatial problem. Such an assumption also is supported by factor analytic studies in which the tactual performance test loaded on the same factor with measures of visuospatial ability (such as the block design subtest of the Wechsler Adult Intelligence Scale) rather than as an independent tactile factor (Fabian and Parsons, 1983; Goldstein and Shelly, 1971; Grant et al, 1984; Silberstein and Parsons, 1981). In a study (Page and Cleveland, 1987) in which aging was a major variable, tactual performance from the Halstead-Reitan Neuropsychological Battery although significantly declining with age, was not among the most discriminating variables related to alcohol use.

Alcohol Abuse and Visual Perception

I have reviewed the body of research in which the visual-perceptual function of abstaining alcoholics has been evaluated. Visual figure-ground and even higher level visuospatial functions frequently have been studied. Research by Wilson and associates (1988) showed that abstaining alcoholics can sustain sensorimotor impairment, a variable that must be controlled in studies of the visual perception of these subjects. In general, when studies have been well designed, results have shown dysfunction in the visuospatial performance of recovering alcohol abusers.

Figure-Ground Perception

The relationship of alcohol abuse to figure-ground perceptual dysfunction has been examined since the 1950s. Kleinknecht and Goldstein (1972) cited two early studies using the Bender-Gestalt Test, which showed essentially no relationship between visual figure-ground dysfunction and alcohol abuse. In a second review (Donovan et al, 1976), two studies were cited comparing alcoholic and nonalcoholic subjects on the Embedded Figures Test, in which no significant differences in performances were observed. More recent reviewers (Lafferty and Kahn, 1986) cited two early studies showing a significant difference in figure-ground perception between alcoholics and nonalcoholics, but in both studies, the Embedded Figures Test was combined with the Rod and Frame Test so that the latter test could have accounted for the difference. Because the Rod and Frame Test is now in question as a figure-ground perception measure (Donovan et al, 1976; Goldstein and Shelly, 1971; Lafferty and Kahn, 1986), its use distorts the interpretation of the earlier study results.

Alterman and associates (1986) used the Embedded Figures Test to compare the performances of 14 alcohol abusers with the performances of 20 control subjects. These subjects were all college students and were defined as problem drinkers if they indicated being intoxicated more than once a month. The alcohol abusers had poorer performance scores than the nonabusers. Whipple and colleagues (1988) studied performances of fathers who were recovering alcoholics of at least 2 years' duration and the performances of their drug-free sons on the Embedded Figures Test. Both groups differed significantly from control subjects on this test.

The Bender-Gestalt and Embedded Figures Tests also have been found to discriminate within the alcoholic population, for example, showing improved performances as time of abstinence increased (Lafferty and Kahn, 1986; Tarbox et al, 1986).

Brandt and associates (1983), using their figure-ground perception test, discriminated between alcoholic and nonalcoholic subjects. These investigators used a timed Embedded Figures Test tachistoscopically presented that was apparently more sensitive than the measures used by others. These researchers also demonstrated that, although scores of alcoholic and nonalcoholic subjects declined with age, alcoholic subjects differed from control subjects regardless of age.

Although inconsistencies in results have been noted, I concluded that visual figure-ground deficits probably are associated with alcohol abuse. The more rigorous and more recent studies supported this relationship.

Complex Visuospatial Functions

Most of the research involving alcohol abuse and perceptual-motor dysfunction includes a major component on visuospatial tasks. This situation probably resulted from the discovery of a relationship between alcohol abuse and visuospatial performance early in the history of this problem. Early studies showed poor performance by alcoholics on space perception–dependent subtests of the Wechsler Adult Intelligence Scale, the Halstead-Reitan

Category and Trail-Making Tests, the Benton Visual Retention Test, Raven's Progressive Matrices, and other tests with similar visuospatial tasks (Goldstein and Shelly, 1971; Jones and Parsons, 1971; Kleinknecht and Goldstein, 1972; Page and Schaub, 1977).

Among the early cross-cultural studies demonstrating that this relationship was not unique to the United States were those by Berglund and associates (1977) (conducted with Swedish subjects) and Clark and Haughton (1975) (conducted with Irish subjects). While evidence was accumulating on the visuospatial dysfunction of alcohol abusers, observations were also being made that showed their verbal and general intellect as measured by the Wechsler Adult Intelligence Scale to be within normal limits (Goldstein and Shelly, 1971; Kleinknecht and Goldstein, 1972).

Reports of studies on visuospatial dysfunction associated with alcohol abuse continued into the 1980s. More cross-cultural studies, from Scotland, Norway, and Canada, verified the relationship (Guthrie and Elliott, 1980; Loberg, 1980; Wilkinson and Carlan, 1980; Wilson et al, 1988).

Studies emphasized the interrelationships of other pertinent variables such as sex, age, education, drinking history, and drinking style (Bolter and Hannon, 1986; Brandt et al, 1983; Burger et al, 1987; Fabian and Parsons, 1983; Gorenstein, 1987; Page and Cleveland, 1987; Silberstein and Parsons, 1981; Tarbox et al, 1986). Regardless of these variables, the relationship between alcohol abuse and visuospatial dysfunction typically remained significant. However, some variation in the degree of the dysfunction has been reported. For example, younger alcoholics have shown a lesser degree of dysfunction than have older abusers (Brandt et al, 1983; Ryan, 1982; Tarbox et al, 1986). Also, evidence has been inconsistent regarding the relationship of drinking style to perceptual dysfunction (Gorenstein, 1987; Page and Cleveland, 1987; Tarbox et al, 1986).

Research showed that, unlike that of control subjects, the alcoholics' perception of visuospatial stimuli was less influenced by global than by local aspects of the stimuli. Thus, the alcoholic subjects who were alcohol-free from 28 to 212 days showed the tendency to match a square composed of small triangles with a triangle composed of small squares rather than matching it with a square made up of small squares. This performance was the opposite of that observed for control subjects (Kramer et al, 1989).

The introduction of the Luria-Nebraska Neuropsychological Battery into alcoholism research did nothing to alter the relationship between visuospatial dysfunction and alcohol abuse (Burger et al, 1987; Chmielewski and Golden, 1980). The visuospatial perception deficit in alcoholics has not varied across measurement tools nor has it varied with time, because recent results are the same in research replication with the same test items shown in earlier studies to detect poor visuospatial perception in alcohol abusers (Kramer et al, 1989).

ETIOLOGY OF PERCEPTUAL DYSFUNCTION

Because investigators now agree that a relationship exists between visual-perceptual dysfunction and alcohol abuse, recent research has focused on why this relationship exists. Researchers have proposed a variety of explanations for this association, but none has been fully verified or universally accepted. Among explanations for perceptual-motor dysfunction being considered by researchers are those pertaining to areas of cerebral damage or "neuropsychological hypotheses" (Parsons and Leber, 1981). Another approach to explaining the perceptual dysfunction of abstaining alcoholics is developmental, including hypotheses of premature aging and childhood brain lesions.

Ethically, human subjects cannot be placed in the kind of experiments that would verify the cause and effect of alcohol abuse and perceptual dysfunction. As Parsons and Leber (1981) have emphasized, we have data only from correlational studies from which to derive hypotheses about etiology. However, researchers have designed projects that can be interpreted to support a specified hypothesis. Because of the difficulties inherent in the researching of this problem, none of the hypotheses has been universally accepted. Although we might attribute the cause of perceptual dysfunction to cerebral damage from alcohol abuse, brain damage could amplify or coexist with the perceptual deficit. It is improbable that the perceptual dysfunction could cause the brain damage.

Finally, perceptual and brain abnormalities could lead to alcoholism (Whipple et al, 1988). Because of the strong genetic component in alcoholism, Whipple and associates (1988) compared perceptual performances of recovering alcoholic fathers and their sons with those of nonalcoholic controls. Electroencephalography results also were analyzed. All the sons participating in the study were reported to be free of drugs, including alcohol. The performances of both alcoholic fathers and their sons were significantly poorer on perceptual tests than those of control subjects. Electroencephalography results also differed from those of control subjects. A discriminant analysis of these results showed that 80% of the sons could be correctly classified, by their electroencephalogram and visual perceptual tests, as experimental or control subjects. There was no relation between performance on tests of memory and the alcohol-related subjects. The fact that boys at risk for alcoholism already showed perceptual dysfunction and reduced brain electrical activity weakens the theory that alcohol abuse leads to perceptual deficits. As Whipple and associates (1988) note, long-term study is required to verify that boys having decreased perceptual skills and different brain activity would actually become alcoholic adults.

Neuropsychological Hypotheses

At the present time, there are two positions on the extent of brain damage associated with the perceptual dysfunction observed in abstaining alcoholics. One view is that damage is limited to the right hemisphere; the other is that there is diffuse impairment. In my opinion, the evidence better supports the latter position.

Right Hemisphere Lesion

Because of the extensive evidence that abstaining alcoholics performed worse than control subjects on tasks requiring the visuospatial function associated with intact right hemisphere, it was hypothesized that alcohol had impaired the right hemisphere of alcohol-abusing subjects. The documented intact left hemisphere functions of alcoholics (ie, their verbal skills) seemed to support this hypothesis. However, reviewers of the research (Ellis and Oscar-Berman, 1989; Parsons and Leber, 1981), investigators examining right hemisphere functions other than visuospatial ones (Cermak et al, 1989), and researchers analyzing measures known to be associated specifically with right or left hemisphere functions (Bolter and Hannon, 1986) have concluded that the evidence failed to support the right hemisphere hypothesis.

Diffuse Impairment

Although there once seemed to be evidence for a frontal system lesion hypothesis, recent opinion suggests that this hypothesis can be absorbed by the proposal that diffuse or generalized brain impairment causes the perceptual dysfunction of alcohol abusers. Ellis and Oscar-Berman (1989) and Parsons and Leber (1981) concluded that, despite the documentation of perceptual deficits associated with right hemisphere impairment and verbal performances indicative of intact left hemisphere functions, rigorous studies have shown performance deficits of alcoholics associated with left hemisphere impairment. When sensitive tools were used to evaluate alcoholic subjects, deficits of left hemisphere function were observed. The anatomical and physiological studies of the brains of alcohol abusers have given inconsistent results.

The fact that many other body systems besides the brain are affected by alcohol abuse complicates the etiology of visuospatial dysfunction. Liver and vascular disease and traumatic brain injury, conditions directly or indirectly related to alcohol abuse, also can affect perception (Eckardt and Martin, 1986; Hillbom and Holm, 1986; Tarter et al, 1986).

Developmental Hypotheses

Some authors discussed the etiology of perceptual dysfunction of the recovering alcoholic from an age perspective. Although childhood lesions were considered, the major discussion has been on various views related to aging and alcoholism.

Childhood Brain Damage

Parsons and Leber (1981) cited some evidence in support of the idea that the hyperactive child with "minimal brain damage" developed into an adult with problems, one of which might be alcohol abuse. The implication was that early structural impairment of the brain could be responsible for later alcoholic behavior. It has been difficult to support this hypothesis, and it is not prevalent in the recent literature.

Aging

The perceptual deficits observed with alcohol abuse resemble the deficits occurring with normal aging. Because of this pattern, considerable attention was focused on the relationship between aging and alcoholism (Burger et al, 1987; Ellis and Oscar-Berman, 1989; Grant et al, 1984; Noonberg et al, 1985; Parsons and Leber, 1981; Ryan, 1982; Tarbox et al, 1986).

Some investigators considered the resemblance a matter of premature aging in alcoholic people, resulting in earlier damage to those brain structures and/or functions that typically do not deteriorate until an older age is reached. As Ellis and Oscar-Berman (1989) expressed it, the alcoholic "becomes old before his time". Others suggested an increased vulnerability of the aging central nervous system. Alcohol toxicity could interact with aging central nervous system processes for a more pronounced performance deficit than shown by the younger central nervous system (Goldman et al, 1983; Tarbox et al., 1986). Another possibility was that perceptual deficits from alcohol abuse could simply be added to those of normal aging (Ellis and Oscar-Berman, 1989).

Recent research has continued to support a hypothesis on the relationship of premature aging and alcohol abuse on perceptual dysfunction. Cermak and colleagues (1989) studied the performance of three groups on tasks processed by the right hemisphere of the brain, tasks that did not involve visuospatial perception. Their study involved alcoholic subjects and groups of younger and older control subjects. The responses of alcoholic subjects were nearer to those of normal older subjects than to patients with right hemisphere damage.

Two other studies, however, failed to lend support to hypotheses on aging and alcohol abuse. Testing subjects' perception of the emotional expression on pictures of human faces, researchers compared responses of younger and older alcoholic subjects with those of younger and older control subjects (Oscar-Berman et al, 1990). Both older control and alcoholic subjects performed more poorly than younger control and alcoholic subjects. Kramer and associates (1989) also found no relationship between age and performance on the visuospatial tasks used in their study.

I have concluded that the associations between age, perception, and alcohol abuse are dependent on the specific kind of performance tasks involved. If aging is a major etiological factor in the visuospatial deficits of alcohol abusers, it is limited to certain kinds of tasks.

ASSESSMENT

Most researchers dealing with perceptual dysfunction and alcohol abuse (see list of references) have used one or more of the following tests: the Block Design, Object Assembly, or Digit Symbol subtests of the Wechsler Adult Intelligence Scale; the Luria-Nebraska Neuropsychological Battery; the Category, Tactual Performance, and Trail-Making components of the Halstead-Reitan Neuropsychological Battery; the Raven Progressive Matrices; the Wisconsin Card Sorting Test; the Bender-Gestalt Test; the Witkin Embedded Figures Test; the Rod and Frame Test; the Rey Figure Test; and several of the Arthur Benton tests.

Most of these tests have a motor skill component. The Bender and Embedded Figures tests assess the subject's ability to separate the foreground figure from distracting background stimuli. The Rod and Frame Test, which also has been used to measure this ability, has been questioned as a figure-ground perception test (Donovan et al, 1976; Goldstein and Shelly, 1971; Lafferty and Kahn, 1986).

Most of the other tests, as well as the Rod and Frame and figure-ground tests, primarily assess visuospatial functions. The obvious exceptions are the Tactual Performance Test of the Halstead-Reitan Neuropsychological Battery and the Tactile Scale of the Luria-Nebraska Neuropsychological Battery, although the former test does have a spatial memory component. The tests involving visuospatial perception vary as to which higher cognitive functions are evaluated: memory, sequencing, abstraction, and ideational flexibility (Eckardt and Martin, 1986; Horton and Wedding, 1984; Page and Cleveland, 1987). I consider all of these tests as measures of complex visuospatial perception.

For a clinical evaluation of perceptual dysfunction of recovering alcoholic patients, appropriate selection of tests depends, first, on the health care professionals involved in the assessment process. Many of the tests available are for use only by clinical psychologists. The tests that measure simple perceptual functions and frequently are administered by occupational therapists to patients with brain lesions would not detect the higher level visuospatial deficits associated with alcohol abuse. Tests of self-care, leisure, and vocational skills that depend on visuospatial performance generally are administered by recreational therapists, occupational therapists, and vocational counselors in a chemical abuse rehabilitation setting. It is essential to observe for any perceptual problems interfering with performance.

TREATMENT

Recovery of Perceptual Function

There is evidence that some cognitive functions may improve in recovering alcohol abusers. Research on this topic has used both longitudinal and cross-sectional designs. Alcoholics who have abstained for several months and as long as 7 years have been studied (Brandt et al, 1983; Cala and Mastaglia, 1981; Ellenberg et al, 1980; Fabian and Parsons, 1983; Goldman, 1983; Goldman, 1986; Goldman et al, 1983; Guthrie and Elliott, 1980; Lafferty and Kahn, 1986; Parsons and Leber, 1981; Yohman et al, 1985). Kleinknecht and Goldstein (1972) concluded that, although many cognitive functions recovered within the first 2 or 3 weeks of abstinence, evidence of reversibility of perceptual dysfunction remained inconsistent. If impaired test performances were still observed 1 month after the patients stopped drinking, visuospatial perception was one of the areas affected (Claiborn and Greene, 1981; Goldman, 1983; Goldman, 1986; Lafferty and Kahn, 1986; Parsons and Leber,

1981). Psychometric studies concluded that older alcoholic subjects regained perceptual functions less readily than did younger subjects (Ellenberg et al, 1980; Goldman et al, 1983). These results were supported by computerized tomography scans of alcoholic patients (Cala and Mastaglia, 1981). Although few computerized tomography (CT) scans of alcoholic subjects have been evaluated for their improvement, those that have been evaluated showed the best recovery in younger patients. Because of the evidence that perceptual deficits were retained after several weeks of abstinence, at least by older recovering alcoholic persons, a number of studies investigated recovery over long time periods. Although some inconsistencies were reported, perceptual dysfunction was still observed in alcoholic subjects abstinent for months and even for years (Brandt et al, 1983; Fabian and Parsons, 1983; Goldman, 1986; Grant et al, 1984; Guthrie and Elliott, 1980; Parsons and Leber, 1981; Yohman et al, 1985).

Rehabilitation

Because the literature has documented retention of visual perceptual deficits despite the spontaneous return of some other cognitive functions in alcoholic patients, it is logical to consider whether or not therapeutic procedures might enhance the recovery of these perceptual processes. This experience-dependent recovery (ie, recovery related to practice) has been studied by Goldman and colleagues in a series of experiments (Ellenberg et al, 1980; Goldman, 1983; Goldman, 1986; Goldman et al, 1983). It was shown that in both younger and older alcohol abusers, practice can improve perceptual test scores on alternate forms beyond improvement caused by time alone (Goldman, 1986). In an experiment with subjects over 40 years of age, training consisted of practice with items similar to, but not the same as, those items used in posttesting. Results showed this type of practice to be effective in older alcoholics.

An alternative training strategy was studied with subjects under 40 years of age (Goldman, 1986). This training task was analyzed into its components, subjects trained on these components, and subjects taught to integrate the components. Using a rigorous 4-group design, it was shown that improved posttest performances were not due to effects of pretesting or to spontaneous recovery over time. The components analysis training strategy was no more effective than was practice with the simple items. Both groups of alcoholic subjects, after their different styles of remediation, performed on a visuospatial task in a manner similar to that of the control subjects.

Goldman (1986) also reported that improvement from a practice exercise was not limited to this exercise but was transferable to other visuospatial tasks. Some degree of transfer was shown on the Wechsler Digit Symbol Subtest, the Trail-Making Test, and the Benton tests of visual retention and line orientation. There was no evidence of learning transfer on the Halstead-Reitan Tactual Perception Test, a finding that indicated that the results of training procedures would transfer only to other visual-perceptual tasks. However, Goldman has provided a beginning research base from which rehabilitation professionals can adopt ideas for clinical programing of alcoholic patients.

McCrady and Smith (1986) have indicated that patients who were less cognitively impaired were more likely than the severely impaired to be successful participants in alcohol rehabilitation programs. Although the focus of their study was on intellectual skills such as memory and problem-solving, the authors' suggestions are readily applicable to the perceptual problems of alcoholic subjects. Skills common to successful recovery following different kinds of alcohol rehabilitation should be identified and measures for these skills developed. It should be determined which, if any, of these skills are related to perceptual function. Appropriate cognitive or behavioral retraining procedures and program evaluations need to be developed. Research should be designed with a view to understanding processes of generalization. Finally, rehabilitation outcome studies can be designed.

Occupational Performance

Several authors have mentioned a potential relationship between decreased occupational function and reduced perceptual status in alcoholic patients. Abbott and Gregson (1981) stated that poor adjustment to daily living tasks is associated with the cortical deficits observed in alcoholic patients. Parsons and Leber (1981) suggested that cognitive deficits (including perceptual deficits) may affect day-to-day functioning, thereby interfering with school or job activities. Finally, Goldman (1986) indicated that rehabilitation of alcohol abusers in cognitive areas could help prepare them for future job responsibilities.

One study with alcoholic subjects found an association between better neuropsychological function and job placement (Walker et al, 1983). Walker and associates (1983) reported various treatment outcomes of male alcoholics in relation to their scores on six neuropsychology subtests and length of hospital stay. Perceptual and conceptual performance was evaluated by four subtests from the Halstead-Reitan Battery with the Digit Symbol and Block Design from the Wechsler Adult Intelligence Scale. One outcome described was employment status of alcoholic patients 6 to 9 months after being discharged from the hospital. Seventy-nine subjects were working full-time, 42 were employed only part-time or inter-mittently, and 46 were unemployed. Employment status was re-lated to perceptual and conceptual performance and to drinking abstinence, but not to length of hospital stay. Those subjects who scored high (average range of the normative group) on the neuro-psychology subtests were more likely to be employed full-time and to have remained abstinent.

Researchers need to document in all age groups whether or not the perceptual dysfunction observed in alcohol abusers is related to deficits in occupational performance (Van Deusen, 1989). Such studies should involve the more complex activities of daily living, such as management of one's financial affairs and maintenance of a balanced lifestyle of work, leisure, and rest. Also, the relationship with work and educational skills should be addressed by the researcher. Raymond (1990) identified these same areas as impor-tant for group work with substance abuse patients. Topics for her Life Management Group included money management, time man-agement (balance of work and play), and work issues.

Researchers also should evaluate the relationship between perceptual performance and early versus late stages of recovery. Rehabilitation may be able to hasten the regaining of normal occupational functioning in recovering alcohol abusers through the early treatment of these patients' perceptual problems.

Many areas are indicated for investigation by the researcher interested in the visuospatial problems of perception in abstaining alcoholics. Of particular importance are studies addressing inter-vention strategies and relating perceptual dysfunction to activities of daily living, leisure, and work activities.

CASE REPORT

Mrs. F is a suburban homemaker diagnosed as having an alcohol abuse problem. Alcoholism is a progressive disease and alcoholics typically progress through 3 stages, each exhibiting a greater degree of dysfunction. Because of her concerned teenaged children and her husband, Mrs. F's problem was diagnosed early, inpatient treatment was not considered necessary, and she was admitted to an outpatient mental health center specializing in chemical abuse. Mrs. F attended therapy groups twice a week at the center as well as participating nightly in Alcoholics Anonymous meetings.

Her chemical abuse counselor became aware of the sensitivity and insight of Mrs. F when she was shown the following poem that Mrs. F had written prior to treatment.

Alcohol—
I wish it had never been discovered.
It makes one dream impossible dreams.
It makes one love when love is absent.
It makes one fight when compromise is possible.
It makes one strong when really one is weak.
It is a crutch—so necessary and so wrong!

In group therapy, Mrs. F's intelligence and creativity continued to be revealed. However, it became apparent that a major area of dysfunction was that of social skills and interpersonal relationships. Mrs. F was referred to groups focusing on this problem area.

Mrs. F was fortunate in that her alcoholic drinking had been essentially confined to home so that, unlike many of her peers, she still retained a driver's license. However, she insisted that her husband or son drive her to social occasions, because she would not be able to adequately park her car. Although knowing that a large part of this problem was Mrs. F's desire to avoid social situations on her own, her counselor also realized that visuospatial problems associated with the abstinence from alcohol in recovering alcoholics could be a realistic factor in Mrs. F's dread of parking. Perceptual screening confirmed her perceptual problem, and Mrs. F's son agreed to help his mother practice parking until compensatory behaviors could be learned. Within a month, Mrs. F had compensated for her perceptual deficit and could no longer use parking as an excuse to avoid socially demanding situations. Mrs. F was able to begin to focus her attention on the interpersonal aspects of her group therapy toward developing a more satisfactory future lifestyle.

References

Abbott MW, Gregson R: Cognitive dysfunction in the prediction of relapse in alcoholics. J Stud Alcohol 42:230–243, 1981.

Alterman AI, Bridges KR, Tarter RE: The influence of both drinking and familiar risk statuses on cognitive functioning of social drinkers. Alcoholism 10:448–451, 1986.

American Psychiatric Association: Diagnostic and Statistical Manual of Mental Disorders (3rd ed). Washington, DC, Author, 1987, pp 165–175.

Ashley MJ: How extensive is the problem of alcoholism? Alcohol Health and Research World 13:305–309, 1989.

Berglund M, Leijonquist H, Horlen M: Prognostic significance and reversibility of cerebral dysfunction in alcoholics. J Stud Alcohol 38:1761–1770, 1977.

Bolter JF, Hannon R: Lateralized cerebral dysfunction in early and late stage alcoholics. J Stud Alcohol 47:213–218, 1986.

Brandt J, Rutters N, Ryan C, Bayog R: Cognitive loss and recovery in long-term alcohol abusers. Arch Gen Psychiatry 40:435–442, 1983.

Burger MC, Botwinick J, Storandt M: Aging, alcoholism, and performance on the Luria-Nebraska Neuropsychological Battery. J Gerontol 42:69–72, 1987.

Cala LA, Mastaglia FL: Computerized tomography in chronic alcoholics. Alcoholism 5:283–294, 1981.

Cermak LS, Verfaellie M, Letourneau L, Blackford S, Weiss S, Numan B: Verbal and nonverbal right hemisphere processing by chronic alcoholics. Alcoholism 13:611–616, 1989.

Chmielewski C, Golden CJ: Alcoholism and brain damage: an investigation using the Luria-Nebraska Neuropsychological Battery. Int J Neurosci 10:99–105, 1980.

Claiborn JM, Greene RL: Neuropsychological changes in recovering men alcoholics. J Stud Alcohol 42:757–765, 1981.

Clarke J, Haughton H: A study of intellectual impairment and recovery rates in heavy drinkers in Ireland. Br J Psychiatry 126:178–184, 1975.

Donovan DM, Queisser HR, O'Leary MR: Group embedded figures test performance as a predictor of cognitive impairment among alcoholics. Int J Addict 11:725–739, 1976.

Eckardt MJ, Martin PR: Clinical assessment of cognition in alcoholism. Alcoholism 10:123–127, 1986.

Ellenberg L, Rosenbaum G, Goldman MS, Whitman RD: Recoverability of psychological functioning following alcohol abuse: lateralization effects. J Consult Clin Psychol 48:503–510, 1980.

Ellis RJ, Oscar-Berman M: Alcoholism, aging, and functional cerebral asymmetries. Psychol Bull 106:128–147, 1989.

Fabian MS, Parsons OA: Differential improvement of cognitive functions in recovering alcoholic women. J Abnorm Psychol 92:87–95, 1983.

Goldman MS: Cognitive impairment in chronic alcoholics. Am Psychol 10:1045–1054, 1983.

Goldman MS: Neuropsychological recovery in alcoholics: endogenous and exogenous processes. Alcoholism 10:136–144, 1986.

Goldman MS, Williams DL, Klisz DK: Recoverability of psychological functioning following alcohol abuse: prolonged visual-spatial dysfunction in older alcoholics. J Consult Clin Psychol 51:370–378, 1983.

Goldstein G, Shelly CH: Field dependence and cognitive, perceptual and motor skills in alcoholics. Q J Stud Alcohol 32:29–44, 1971.

Gorenstein EE: Cognitive-perceptual deficit in an alcoholism spectrum disorder. J Stud Alcohol 48:310–318, 1987.

Grant I, Adams KM, Reed R: Aging, abstinence, and medical risk factors in the prediction of neuropsychologic deficit among long-term alcoholics. Arch Gen Psychiatry 41:710–718, 1984.

Guthrie A, Elliott WA: The nature and reversibility of cerebral impairment in alcoholism. J Stud Alcohol 41:147–155, 1980.

Hillbom M, Holm L: Contribution of traumatic head injury to neuropsychological deficits in alcoholics. J Neurol Neurosurg Psychiatry 49:1348–1353, 1986.

Hilton ME: Drinking patterns and drinking problems in 1984: results from a general population survey. Alcoholism 11:167–175, 1987.

Hochla NAN, Parsons OA: Premature aging in female alcoholics. A neuropsychological study. J Nerv Ment Dis 170:241–245, 1982.

Horton AM Jr, Wedding D: Clinical and Behavioral Neuropsychology. New York, Praeger, 1984.

Jones B, Parsons OA: Impaired abstracting ability in chronic alcoholics. Arch Gen Psychiatry 24:71–75, 1971.

Kramer JH, Blusewicz MJ, Robertson LC, Preston K: Effects of chronic alcoholism on perception of hierarchical visual stimuli. Alcoholism 13:240–245, 1989.

Kleinknecht RA, Goldstein SG: Neuropsychological deficits associated with alcoholism. Q J Stud Alcohol 33:999–1019, 1972.

Lafferty P, Kahn MW: Field dependence or cognitive impairment in alcoholics. Int J Addict 21:1221–1232, 1986.

Loberg T: Alcohol misuse and neuropsychological deficits in man. J Stud Alcohol 41:119–128, 1980.

McCrady BS, Smith DE: Implications of cognitive impairment for the treatment of alcoholism. Alcoholism 10:145–149, 1981.

Moore DT: Reversal of alcohol effects, acute and chronic conditions. Alcohol Health and Research World 11:52–59;78, 1986.

Noonberg A, Goldstein G, Page HA: Premature aging in male alcoholics: "accelerated aging" or "increased vulnerability"? Alcoholism 9:334–338, 1985.

Oscar-Berman M, Hancock M, Mildworf B, Hutner N, Weber DA: Emotional perception and memory in alcoholism and aging. Alcoholism 14:383–393, 1990.

Page RD, Cleveland MF: Cognitive dysfunction and aging among male alcoholics and social drinkers. Alcoholism 11:376–384, 1987.

Page RD, Schaub LH: Intellectual functioning in alcoholics during six months' abstinence. J Stud Alcohol 38:1240–1246, 1977.

Parsons OA, Leber WR: The relationship between cognitive dysfunction and brain damage in alcoholics: Causal, interactive, or epiphenomenal? Alcoholism 5:326–343, 1981.

Raymond M: Life skills and substance abuse. Mental Health Special Interest Section Newsletter 13(3):1–2, 1990.

Robins LN, Helzer JE, Weissman MM, et al: Lifetime prevalence of specific psychiatric disorders in three sites. Arch Gen Psychiatry 41:949–958, 1984.

Ryan C: Alcoholism and premature aging: a neuropsychological perspective. Alcoholism 6:22–30, 1982.

Silberstein JA, Parsons OA: Neuropsychological impairment in female alcoholics: replication and extension. J Abnorm Psychol 90:179–182, 1981.

Tarbox AR, Connors GJ, McLaughlin EJ: Effects of drinking pattern on neuropsychological performance among alcohol misusers. J Stud Alcohol 47:176–179, 1986.

Tarter RE, Hegedus AM, Van Thiel DH, Gavaler JS, Schade RR: Hepatic dysfunction of neuropsychological test performance in alcoholics with cirrhosis. J Stud Alcohol 47:74–77, 1986.

Van Deusen J: Alcohol abuse and perceptual-motor dysfunction: the occupational therapist's role. Am J Occup Ther 43:384–390. 1989.

Walker RD, Donovan DM, Kivlahan DR, O'Leary MR: Length of stay, neuropsychological performance and aftercare: influences on alcohol treatment outcome. J Consult Clin Psychol 51:900–911, 1983.

Whipple SC, Parker ES, Noble EP: An atypical neurocognitive profile in alcoholic fathers and their sons. J Stud Alcohol 49:240–244, 1988.

Wilkinson DA, Carlen PL: Neuropsychological and neurological assessment of alcoholism. J Stud Alcohol 41:129–139, 1980.

Wilson JTL, Wiedmann KD, Phillips WA, Brooks DN: Visual event perception in alcoholics. J Clin Exp Neuropsychol 10:222–234, 1988.

Yohman JR, Parsons OA, Leber WR: Lack of recovery in male alcoholics' neuropsychological performance one year after treatment. Alcoholism 9:114–117, 1985.

NEUROBEHAVIORAL PERSPECTIVES ON SCHIZOPHRENIA

This chapter examines schizophrenia and the assessment and rehabilitation strategies designed to be responsive to patients' underlying cerebral defects, perceptual and cognitive deficits, processing strategies, and characteristic vulnerabilities to stress. This chapter does not, however, focus on specific deficits in body image and visual or somesthetic perception. Perceptual deficits reflecting problems in the interpretation of sensory input are but one dimension of the complex interpretive failures that plague the schizophrenic patient. Therefore, this chapter moves beyond approaches that focus on perceptual deficits to emphasize the *interactive* nature of sensory, attentional, perceptual, cognitive, metacognitive, affective, and environmental factors in occupational performance and the rationale for an interactive process-oriented approach to rehabilitation. Although the author believes this to be the approach of choice for meeting the complex biopsychosocial needs of the schizophrenic population, it is a valuable model for other diagnostic groups as well. Practitioners working outside of the mental health field are, therefore, encouraged to read this chapter and use the resources cited in the bibliography. They represent the multidisciplinary efforts of researchers and clinicians working in physical as well as psychosocial specialties.

INTRODUCTION

For those who struggle with episodic or persistent symptoms of schizophrenia, occupational performance is often an elusive and overwhelming phenomenon. The most rudimentary tasks of daily living may represent enormous challenges for 2 million Americans diagnosed with this illness. These challenges do not arise from an absence of intellect, atrophied muscles, a conscious desire to languish unproductively, or the "split personality" erroneously ascribed to schizophrenia; they are the result of a variety of acute and chronic phenomena of uncertain etiology that influence thought processes, reality orientation, and social behavior; diminish abilities to maintain a productive life; and contribute to poor treatment response and high relapse rates. Personal accounts that characterize the illness as "mostly painful," "a journey of fear," and "often paralyzing" (McGrath 1984) suggest that emotional survival, for some patients, is a far more fundamental issue than productivity.

The challenge of schizophrenia is not only a personal one for the afflicted. It has a significant impact on families, communities, and the health and social welfare systems. Social and economic costs, estimated to be 30 billion dollars per year, render it a major public health problem. Keith (1988) reports that ". . . of the major health problems of the 20th century, none combines the frequency of occurrence, degree of disability, and squandered human potential that characterizes schizophrenia. . . . It is five times more common than multiple sclerosis, six times more so than insulin dependent diabetes and 60 times more so than muscular dystrophy." Treatment costs exceed 7 billion dollars annually, and indirect costs (social services, loss of productivity, and premature mortality) account for at least twice that amount. In spite of advances in the management of psychotic symptoms, recurrent acute episodes and persistent functional residuals continue to defy psychopharmacology and most other treatment efforts. Keith suggests that a 10% reduction in number, duration, or intensity of episodes would save 700 million dollars in treatment costs alone. The need for innovative and more effective methods for managing schizophrenia is evident.

The neuroscientific findings of the past two decades and growing interdisciplinary interest in the interaction among central nervous system development, environment, and illness hold great promise for stimulating more effective methods. Investigations from the basic behavioral sciences and clinical fields provide insight into etiology, symptoms, and residual deficits. Consequently, rehabilitation specialists have an expanding scientific base from which to evaluate patients' failures to function and their own failure to rehabilitate, examine the rationale for current practice, define more substantive treatment models, and develop and study new strategies.

THE SCHIZOPHRENIAS

Schizophrenia is a complex grouping of disorders characterized by psychotic features (ie, hallucinations, incoherence, delusions), symptoms involving multiple psychological processes (content and form of thought, perception, affect, sense of self, volition, relationship to the external world, and psychomotor behavior), deterioration from a previous level of functioning, onset before age 45, and a duration of at least 6 months (APA, 1986). Although these criteria are part of a uniform diagnostic system (DSM III-R), they should not be viewed as a fixed formula for understanding the boundaries and patterns of this illness. Schizophrenia is not all of one piece. No patient manifests all symptoms at a given time or in the full course of the illness; there are great variations in symptom configuration, severity, and duration. Because these symptoms are not unique to this condition, efforts to understand their pathogenesis, predict their course, or provide effective treatment are made more complex.

The heterogeneity of schizophrenia has been acknowledged and debated by many (Sommers, 1985). Should it be defined by its phenomenological characteristics or by a biotype that transcends specific clinical symptoms (Andreason, 1987)? Recent efforts to delineate positive and negative symptom syndromes have served to integrate both perspectives and give much needed attention to the perplexing residual deficit behaviors that impact on occupational performance (Andreason, 1982a, 1982b, 1985; Carpenter et al, 1973).

Positive symptoms are characterized by prominent delusions, hallucinations, a formal thought disorder, and persistently bizarre behavior. These more florid manifestations are viewed as distortions of normal function. Patients with only these symptoms generally have a better premorbid adjustment, better overall function, and normal sensoria and show no evidence of cerebral atrophy (Andreason, 1982b). The negative symptom cluster, in contrast, is characterized by a loss of normal function: affective flattening, alogia (poverty of speech), avolition, anhedonia (difficulties in experiencing interest or pleasure), and attentional impairments. These patients, previously referred to as process schizophrenics, demonstrate poor premorbid adjustment, lower overall levels of function, impaired cognition, previous brain injury, and cerebral atrophy (Andreason 1982a). These syndromes may be concurrent or independent. Early positive episodes may progress to the negative deficit state. The presence of negative symptoms during acute episodes may be prognostic of later poor functioning (Pogue-Geile and Harrow, 1985). Carpenter and associates (1985) urge care in diagnosing negative symptoms, because similar behaviors may be secondary to medication, a defensive reaction to the psychosis, depression, demoralization, and under- or overstimulating environments. Each needs to be considered before a rational treatment plan can be initiated.

The behaviors identified in Andreason's (1983) Scale for the Assessment of Negative Symptoms reflect key areas of attentional and information processing deficits known to impede occupational performance in schizophrenics. These include difficulties in sustaining focused attention (Wohlberg and Kornetsky, 1973), distractibility (McGhie et al, 1965), slowness in initial processing of information in sensory memory (Saccuzzo et al, 1974), impaired detection of relevant stimuli imbedded in irrelevant noise (Rappaport et al, 1972), and inefficient active organization of information in short-term memory (Koh, 1978). The behavioral sequelae of these phenomena are familiar to rehabilitation specialists. They are underscored in the Iowa City study of 52 schizophrenic patients, in which only 6% with negative symptoms, 41% with mixed schizophrenia, and 55% with positive symptoms alone were employed (Andreason 1982a).

NEUROSCIENTIFIC FINDINGS

Although clinicians and experimental psychologists have long documented the presence of perceptual and cognitive deficits and inferred a neurobiological basis for schizophrenia, neuroscientists with access to advanced technology have only recently produced respectable supportive data. Abnormalities in ventricular and limbic systems, the frontal cortex, and left hemispheric areas and variations in neurochemical activity have been identified as likely sources of the various cognitive impairments and aberrant social behaviors associated with this illness.

Evidence of reduced brain mass produced by ventricular enlargement and cortical atrophy in negative symptom patients has been reported by various investigators (Meltzer, 1987; Owens et al, 1985). Such anomalies produce concreteness, impaired attention, problems in ignoring irrelevant visual and auditory stimuli, decreased spontaneity of speech, difficulties in shifting sets, and indifference to people and things in the environment—phenomena characteristic of traumatically brain injured individuals as well.

The frontal lobe is implicated in investigations showing schizophrenic failures to manifest the same increase in cerebral blood flow as normal individuals during cognitive tasks assessing abstraction and learning efficiency (Weinberger et al, 1986). Weinberger links this difficulty in "turning on part of the frontal lobe" to the withdrawal, impaired cognition, and muteness characteristic of negative symptom patients. This is most evident when tasks such as problem-solving or keeping schedules place a premium on prefrontal cortical activities.

Other investigations specify greater left hemispheric involvement against a background of diffuse cerebral abnormalities (National Institute of Mental Health, 1988). Gazzaniga (1988) aptly describes schizophrenia as a disease in which the left hemisphere, the brain's interpreter, goes wild in its attempts to bring order out of the chaos produced from poor "wiring" at many levels and the individual's misreading of environmental stimuli. The interaction of various brain systems also is demonstrated through the dopamine hypothesis (Meltzer and Stahl, 1976). A deficit of this neurotransmitter is linked with negative symptoms, and an excess is associated with positive symptoms, particularly when abnormalities occur at such anatomical sites as the basal ganglia or limbic system. Because the latter serves to integrate cortical centers with senso-

rimotor systems and more primitive visceral and reticular structures, any alteration in neurochemical activity will impact on
abilities to integrate meaningful environmental data and prepare
an adequate response from cortical areas. New medications, such
as clozapine, are believed to produce symptomatic relief with fewer
extrapyramidal effects for neuroleptic-resistant patients by regulating dopaminergic activity in the mesolimbic system (Meltzer,
1991).

Additional support for neurochemical links to schizophrenia is
summarized in McKenna's (1987) discussion of relationships between dopamine and irregularities of motor activity. Of particular
interest is research relating eyetracking dysfunction and schizophrenic "thought slippage" (Holtzman, 1985). The prevalence of eye
movement disorders in schizophrenics and their first degree relatives has been described as a neurophysiological disturbance of
cognitive centering. Schizophrenics have less accurate smooth pursuit movements and appear to rely more on head movement for
scanning and watching moving objects than normal subjects. In
addition, saccadic movements (enabling rapid shifts of gaze and the
ability to focus on interesting targets or stationary objects) are
highly sensitive to variations in motivation and attention. Eye
movement disorders may be caused by attentional dysfunctions or
problems of proprioceptive or interoceptive feedback. The impact of
such disorders is important, because smooth pursuit and saccadic
movements are two of the six functional eye movement classes that
need to work in concert to allow for accurate perception (Leigh and
Zee, 1983). This component of occupational performance has not
been adequately addressed by mental health practitioners attempt-
ing to enhance function in this population.

Differences in gender and the preponderance of males among
the chronically mentally ill addresses several of these neuroscientific issues (Flor-Henry, 1990). Hogarty (1985) suggests that biological as well as social factors contribute to the higher clinical
visibility and lower rehabilitation success of males. He ascribes
difficulties in outcome to a combination of greater left hemispheric
vulnerability and more developmental disabilities in males, in
general, and greatly reduced blood flow to the left hemisphere of
schizophrenics, specifically. He further suggests that challenges to
left hemisphere integrity, reflected in task stress and implied or
real criticism of performance, may precipitate more psychotic episodes and symptom exacerbations in schizophrenic men. Women,
usually with later onset of illness, better premorbid history, and
less typical schizophrenic features, appear to be less specialized
hemispherically and perhaps more bilateral and adaptable (Goy
and McEwen, 1980).

The presence of structural and neurochemical abnormalities must not be used to dismiss potentials for change. There is some evidence to suggest that well-conceived interventions can promote more efficient function. The areas of investigation summarized earlier provide a valuable context for the work of rehabilitation specialists. They help to explain clinical phenomenology and should serve to focus and intensify treatment and research efforts. This should involve a conceptual framework that ties together brain abnormalities with the personal reality of an individual's mind. Gazzaniga (1988) reminds us that "endogenous brain changes create new circumstances to which the brain's interpreter must react. That reaction, in turn, produces memories that can become powerful guides for the mental outlook of the individual." Schizophrenia serves as an imposing model of what can happen to the human mind when exposed to long-term distortions of reality, the stigma of the disease, recognition of the impact of the disorder on self and others, and the destruction of a basic life context (Strauss, 1990). The relevance of this for biopsychosocial theory and practice with all disabilities is considerable.

OPERATIONAL MODELS

The growth of brain-behavioral hypotheses has stimulated several operational models for schizophrenia that are of particular interest to those who believe that occupational performance is mediated by a broad range of biological, psychological, social, and environmental factors.

The Diathesis-Stress-Interaction Model

The Diathesis-Stress-Interaction (DSI) model suggests that schizophrenic symptoms arise when an individual with pre-existing areas of vulnerability is confronted with life stressors, and the valence between stressor and problem-solving capacity is unevenly matched (Zubin and Spring, 1977). The existence of low thresholds for disorganization contributes further to vulnerabilities. Environmental and internal stresses increase arousal and introduce many competing responses of equal strength. These, in turn, often lead to the eruption of inappropriate responses such as withdrawal, inattention, poor judgment and problem-solving, anger, and florid symptoms.

Stressors that impact on the individual's social network appear to be the most powerful and disruptive. Investigators have demonstrated higher relapse rates among patients who experience their families as critical and intrusive (Anderson et al, 1986).

DSI also underscores the need to develop clinicians and treatment strategies that do not induce stress. This requires an appreciation of the interaction among the task and interpersonal demands of treatment and the underlying cognitive and social capacities of the patient. The information processing paradigm provides such a structure.

The Information Processing Paradigm

Information processing theory is a conceptual framework of the mind that organizes how one adds information to existing knowledge, how one accesses the information again, and how one uses it in all aspects of human activity (Mayer, 1988). It focuses on sensory cues that capture and sustain attention; associations and interpretations requiring memory, language, and complex organizational processes; and behaviors evidenced in voluntary motor activity.

There is support for the belief that basic pathology in schizophrenia is derived from either defective analysis of incoming sensory signals or a defect in their interpretive reconstruction at higher levels of information processing (Braff and Saccuzzo, 1985; Neuchterlein and Dawson, 1984; Wallace and Boone, 1983). Research has documented the presence of deficits in every element of information processing. Attention appears to be implicated in many of these deficits, because it plays a dominant role as a filter, sorting relevant and irrelevant data. It is not a single process, but rather a complex set of phenomena in which sensory cues interact with the individual's intentions and expectations and the context in which stimuli occur. Orienting, selective attention, concentration, preparation capacity, and controlled processing are dimensions of attention needed for tasks of daily living. The exact cause of attentional deficits in the schizophrenic population is inadequately understood. Relationships between specific attentional deficits and specific neuroanatomical loci and the competing demands of other thought processes have been emphasized by some researchers.

Similarly, problems in the higher integrative processes involving perception, flexibility, and problem-solving are not fully understood. Network models that describe the encoding, elaboration, and recording of sensory input are gaining in popularity and need to be studied and applied. Gibson's (1986) innovative work with visual perception translates traditional neurophysiological constructs into a theory of affordances—an action-in-the-environment model in which sensory information is given meaning through experience in the real world (Pierce, 1991). Toglia's (1992) dynamic interactional model of cognition also fosters a network model. It moves beyond traditional skill-specific views of dysfunction to address underlying conditions, processing strategies, and environmental situations that influence performance.

One should not, therefore, isolate attentional, perceptual, or information processing defects from the social-interpersonal field. Attention deficits produce a tendency to drift off the topic, decrease awareness of nonverbal and verbal reactions, limit the ability to listen, and allow for only a partial awareness of social situations. Self-monitoring deficits produce problems with speed of reactions, tone of voice, and management of emotions. Characteristic rigidity of thought produces a limited ability to see another's point of view or to come up with alternatives for solutions to social problems (Toglia and Golisz, 1990). These phenomena have a significant impact on role performance and overall adaptive potential. Clinical implications of these phenomena are addressed in the case material appended to this chapter.

ISSUES IN REHABILITATION: THE STATE OF THE ART

Interest in rehabilitation and the functional capacities of the mentally ill has peaked in the past 2 decades, after a long hiatus in which psychodynamics and medication management were favored modalities (Fine, 1980). At the present time, psychiatric rehabilitation has achieved greater status and visibility as a systematic means of facilitating "the physical, emotional and intellectual skills necessary to live, learn and work in [one's] own particular environment" (Anthony and Nemec, 1984). In combination with appropriate medication and social support, psychiatric rehabilitation can enhance coping capacities needed to neutralize the negative interaction of stress and vulnerability (Liberman, 1988). Social skills training and other techniques based on social learning principles and "learning by doing" have assumed particular importance in contemporary practice (Fine, 1980; Greenberg et al, 1986; Hersen and Bellack, 1976; Liberman, 1988). A growing body of literature and research, as well as more training opportunities, has enhanced services and brought psychiatric rehabilitation to the attention of a larger community of health professionals, consumers, advocates, and funding resources.

In spite of these significant efforts to meet the needs of the chronically mentally ill and cultivate a coherent body of knowledge, rehabilitation frequently is judged on the basis of interventions that fail. Failure is particularly evident among patients with persistent deficit symptoms. There are those who believe that poor outcome and patient resistance to rehabilitation reflect a glaring lack of fit between patient capacities and rehabilitation goals and techniques. Hogarty (1985) cites ". . . premature expectations for change or the prescription of therapeutic tasks which require adaptive efficiency, cognitive integration and insight development beyond the capability of the patient." Even highly lauded social skills training programs often fail to adequately consider the underlying cognitive deficits that influence social capacities and predict readiness and accessibility for a given treatment strategy. For example, role playing (a core technique in such interventions) often requires the ability to deal with more than one perspective at a time, a highly elusive cognitive skill for many participants. Trying to learn social skills in a demanding social milieu requiring complex processing appears to compound problems rather than solve them. For some, the side effects of medication and the rehabilitation process itself undermine outcome, limit potentials for learning and generalizing skills, and actually precipitate symptom exacerbation.

Current knowledge compels us to consider the relationships among cerebral defects, cognitive deficits, medication effects, vulnerabilities to stress, pervasive difficulties in occupational performance, and treatment response. The remaining sections of this chapter focus on strategies that attempt to address these issues. Although no substantive research data are currently available to demonstrate the predictable efficacy of these techniques with the schizophrenic population, a confluence of factors support their application and careful study.

RATIONALE AND OBJECTIVES FOR REHABILITATION

Brain behavioral models provide useful contexts for understanding the occupational performance of schizophrenics and establishing a framework for treatment objectives and strategies. DSI considers the patient's difficulties within a field involving neurobiological and affective capacities, the demands of a given role and task, and the expectations and dynamics of the social-environmental press. It serves an integrative role in bringing together a variety of biopsychosocial perspectives. Information processing theory, in turn, magnifies a central component of this transaction. It directs our attention to the infrastructure of thought and action: the states of arousal, attention, perception, retention, organization, mental strategies, response patterns, and executive functions needed to negotiate task and environment. Both are of importance in developing meaningful interventions.

Spaulding and colleagues (1986) provide a useful structure for conceptualizing treatment within a framework that acknowledges vulnerability, stress, information processing overload, hyperarousal, and social-interpersonal deficits. They focus rehabilitation on (1) reducing arousal from levels that produce acute disorganization, (2) raising the threshold for disorganization, and (3) providing environmental conditions and learning experiences that favor organization. These objectives are derived from the belief that information processing capacity is greatly reduced when there are too high a demand and too many competing responses of equal strength.

THE FUNCTIONAL ASSESSMENT

Identifying these phenomena within the context of an individual's unique configuration of deficits, strengths, life roles, social network, and environmental demands is critical to any thoughtful rehabilitation effort. A functional assessment, defined as a planned process of obtaining, interpreting, and documenting the current and changing status of an individual's capacities to perform work, self-care, recreation, and leisure tasks (American Occupational Therapy Association, 1989), addresses those requirements. The reader will find a highly relevant, comprehensive approach to the functional assessment process in the AOTA Self Study Series: Assessing Function (Royeen, 1989). Its focus on occupational performance and a multidimensional person-task-environment approach to assessment makes it an extremely useful basic resource.

Generating meaningful data about occupational performance and functional living skills requires knowledge of the patient's needs, priorities, and personal perspective as well as skill in using a range of evaluative methods. Burke (1989) emphasizes the importance of acquiring intimate knowledge of the individual's role and daily life as the starting point for assessment. This should include the patient's view of himself or herself and the chronic illness that defines so much of his or her daily life, because how one interprets life experiences is often more crucial to adaptation than the actual situations themselves (Fine, 1990a). This process establishes an important collaborative set and an initial view of the individual that clarifies priorities, influences the therapist's clinical reasoning, and establishes a context that guides the selection of evaluation tools.

An interactional view of schizophrenia requires a broad range of assessment resources. One need not use them all, but knowing what they are capable of doing can facilitate decision-making and data collection. There are global assessments of major life roles, tests of daily living competencies such as hygiene, budgeting, and social skills; task analysis; and measures of psychobiological processes, reinforcers, stress, and environment (Asher, 1989; Hemphill, 1988; Kielhofner, 1985; Liberman, 1988). Instrument choice utimately reflects the fit between individual priorities and characteristics such as content, format, psychometrics, the constraints of time and money, and the patient's capacities to tolerate such investigations. Although standardized, valid methods are of great importance, observations of the individual involved in valued tasks in his or her natural environment should not be neglected. The Routine Task Inventory is an observational guide for determining the severity of disability in personal activities of daily living (Allen, 1985). Clearly, the art of assessment requires the capacity to narrow the focus and magnify particular components of performance without losing sight of the bigger biopsychosocial picture.

Our focus, information processing capacities, is no less complex an area for clinical decision-making. Therapists need to familiarize themselves with tools that identify specific cognitive deficits, measure levels of cognition, identify difficult tasks and task components, measure processing skills, and provide prognostic data. Toglia (1989a) provides an overview of cognitive assessment methods used with brain-injured adults, many of which are highly relevant to the schizophrenic population. Of particular interest are tests of attention, perception, visuomotor performance, organization, and problem-solving. The Southern California Sensory Integration Test, used principally with physically challenged and learning-disabled children, also has been applied to schizophrenic adults for purposes of examining underlying nervous system functions that influence cortical operations (Ayres, 1972; King, 1974; Pierce, 1991). Other tests developed by occupational therapists specifically for psychiatric populations include the Allen Cognitive Levels Test (Allen, 1985), the Bay Area Functional Performance Evaluation (Bloomer and Williams, 1987), and the SBC Adult Psychiatric Sensory Integration Evaluation (Schroeder et al, 1983). Lezak's (1984) classic Neuropsychological Assessment and Kendall and Hollon's (1981) Assessment Strategies for Cognitive-Behavioral Interventions review assessment issues and describe relevant standardized instruments that measure elements of information processing capacity. Computerized cognitive diagnostic batteries derived from experimental psychopathology methods have been developed by Bracy (1983), Magaro and associates (1986), and Spaulding and associates (1986, 1989) to assess functional levels across the broad spectrum of information processing stages. The last two systems have been designed to generate measures associated with abilities known to be impaired by schizophrenia.

Experimental psychopathologists have focused on the structural processing or capacity dimensions of cognition, with content traditionally playing a minor role. As a result, many assessment methods used for schizophrenia and brain disease are a seemingly arbitrary sample of content or tasks: geometric shapes, strings of letters and digits. This approach "tests the engine" irrespective of "the fuel." For clinicians who place emphasis on the interactive nature of person and task and who want a broader range of personal cognitive-behavioral data, such strategies may be disarming and inadequate if used in isolation (Kihlstrom and Nasby, 1981). Nonetheless, they represent a legitimate approach to the process of estimating what an individual can and cannot do. Like other static assessment methods, they are useful in identifying the need for treatment and establishing a performance baseline.

They do not, however, provide information about what the individual's potentials for change are, an issue of growing importance to rehabilitation specialists, administrators, and third-party payers. How quickly does the patient learn new materials, and how well does he or she retain them? How does he or she go about organizing new information? How does he or she proceed with decisions in response to environmental demands? How orderly and comprehensive are the patient's problem-solving strategies? How good a sense does he or she have of the fitness and adequacy of his or her solutions? (Erikson and Binder, 1986). These questions are basic to Toglia's (1989a) formulation of a "dynamic investigative approach" to cognitive assessment. Used as a supplement to traditional static techniques with traumatically brain-injured individuals, it addresses learning potential, analyzes individual processing strategies and style, and provides important guidelines for treatment. Dynamic assessment, derived from the work of Vygotsky (1978) and Feuerstein (1979), generates the best possible performance by altering test procedures or materials with cuing, task modification, changes in the environmental context, and questions. Strategy investigation involves probing patients' performance response by pursuing ambiguities and clarifying the clinician's hypotheses about the patient's style through a line of questioning adapted from Piagetian techniques. (Standardization of a prompting procedure and scoring format is currently under way at New York Hospital-Cornell Medical Center by Toglia and colleagues.)

Estimating potentials for change and identifying conditions that facilitate performance are of particular importance for schizophrenics, with many deficits that dominate the clinicians's field of inquiry and obscure capacities. Preliminary work with a small cohort of chronic schizophrenics at The Payne Whitney Clinic of New York Hospital-Cornell Medical Center supports the value of Toglia's method in clarifying behavioral idiosyncrasies, identifying basic processing and self-monitoring strengths and deficits, and developing meaningful treatment goals. The case material at the conclusion of this chapter provides examples of this process.

REHABILITATION STRATEGIES

Treatment strategies that are responsive to patients' underlying cerebral defects, perceptual and cognitive deficits, processing style, and vulnerabilities to stress also, by definition, must be sensitive to changes in positive and negative symptoms over the course of a given individual's illness. Because schizophrenia is not all of one piece, rehabilitation specialists must be knowledgeable and adaptive in the face of changing needs, treatment environments, and time frames. Although our overall mission is enhanced role performance in keeping with individual potentials, acute and chronic stages require different goals and different strategies. Short-term or preliminary goals often address the mastery of microscopic elements of that larger objective (ie, more focused attention, better problem-solving capabilities, more effective communication). Because some treatment activities may appear unrelated to the manifest problems that confront patients, we often find ourselves struggling to justify what we do, where we do it, and whether or not it is a reasonable and relevant thing to do during a particular phase of an illness. How intensive should rehabilitation be during acute episodes? What should its frequency and duration be in the community? What should it address, and how can it best be implemented? What evidence is there to support its value? These are increasingly important issues from both clinical and cost-benefit perspectives.

Schizophrenic arousal, low thresholds for disorganization, and pervasive cognitive impairments are core problems that provide a useful framework for phase-specific rehabilitation planning and research activity. Their impact on occupational performance and their relationship to prevailing views of schizophrenia allow us to respond to our patients' functional dilemmas while participating in a larger professional effort to generate meaningful answers to some of the aforementioned questions.

Reducing and Regulating Arousal

Antipsychotic drugs are, at the present time, the most potent means for reducing and regulating arousal in the schizophrenic patient. During acute psychotic states, potentials for hyperarousal and competing responses also may be modulated by minimizing stimulation and distractions. Some activity and milieu therapy techniques have been discredited during short-term acute hospitalizations because of the ambiguous, stimulating nature of group encounters for patients with impaired cognition and tenuous control (Drake and Sederer, 1986). However, this should not be interpreted as a negation of well-planned, controlled interventions that are attentive to contemporary knowledge about patient capacity. Carefully titrated brief contacts that are structured but not overly stimulating, explicit repetitive instructions, clear feedback about the consequences of behavior, and the calculated management of the milieu can create a holding environment, promote reality orientation, and address relevant, manageable short-term goals (Kahn and White, 1989; Kaplan, 1988).

Fine (1989) has conceptualized such interventions as "brief focused rehabilitation"—the time-limited, task and goal–centered means of acquiring self-management skills. Feeling in control of oneself, working toward meaningful, manageable goals, learning that problems are solvable, and cultivating some competencies and resources with which to solve them are essential features of self-management. They are also an important means for regulating arousal that cannot be achieved through medication alone. High rates of relapse and rehospitalization attest to the need for thoughtful interventions that modulate response to environmental stress. Poor medication response, severe side effects, and noncompliance make alternative means of stabilizing patients an important option. Carpenter and associates (1977) report positive results in the use of highly structured psychosocial strategies without medication. Longitudinal studies are currently under way to measure the efficacy of combining low-dose medication with family psychoeducation to manage the arousal effects of high expressed emotion relationships (Schooler, 1991).

Some patients can be taught to manage their own arousal during nonacute stages of their illness. Benson's (1975) relaxation response, systematic induction of proper breathing, and passive relaxation with imagery have been used to reduce the effects of stress and create less stressful environments (Lukoff et al, 1986; Stein and Nikolic, 1989). The reduction of arousal is believed to have both biological and psychological effects. The patient's sense of being in control of himself or herself plus the focused effort required to do these procedures are believed to produce neurochemical activity that protects the immune system and may stimulate the production of dopamine. The implications of this hypothesis for other activities that require meaningful focused effort and promote self-control are of great interest and merit continued investigation.

Although some practitioners report success with relaxation strategies, it is not an appropriate intervention for all schizophrenic patients, particularly during acute phases of the illness. Even during more stable periods, care must be taken in establishing a comfortable threshold for "letting go" and managing imagery and sensations brought to awareness without stimulating undue anxiety in patients with fluid boundaries and impaired body image. An individualized, carefully managed approach to relaxation with this population is demonstrated by the case of Sara. Her experience is described in Case Report 2.

Raising Thresholds for Disorganization: Movement as an Organizer for Higher Cognitive Functions

The schizophrenic's propensity for disorganization is a core dimension of his or her inability to function. If one were able to elevate that threshold and protect the individual from the collision of stress and vulnerability, it seems likely that a great deal more could be accomplished. The protection derived from social support, skill competencies within the treatment environment, and medication often is not adequate for generalization under the duress of community living. Other means for deterring disorganization are needed. Sensori-integrative strategies provide an appealing, but heretofore unfulfilled, possibility.

Under normal conditions, the brain's sensory integrative processes transform sensory information about external and internal environments into a simplified, meaningful representation of events. One might well identify sensory integration as a linchpin for information processing. Deficits in sensory or integrative functions in some schizophrenics interfere with that basic level of processing. King's (1974) application of sensory integrative therapy with process schizophrenics was based on a belief that adaptive movement is one of the most powerful organizers of sensory input (Ayres, 1972). Although sensory integration requires constant interaction of all systems, it is believed to be managed by the cerebellum and brain stem. Such subcortical regulation, in turn, depends on adequate sensory stimulation and arousal.

King used a range of pleasurable but nondemanding sensory and gross motor activities with chronic patients with affective flattening, postural irregularities, and poor movement patterns to normalize movements, strengthen upper trunk stability, and enhance arousal and motor planning capacities. Jorstad and associates (1977) report improvements in sensory dysfunction, socialization capacities, affect, self-esteem, and general functioning with a small sample of process schizophrenics who were seen twice daily, five times a week, for up to 6 months. Other clinicians have reported varying degrees of response to their adaptations of King's method (Crist, 1979; Rider, 1978; Ross and Burdick, 1981). However, little substantive research has been generated to support the promise of this approach. Although new scientific findings and our culture's commitment to exercise as an antidote for stress and disorganization provide renewed impetus for applying movement strategies to schizophrenia, controlled studies are needed to identify the value and the limits of the technique. Important questions have been raised regarding the linkage of change at the brain stem with changes at the cortical level (Ottenbacher, 1982). We need to know more about the impact of sensory integration strategies during and after treatment. What measurable gains are achieved in cognitive and social adaptation? Is it reasonable to expect a direct effect, or should cognitive and social adaptation be perceived, instead, as an initial intervention that prepares the central nervous system for the next level of information processing remediation? It appears to be an appropriate time to put King's (1990) belief in "moving the body to change the mind" to the test of more vigorous clinical trials.

Learning Experiences That Favor Organization: Cognitive Rehabilitation

Although sensorimotor approaches seek order by stimulating integration at the lower levels of the central nervous system, interventions directed at organizing higher level cortical activities have gained in popularity. Cognitive therapies have proliferated for virtually all of the major mental illnesses. Most focus on the content and dynamics of thought, whereas others use social learning strategies to stimulate problem-solving and social interpersonal behaviors. In contrast, cognitive perceptual rehabilitation—used principally with traumatic brain injuries—addresses the infrastructure and process of thought and action. It systematically stimulates and organizes the individual's capacity to handle information by improving mental strategies and developing a greater behavioral repertoire with which to learn, perceive, and interact with the environment (Abreu and Toglia, 1987). If negative symptoms truly reflect defects in the structural and neurochemical integrity of the brain, there is an inherent logic in applying cognitive rehabilitation to schizophrenia (Carpenter, 1985; Magaro, 1986; Spaulding et al, 1986, 1989). Although one cannot assume equivalency of traumatic brain injuries with the longer term anomalies of schizophrenia, theories of neuroplasticity, work with the learning disabled, and reports of functional gains in stroke patients long after the traditional window of opportunity for recovery has closed provide food for thought.

Cognitive rehabilitation is based on the assumption that brain damage rarely eliminates the total capacity to perform a task. Although efficiency may be diminished, the human brain provides more avenues for function to emerge (Bach-y-Rita, 1980, 1989; Luria, 1980). Recovery of function has been credited to a variety of conditions: the spontaneous release of compensatory skills with lower brain areas assuming control, the substitution of intact cognitive skills and behavioral strategies, the interaction of different brain areas, or through a planned reorganization of functional systems (Bracy, 1986). Luria's theories of planned reorganization of functional systems are based on the uniquely adaptive behavior of the human cortical system in interaction with the environment over time. Motivation, meaningful activity, and conscious compensation are critical aspects of this adaptation. "In human activity, recognition of the aim during the completion of activity allows reorganization across different levels of cortical functions which otherwise would not have been connected" (Armstrong, 1989). Long periods of training and considerable effort are required to stimulate new functional systems, with short frequent contacts yielding the most effective results. Luria's (1963; 1973; 1980) retraining methods employ systematic repetitive exercises that place demands on the individual to perform the impaired skill through the mastery of increasingly complex skill components. His theories and methods should be required reading for task-oriented practitioners irrespective of their area of specialization. Readers unfamiliar with the range of cognitive rehabilitation theories and methods also are referred to Abreu and Toglia (1987), Ben-Yishay and Diller (1983), Dougherty and Randomski (1987), Meier and associates (1987), Prigatono (1985), Sohlberg and Mateer (1989), and Trexler (1987).

The practitioner with experience with brain injuries is familiar with the problems that occur in transferring acquired skills from the clinic to the real world. It does not occur automatically. It is part of the learning process and must be addressed throughout treatment. A multicontextual treatment approach designed to facilitate the process of generalization should be of interest to practitioners in all specialties (Toglia, 1991). Toglia has applied contemporary cognitive psychology concepts to the problem by systematically identifying criteria for transfer, emphasizing information processing and metacognitive training, using meaningful activities, and integrating multiple environments into treatment planning. With these factors in mind, the goal of improving abilities to explore the environment for relevant information for a patient with attentional deficits will remain constant while the environment, movement requirements, and physical characteristics of the treatment task gradually will be altered. This approach is amplified in the Case Reports for Roger and Beatrice located at the conclusion of this chapter.

Carpenter (1985) has identified cognitive rehabilitation techniques of particular relevance to negative symptoms. They are (1) problem-solving strategies stressing use of formalized programs to develop stepwise solutions to complex tasks; (2) articulated feedback to help patients assess consequences of incorrect solutions to complex tasks; (3) exercises to develop verbal fluency and instill intellectual flexibility; (4) training that enables patients to use verbal programs from others to regulate behavior no longer controlled by unconscious and automatic schemata that rely heavily on frontal lobe integrity; and (5) training to analyze behavior and anticipate consequences.

Although these capacities are regulated by the interaction of many cognitive elements, attention plays a significant role in the overall organizational integrity of the individual's thoughts and actions. Spaulding and colleagues (1986) consider "environmental structure (ie, establishing time limits), enriched informational input, and feedback on performance" as important elements in the remediation of attentional deficits and the development of a more resilient organizational set. Self-talk and self-instructional strategies during task performance (Meichenbaum and Cameron, 1973) and interventions focused on continuous work performance are reported to improve attentional capacities in schizophrenic patients. Although a variety of therapeutic modalities fulfill Carpenter's and Spaulding's criteria, computer-based interventions are particularly well suited to facilitating attention and overall cognitive organization.

Armstrong (1989) describes the use of computer-based interventions with brain-injured individuals as "an exploration into the inter-system and inter-functional forms of conscious, goal-oriented reorganization. Mental control, conceptual organization and goal-awareness can be stimulated by interactions with computer programs." In recognition of such potential, the production of specialized software programs has developed into a growth industry, with resource manuals and program analyses formats available to assist the clinician in establishing an appropriate fit between task and patient needs (DLM Teaching Resources, 1989; Goldojarb, 1985; Kreutzer et al, 1987; Shaw and McKenna, 1989).

The special properties of computers also have attracted mental health practitioners involved in cognitive retraining of schizophrenic patients. Magarow (1986) has applied commercially available games to this population, emphasizing the motivational characteristics of the software and the task and the infinite patience of the machine. Fine (1990b) has used a graded range of remedial, educational, and recreational programs to stimulate attentional, memory, problem-solving, and role-taking behaviors in negative symptom patients. The highly interactive but modifiable nature of the computer gives patients external support needed to develop independent work habits. It can provide continuous and immediate feedback through a hierarchy of visual and auditory cues. Because many software packages permit graded levels of difficulty, the patient has more control over what and how much goes on in each session. Such control, and opportunities for repetition, support the integration of skills through overlearning, a seemingly necessary phenomenon for those with diffuse defects. Although the therapist plays a central role in designing and directing treatment, inducting the patient into the world of high technology, providing additional prompts and cues, and reinforcing the growth of cognitive capacities, the interpersonal demands of this method are far more controllable than are group treatments.

Task-Oriented Learning Therapy: A Sequential Graded Treatment Package

Cognitive retraining for schizophrenia must be viewed as part of a comprehensive systematic rehabilitation program that is sensitive to patients' readiness to experience and respond to increasingly complex stimuli and real life situations. A growing trend toward supplementary social group treatments for the brain injured supports this belief. A graded treatment package (Task-Oriented Learning Therapy) combining cognitive rehabilitation and social skills training for patients with negative deficit symptoms has been developed by occupational therapy staff at The Payne Whitney Clinic (Fine, 1990b). The Computer-Based Skill Acquisition Program (CBSAP) and a group-centered psychoeducational program called the Life Skills Curriculum provide an opportunity to put skill acquisition into a meaningful perspective. As indicated above, the CBSAP is designed to address basic attentional, information processing, and role-taking deficits that influence higher level cognitive and interpersonal function. Software programs, selected and graded to meet individual needs, are administered several times a week for periods determined by patient response patterns. This phase of the treatment package provides manageable learning experiences that stimulate and organize basic cognitive skills that prepare patients for the more demanding social skills group strategy. "The key to delivering interventions systematically is to treat the most molecular defects first, whenever possible. . . . If an intervention is aimed at a molar deficit that is mediated by a molecular deficit (eg, social skills training attempted with patients having severe attentional deficits), the effect of the intervention can be suboptimal" (Spaulding, 1986).

The Life Skills Curriculum applies social learning principles and graded, goal-directed activities to the acquisition of problem-solving and communication skills in a group setting (Fine and Schwimmer, 1986). Like other social learning applications, frequent practice, repetition, reinforcement, modeling, and feedback are core tools for fostering desired behaviors. They are promoted in a classroom milieu through the use of lectures, group discussion, role playing, game playing, video and audio resources, paper and pencil exercises, and homework assignments. Although the manifest content of a class or series of classes may be goal setting, stress and time management, leisure-time planning or social skills, problem solving, and communication are core objectives for all sessions. Instructional components are selected and graded to match attention, memory, and learning styles as best as one can within a group context. Multimodal techniques that tap visual, auditory, and motor capacities also are important components of the curriculum. Pre- and postcourse self-assessments such as the Payne Whitney Clinic Life Skills Learning Needs Assessment or Bienvenu's (1976) Interpersonal Communication Inventory reinforce a central assumption that participants are capable of identifying their own learning needs and monitoring changes in their own behavior. Commitment to encouraging patients' self-management capacities is further reinforced by their input into content, sequence, and duration of learning modules (Greenberg et al, 1986).

Both strategies are based on principles deemed particularly important to the population under consideration.

1. Behavior is more than it appears to be. Clinicians must look beneath the surface of manifest behaviors to understand and promote behavioral change. The cognitive underpinnings of social competency are central themes in this treatment package.

2. Learning by doing is a powerful instrument for change if designed and applied appropriately. A manageable balance of task and talk is essential.

3. Graded skill acquisition, directed at the optimal match between level of function and level of arousal (Kaplan, 1988) and presented at the patient's pace, is most likely to yield an adaptive response.

4. Essential opportunities for repetition, practice, and feedback must provide manageable novelty and reflect the interests and values of the patient if engagement is to be sustained.

5. Increased self-monitoring and self-management capacities facilitate the application of cognitive and social skills outside of the treatment environment.

Fine and colleagues (1990b) believe that the Task Oriented Learning Therapy package, along with appropriate medication, is more responsive to the biological vulnerability, high arousal potentials, low thresholds of disorganization, cognitive deficits, and social impairments that characterize the negative symptom syndrome.

RESEARCH OPPORTUNITIES

The functional impairments associated with the schizophrenias represent rich and compelling areas of investigation for clinicians. Rehabilitation specialists must take the initiative in evaluating the efficacy of their modalities if the promise of these interventions is to be fulfilled and current commitments to rehabilitation are to be sustained. The National Institute of Mental Health (1987) Schizophrenia Research Panel underscores the need for an expanded base of knowledge in many relevant areas. These include

Isolating and defining specific deficits and designing focused strategies specifically aimed at overcoming them.

Assessing the impact of short- and long-term rehabilitation strategies with sub-groups of schizophrenic patients with different symptom patterns and functional deficits.

Defining treatment and rehabilitation requirements at different phases of the illness.

Identifying environmental settings and conditions that facilitate the treatment and rehabilitation process.

Studying the interaction of drug, neuropsychological, and social-learning interventions.

CONCLUSION

Schizophrenia represents a complex heterogeneous grouping of disorders, among them a particularly refractory sub-group whose negative deficit symptoms represent functional disabilities of major proportions. The emergence of relevant neuroscientific data provides us with challenging opportunities to broaden our vision of mental health practice, better understand the intransigent behaviors of many patients, develop innovative strategies, and design controlled outcome studies.

The vulnerability-stress model provides a particularly useful formula for observing the interaction among brain, mind, and environment, because neither the patient nor the presenting problems are unidimensional. In espousing the integration of biological, psychological, and social perspectives, we are addressing a basic characteristic of schizophrenia—the need for integration. Strauss (1986) suggests that rehabilitation may not simply help compensate for deficits but may contribute in extremely important ways to the recovery process by fostering the "reintegration of self." That can be understood as a more focused, goal-oriented self emerging from increased control over disorganization and competing responses; a more empowered, accepting self emerging from the acquisition of self-monitoring and self-management skills; and a more socially competent self able to respond with greater flexibility to the demands of the environment. Such goals are best met by strategies that are sensitive to existing levels of capacity, emphasize an appropriate fit between capacity and the demands of treatment, and above all, reflect a belief that the patient is more than his or her illness (Fine, 1980).

CASE REPORT 1

Beatrice: Transferring Skills to the Real World

Presenting Problem. Beatrice, an intelligent but functionally impaired 50-year-old woman with a lengthy history of positive and negative symptoms, was increasingly preoccupied with her slowness and difficulties with self-care and home-management activities (Fine and Toglia, 1990). Her high anxiety and demoralization in response to these problems were partially linked to the earlier painful loss of an apartment and personal possessions during a prolonged psychotic episode. The stress provoked by these memories appeared to limit already compromised problem-solving capacities. Various skill acquisition techniques were used, practiced, and mastered in one-to-one and group occupational therapy sessions. However, these methods failed her at home, where they mattered most.

Occupational Therapy Objectives

1. Clarify issues that influence this patient's inability to transfer learned behaviors in the clinic to the natural environment in which the skills are needed; estimate her potential for change.

2. Develop and implement a rehabilitation service plan that will modify the conditions that currently undermine her personal goals and functional capacities.

Occupational Therapy Evaluation. Dynamic investigative assessment techniques were introduced to identify factors contributing to her inability to generalize acquired skills and to ascertain the modifiability of her exhausting routines. Personality and emotional factors were already well known to the therapist. Task and environment variables were reviewed through observation and analysis in her home. A battery of assessments, focused on internal processing strategies and incorporating cuing and investigative questions, was chosen to identify deficits and conditions that maximize performance. This included the Contextual Memory Test, the Dynamic Visual Processing Assessment, and the Category Flexibility and Deductive Reasoning Test (Toglia, 1992). Surprisingly, most of Beatrice's difficulties were chiefly those of style rather than capacity. Visuomotor skills, attention, short-term memory, and basic organizational capacities were sufficiently intact but not always accessible because of a lack of efficiency (eg, overattentiveness to detail, difficulty disengaging from a task) and inadequate self-monitoring skills. During assessment sessions, she was responsive to cuing, able to retain information, apply it to subsequent assessment tasks that looked different, and improve the efficiency of her cognitive operations. Prior assessments and rehabilitation efforts had not made those distinctions. Beatrice found great comfort in learning that there were significant strengths where she and her succession of mental health therapists believed there to be principally deficits.

Occupational Therapy Service Plan. As a result of these data, efforts to engage her potential were shifted from skill training groups to techniques that enhance her ability *to monitor her own tendencies* to overfocus on details, make unecessary work for herself, and take too much time to complete tasks.

With self-monitoring skills as the mental strategy we wished to address at this juncture in treatment, therapist and patient developed a simple self-assessment form that she could use each morning to track how much time she actually used for bathing, cleaning, and eating breakfast. Because her slow pace and overattention to detail were a problem, realistic time frames for each task were established in advance. The evaluation, written as a questionnaire, also was designed to internalize necessary cues and prompts and reduce the potency of her external locus of control orientation. It posed such questions as: How much time did my breakfast take? Did I meet the goals I set? If not, what got in the way? Was there anything I could have done differently? Could two things have been done at the same time (eg, listen for the weather forecast while eating)? Did my thoughts about my past get in the way?

Beatrice was also given written guidelines to help her organize her thoughts before initiating any task. Although this approach may not be suitable for all patients, her basic intellect, motivation for increased autonomy, and her affinity for techniques that she associates with school and the structure they provide made this strategy a reasonable and fruitful one. Within the context of each self-care or home-management activity, the guidelines asked her to

1. Visualize a job well done. Imagine what you need to do, step by step, to get this done in the most efficient way.

2. Avoid unecessary actions—don't get caught in all of those extra details.

3. Don't get stuck with thoughts about the past. You are working on today and tomorrow!

4. Use your time as efficiently as you can.

The same techniques were applied to a succession of other meaningful activities: cooking tasks requiring recipe selection, shopping, budgeting, and meal preparation; making holiday cards on a computer with software that requires independent decision-making; writing a letter in response to a simulated life event that would ordinarily set her off (eg, to the Internal Revenue Service, Social Security Administration, her mother). In each instance, the behaviors she wishes to monitor are identified, and manageable goals, questionnaires, and guidelines are developed. These activities, and the outcome of the preceding week's "homework," are reviewed with the therapist in weekly sessions. The patient's responsiveness to this approach has been notable; she has chosen independently a similar process to successfully curtail her long-term smoking habit.

CASE REPORT 2

Sara: Managing Stress and Arousal

Presenting Problem. Sara is a 32-year-old single woman whose physical presence alone conveys the essence of a 15-year struggle with chronic schizophrenia and the effects of multiple hospitalizations and neuroleptics. Although medication helps sustain her in the community, it in no way insulates her from constant anxiety and emotional pain. Her level of stress and arousal is usually palpable when she arrives at her occupational therapist's office for sessions intended to address activities of daily living. Her large, overstuffed purse is usually anchored across hunched shoulders; her house keys are clutched in a wad of tissues to disguise them from threats of the street; and her pained expression clearly conveys that she has exceeded her limits for coping with internal and external stimuli. The therapist's first challenge is to reduce the degree of arousal before pursuing any other goals.

Occupational Therapy Intervention. Effective stress reduction strategies with Sara follow a particular pattern that has emerged after numerous years of work together. Finding the right strategy for individuals with schizophrenia is complex. Relaxation techniques are not always appropriate for this population. However, a variety of factors contribute to the success of regulated breathing, muscle relaxation, and self-selected imagery with this particular individual. One is the long-term nature of her therapeutic alliance with the therapist; a second is the degree to which the patient's need to maintain control over the situation is honored. For Sara, relaxation activities are almost always preceded by the presentation of some small unsolicited gift to the therapist (usually several new postage stamps), angry ranting over old traumas and injustices (as if they had occurred just moments ago), or both.

Establishing control (first with her gift and then by letting off some emotional steam) appears to be an essential prelude to the actual relaxation process that enhances her ability to use it productively. They are all important parts of the process of regulating the arousal that everyday events provoke. They appear to create a focus and structure for the competing responses that otherwise flood her and make her inaccessible to any interventions. They provide access to her basic information processing capacities and allow her to put her preoccupations into the perspective of the here and now and proceed with other aspects of her rehabilitation program.

CASE REPORT 3

Roger: Attending to the Details of Work and Social Relationships

Presenting Problem. This 28-year-old single junior college graduate has been referred to an occupational therapist for a consultation regarding his current functional status and longer term vocational and social potential. Roger recently was discharged from his third brief psychiatric hospitalization in 4 years. He is unemployed, without significant friendships, and living with his parents. He is eager to find a respectable place for himself in the work force but is unrealistic about his career goals, as he strives to match his high-achieving siblings. He is demoralized by the recurrence of his illness, his inability to support himself, the absence of friendships and romance, and his mother's style of anxious caretaking. He is well-groomed, but stiff and awkward in the management of his body. He is likable and capable of humor, but his affect is generally flat and stereotypal. Most notable is his vagueness, disorganization, tendency to answer questions without sufficient thought, and inability to sustain conversations or follow through on his own goals.

Personal History. Roger has a long-standing history of adjustment problems, manifest since childhood in poor social and academic performance: "I was slower at learning than others." Although classroom difficulties strongly suggested a significant learning disability, his neurobehavioral problems were never formally diagnosed until adulthood. At the present time, he also carries a psychiatric diagnosis of schizophrenia, with both florid and deficit symptoms. Depression also surfaces after each psychotic episode, making the recovery period more difficult and potentially risky. He has worked as a messenger, hospital aide, and security guard but aspires to something with more status in the health care or legal field.

Occupational Therapy Objectives

1. Identify patient's potential for vocational and social adjustment.

2. Develop manageable short- and long-term goals with the patient.

3. Propose a rehabilitation plan.

Occupational Therapy Evaluation. In an initial interview, Roger provided an adequately detailed—albeit slow—report of his educational, vocational, and psychiatric trials and tribulations. Although he strongly emphasized his desire to obtain respectable, meaningful work, he had no real plan for pursuing this goal; prior jobs had simply "come up." His social disabilities were most evident in more open-ended conversation or when the therapist posed a moderately complex question. His responses were punctuated by "I lost you" or by a glazed expression. These social-interpersonal behaviors and his inability to make his goals operational warranted closer scrutiny. Summaries of prior neuropsychological testing documented the presence of a developmental learning disability and emphasized problems with sustained attention and concentration but said little else. For this assessment, Toglia's (1992) Dynamic Visual Processing Assessment, Contextual Memory Test, and Category Flexibility and Deductive Reasoning Test were chosen to elicit more specific information about processing style and strategies, to estimate his potential for change, and to guide treatment planning.

Roger demonstrated good attention, flexibility, and organizational skills on concrete tasks in which he was able to externally manipulate information. His characteristic difficulties emerged when internal planning, decision-making, and deductive reasoning were called for. He would become more disorganized, lose track of information, overfocus on some parts of the situation, and miss the "bigger picture." Performance on complex tasks was impulsive and characterized by trial and error; he tended to overestimate his own abilities. He was able to use verbal cues and external structure to correct situations in which he omitted essential information. Tasks involving procedural learning generated good results. However, in situations requiring logic or the management of simultaneous facts, verbal cuing did not help.

Although this patient's functional impairments were already observable, these findings addressed their specific nature and provided greater clarity about probable fixed limitations and those that might be changed. This information was shared with the referring psychiatrist and used for counseling the patient and his family as well as for formulating an initial treatment strategy directed at underlying information processing skills needed to maximize vocational and social role potentials.

Occupational Therapy Intervention. A brief, focused, written outline of these findings was shared with the patient. Emphasis was placed on what he did best, what he could improve, and how treatment might help him with work and socialization. He agreed to work on his tendency to ignore important facts in problem-solving situations and learn how to check himself along the way and was particularly pleased to learn that the computer would be used in the process. A graded treatment package (Task Oriented Learning Therapy) combining cognitive rehabilitation strategies (Computer-Based Skill Acquisition Program) and social skills training (Life Skills Curriculum) will be used to cultivate these capacities. Initially, selected computer exercises and games will be used twice weekly to expand Roger's capacities for attending to details, considering situations more carefully, and cultivating self-monitoring skills. These skills will be reinforced with homework assignments formulated around information gathering about independent living facilities or jobs that are of interest to him. As in the case of Beatrice, simple written guidelines and other structured formats will be developed to assist him within and outside of the clinic. The Life Skills Curriculum will be introduced when he demonstrates an understanding and ability to transfer these processing strategies to the more complex demands of social skills development and group interaction. Both strategies will then be used concurrently until maximum benefit is achieved. Progress will be reviewed on a monthly basis.

References

Abreu B, Toglia JP: Cognitive rehabilitation: a model for occupational therapy. Am J Occup Ther 41:439–448, 1987.

Allen CK: Occupational therapy for psychiatric diseases: measurement and management of cognitive disabilities. Boston, Little, Brown & Co, 1985.

American Occupational Therapy Association (AOTA): Uniform terminology for occupational therapy (2nd ed). Am J Occup Ther 43:808–815, 1989.

American Psychiatric Association: Diagnostic and statistical manual of mental disorders (3rd ed rev). Washington, DC, 1986.

Anderson CM, Reiss DJ, Hogarty GE: Schizophrenia and the family. New York, Guilford, 1986.

Andreason N: The diagnosis of schizophrenia. Schizophr Bull 13(1):9–22, 1987.

Andreason N: Positive vs negative schizophrenia: a critical evaluation. Schizophr Bull 11(3):380–389, 1985.

Andreason N: The scale for the assessment of negative symptoms (SANS). Iowa City, Iowa, University of Iowa, 1983.

Andreason N: Negative symptoms in schizophrenia: definition and reliability. Arch Gen Psychiatry 39:784–788, 1982a.

Andreason N: Negative vs positive schizophrenia: definition and validation. Arch Gen Psychiatry 39:789–794, 1982b.

Anthony WA, Nemec P: Psychiatric Rehabilitation. In Bellack AS (ed): Schizophrenia Treatment, Management and Rehabilitation. New York, Grune & Stratton, 1984.

Armstrong C: Luria's theory of brain function recovery with applications to the use of computers in cognitive retraining. Cognitive Rehabilitation, January/February:10–15, 1989.

Asher IE: An Annotated Index of Occupational Therapy Evaluation Tools. Rockville, MD, American Occupational Therapy Association, 1989.

Ayres AJ: Sensory Integration and Learning Disabilities. Los Angeles, Western Psychological Services, 1972.

Bach-y-Rita P (ed): Recovery of Function: Theoretical Considerations for Brain Injury Rehabilitation. Bern, Switzerland, Hans Huber, 1980.

Bach-y-Rita P (ed): Traumatic Brain Injury. New York, Demos, 1989.

Ben-Yishay Y, Diller L: Cognitive Remediation. In Rosenthal M (ed): Rehabilitation of the Head Injured Adult. Philadelphia, PA, FA Davis Co, 1983, pp 367–380.

Benson H: The Relaxation Response. New York, William Morrow, 1975.

Bienvenu MJ: An interpersonal communication inventory. J Communication 21(4):381–388, 1971.

Bloomer JS, Williams SK: The Bay Area Functional Performance Evaluation. Palo Alto, CA, Consulting Psychologists Press Inc, 1987.

Bracey O: Computer based cognitive rehabilitation. Cognitive Rehabilitation 1(1):7–8, 1983.

Bracey O: Cognitive rehabilitation: a process approach. Cognitive Rehabilitation 4(2):10–17, 1986.

Braff D, Saccuzzo D: The time course of information processing deficits in schizophrenia. Am J Psychiatry 142:170–174, 1985.

Burke JP: Selecting evaluation tools. In Royeen CB (ed): Self Study Series: Assessing Function. Rockville, MD, American Occupational Therapy Association, 1989.

Carpenter W: Thoughts on the treatment of schizophrenia. Schizophr Bull 12:527–539, 1986.

Carpenter WT, Heinrichs DW, Alphs SD: Treatment of negative symptoms. Schizophr Bull 11(3):440–452, 1985.

Carpenter WT, McGlashan T, Strauss JS: The treatment of acute schizophrenia without drugs. Am J Psychiatry 134:14–20, 1977.

Carpenter WT, Strauss JS, Bartko JJ: Flexible system for the diagnosis of schizophrenia: report from the WHO International Pilot Study of Schizophrenia. Science 182:1275–1277, 1973.

Crist P: Body image changes in chronic non-paranoid schizophrenics. Can J Occup Ther 42(2):61–65, 1979.

DLM Teaching Resources: Apple computer resources in special education. Texas, Allen, 1989.

Dougherty PM, Randomski MV: Cognitive Rehabilitation Workbook. Rockville, MD, Aspen Publishers, 1987.

Drake RE, Sederer LI: Inpatient psychosocial treatment of chronic schizophrenia: negative effects and current guidelines. Hosp Community Psychiatry 37:897–901, 1986.

Erickson RC, Binder LM: Cognitive deficits among functionally psychotic patients: a rehabilitative perspective. J Clin Exp Neuropsychol 8(3):257–274, 1986.

Fine SB: Clinical Casebook II: Psychosocial Issues and Adaptive capacities. In Royeen CB (ed), Self Study Series: Assessing Function. Rockville, MD, American Occupational Therapy Association, 1990a.

Fine SB: Task oriented learning for deficit symptoms: putting skill acquisition into proper perspective. Symposium: treatment of negative symptoms of schizophrenia. American Psychiatric Association 143rd Annual Meeting, New York, 1990b.

Fine SB: Brief focused rehabilitation: strategies for short-term psychiatric settings. Presentation at American Occupational Therapy Conference, Baltimore, MD, April, 1989.

Fine SB: Psychiatric treatment and rehabilitation: what's in a name? Psychiatric Hospital 12:8–13, 1980.

Fine SB, Schwimmer P: The effects of occupational therapy on independent living skills. Mental Health Special Interest Newsletter, Am Occup Ther Assoc 9:1–3, 1986.

Fine SB, Toglia JP: Applying cognitive rehabilitation to mental health practice: assessment and treatment strategies for schizophrenia. Conference at New York Hospital-Cornell Medical Center, November 3, 1990.

Flor-Henry P: Influence of gender in schizophrenia as related to other psychopathological syndromes. Schizophr Bull 16(2):211–227, 1990.

Feuerstein R: The Dynamic Assessment of Retarded Performers: The Learning Potential Device, Theory, Instruments and Techniques. Baltimore, University Park Press, 1979.

Gazzaniga MS: Mind Matters: How Mind and Brain Interact to Create Our Conscious Lives. Boston, Houghton Mifflin, 1988.

Gibson JJ: The Ecological Approach to Visual Perception. Hillsdale, NY, Lawrence Erlbaum Associates, 1986.

Goldojarb M: Software classification form: organizing computer software. Cognitive Rehabilitation, September/October, 1985.

Goy RW, McEwen BS: Sexual differentiation of the brain. Cambridge MA, MIT Press, 1980.

Greenberg L, Fine SB, Cohen C, et al: An interdisciplinary psychoeducational program for schizophrenic patients and their families in an acute care setting. Hosp Community Psychiatry 39(3):277–282, 1986.

Hemphill B (ed): Mental Health Assessment in Occupational Therapy. Thorofare, NJ, Slack, 1988.

Hersen M, Bellack AS: Social skills training for chronic psychiatric patients: rationale, research findings, and future directions. Comprehensive Psychiatry 17:559–580, 1976.

Hogarty GE: Treatment resistance of schizophrenic patients to social and vocational rehabilitation: the nature of the problem and model of treatment. Presentation at International Symposium on Schizophrenia, Munich, Germany, October, 1985.

Holtzman PS: Eye movement dysfunctions and psychosis. Int Rev Neurobiol 27:179–205, 1985.

Jorstad V, Wilbert DE, Wirrer B: Sensory dysfunction in adult schizophrenia. Hosp Community Psychiatry 28(4):280–283, 1977.

Kahn EM, White EM: Adapting milieu approaches to acute inpatient care for schizophrenic patients. Hosp Community Psychiatry 40(6):609–614, 1989.

Kaplan K: Directive Group Therapy. Thorofare, NJ, Slack Inc, 1988.

Keith S: A national plan for schizophrenia research: report of the National Advisory Mental Health Council. (DHHS Publication No ADM 88–1571), Rockville, MD, National Institute of Mental Health, 1988.

Kendall PC, Hollon SD: Assessment Strategies for Cognitive Behavioral Interventions. New York, Academic Press, 1981.

Kielhofner G (ed): Instrument Library. A Model of Human Occupation. Baltimore, MD, Williams & Wilkins, 1985.

Kihlstron JF, Nasby W: Cognitive Tasks in Clinical Assessment: An Exercise in Applied Psychology. In Kendell PC, Hollon SD (eds): Assessment Strategies for Cognitive Behavioral Interventions. New York, Academic Press, 1981.

King LJ: A sensory-integrative approach to schizophrenia. Am J Occup Ther 28:529–536, 1974.

King LJ: Moving the body to change the mind: sensory integration therapy in psychiatry. Occup Ther Practice 1(4):12–22, 1990.

Koh SD: Remembering of Verbal Materials by Schizophrenic Young Adults. In Schwartz S (ed): Language and Cognition in Schizophrenia. Hillsdale, NJ, Erlbaum, 1978.

Kreutzer JS, Hill MR, Morrison C: Cognitive Rehabilitation Resources for the Apple II Computer. Indianapolis, IN, NeuroScience Publishers, 1987.

Leigh RJ, Zee DS: The Neurology of Eye Movements. Philadelphia, FA Davis Co, 1983.

Lezak MD: Neuropsychological Assessment (2nd ed). New York, Oxford University Press, 1984.

Liberman R: Psychiatric Rehabilitation of Chronic Mental Patients. Washington, DC, American Psychiatric Press, 1988.

Lukoff D, Wallace CJ, Liberman RP, Burke K: A holistic program for chronic schizophrenic patients. Schizophr Bull 12:274–282, 1986.

Luria AR: Restoration of Function After Brain Injury. New York, MacMillan Co, 1963.

Luria AR: The Frontal Lobes and the Regulation of Behavior. In Pribram K, Luria AR (eds): The Psychophysiology of the Frontal Lobes. New York, Academic Press, 1973.

Luria AR: Higher Cortical Functions in Man. New York, Basic Books, 1980.

Magaro PA, Johnson MH, Boring R: Information Processing Approaches to the Treatment of Schizophrenia. In Ingram R (ed): Information Processing Approaches to Clinical Psychology. New York, Academic Press, 1986.

Mayer MA: Analysis of information processing and cognitive disability theory. Am J Occup Ther 42(3):176–183, 1988.

McKenna PJ: Pathology, phenomenology and dopamine hypothesis of schizophrenia. Br J Psychiatry 151:288–301, 1987.

McGhie A, Chapman J, Lawson JS: The effect of distraction of schizophrenic performance: Z. Psychomotor ability. Br J Psychiatry 111:391–398, 1965.

McGrath ME: First person accounts. Where did I go? Schizophr Bull 10:638–640, 1984.

Meichenbaum D, Cameron R: Training schizophrenics to talk to themselves: a means of developing attentional controls. Behavior Therapy 4:515–534, 1973.

Meier M, Diller L, Benton A (eds): Neuropsychological Rehabilitation. New York, Guilford Press, 1987.

Meltzer H: The mechanism of action of novel antipsychotic drugs. Schizophr Bull 17(2):263–287, 1991.

Meltzer H: Biological studies in schizophrenia. Schizophr Bull 13(1):77–111, 1987.

Meltzer H, Stahl SM: The dopamine hypothesis of schizoprhenia: a review. Schizophr Bull 2:19–76, 1976.

National Institute of Mental Health: A national plan for schizophrenia research: report of the National Advisory Mental Health Council (DHHS Publication No ADM 88–1571), Rockville, MD, 1988.

Neuchterlein KH, Dawson MC: Information processing and attentional functioning in the developmental course of schizophrenic disorders. Schizophr Bull 10:160–203, 1984.

Oltmanns TF: Selective attention in schizophrenia and manic psychosis: the effects of distraction on information processing. J Abnorm Psychol 87:212–225, 1978.

Orzack MH, Kornetsky C: Attention dysfunction in chronic schizophrenia. Arch Gen Psychiatry 14:323–326, 1966.

Ottenbacher K: Sensory integration therapy: affect or effect. Am J Occup Ther 36:571–578, 1982.

Owens DG, Johnstone EC, Crow TJ, Frith CD, Jagoe JR, Kreel L: Lateral ventricular size in schizophrenia: relationship to the disease process and its clinical manifestations. Psychol Med 15:27–41, 1985.

Pierce D: Cognition: Temporal Orientation and Organizational Capacity. In Royeen CB (ed): Self-Study Series: Neuroscience Foundations of Human Performance. Rockville, MD, American Occupational Therapy Association, 1991.

Pogue-Geile MF, Harrow M: Negative symptoms in schizophrenia: their longitudinal course and prognostic importance. Schizophr Bull 11(3):427–439, 1985.

Prigatono G: Neuropsychological rehabilitation after brain injury. Baltimore, MD, Johns Hopkins University Press, 1985.

Rappaport M, Hopkins HK, Hall K: Auditory signal detection in paranoid and nonparanoid schizophrenics. Arch Gen Psychiatry 27:747–752, 1972.

Rider B: Sensorimotor treatment of chronic schizophrenics. Am J Occup Ther 32(7):451–455, 1978.

Royeen C (ed): Self-Study Series: Functional Assessment. Rockville, MD, American Occupational Therapy Association, 1989.

Ross M, Burdick D: Sensory Integration. Thorofare, NY, Slack Inc, 1981.

Saccuzzo DP, Hirt M, Spencer T: Backward masking as a measure of attention in schizophrenia. J Abnorm Psychol 83:512–522, 1974.

Schooler NR: Maintenance medication for schizophrenia: strategies for dose reduction. Schizophr Bull 17(2):311–324, 1991.

Schroeder CV, Block MP, Trottier EC, Stowell MS: SBC Adult Psychiatric Sensory Integration Evaluation (3rd ed). Kailua, Hawaii, Shroeder Publishing & Consulting, 1983.

Shaw C, McKenna K: Microcomputer activities for attention training. Cognitive Rehabilitation, January/February, 18–20, 1989.

Sohlberg MM, Mateer CA: Introduction to Cognitive Rehabilitation: Theory and Practice. New York, Guilford Press, 1989.

Sommers AA: Negative symptoms: conceptual and methodological problems. Schizophr Bull 11:3:364–379, 1985.

Spaulding WD, Garbin CP, Crinean WJ: The logical and psychometric prerequisites for cognitive therapy of schizophrenia. Br J Psychiatry 155(5):69–73, 1989.

Spaulding WD, Storms L, Goodrich V, Sullivan M: Experimental psychopathology in psychiatric rehabilitation. Schizophr Bull 12(4):560–577, 1986.

Stein F, Nikolic S: Teaching stress management techniques to a schizophrenic patient. Am J Occup Ther 43(3):162–169, 1989.

Strauss JS: Psychological and social etiologies. Negative symptoms of schizophrenia:

highlights of a symposium. Sponsored by Sandoz Pharmaceuticals, New York City, May, 1990.

Strauss JS: Discussion: what does rehabilitation accomplish? Schizophr Bull 12:720–723, 1986.

Toglia JP: A Dynamic Interactional Approach to Cognitive Rehabilitation. *In* Katz N (ed): Cognitive Rehabilitation: Models for Intervention in Occupational Therapy. Boston, MA: Andover Medical Publisher, 1992.

Toglia JP: Generalization of treatment: a multicontextual approach to cognitive perceptual impairment in the brain injured adult. Am J Occup ther 45(6):505–516, 1991.

Toglia JP: Approaches to cognitive assessment of the brain injured adult: traditional methods and dynamic investigation. Occup Ther Practice 1(1):36–55, 1989a.

Toglia JP: Visual perception of objects: an approach to assessment and intervention. Am J Occup Ther 44:578–595, 1989b.

Toglia JP, Golisz K: Cognitive Rehabilitation: Group Games and Activities. Tucson, Arizona, Therapy Skill Builders, 1990.

Trexler LE (ed): Cognitive Rehabilitation: Conceptualization and Intervention. New York, Plenum Press, 1982.

Vygotsky LS: Mind in Society: The Development of Higher Psychological Processes. Cambridge, MA, Harvard University Press, 1978.

Wallace CJ, Boone SE: Cognitive Factors in Social Skills of Schizophrenic Patients: Implications for Treatment. *In* Spaulding WD, Cole JK (eds): Theories of Schizophrenia and Psychosis. Lincoln, University of Nebraska Press, 1983.

Wallace CJ: Functional assessment in rehabilitation. Schizophr Bull 12(4):604–624, 1986.

Weinberger DR, Berman KF, Zec RF: Physiologic dysfunction of dorsolateral prefrontal cortex in schizophrenia: I. Regional cerebral blood flow evidence. Arch Gen Psychiatry 43:114–124, 1986.

Wohlberg G, Kornetsky C: Sustained attention in remitted schizophrenics. Arch Gen Psychiatry 28:533–537, 1973.

Zubin J, Spring G: Vulnerability: a new view of schizophrenia. J Abnorm Psychol 86:103–126, 1977.

INTRODUCTION TO BODY IMAGE DYSFUNCTION

DEFINITIONS

In Part II of this book, body image disturbances, including those involving inattention, are addressed. Body image is a complex construct and is defined to include the relevant psychological and sociological meanings of the body as well as the neural schema (Lacey and Birtchnell, 1986; Siev et al, 1986).

Body Schema

Body schema refers to the integration of proprioceptive, tactile, and pressure input making up the neural postural model. This schema is the neural foundation for perception of body position and the relationships of the body and its parts.

Body Image

Body image is a dynamic synthesis of the body schema and those environmental inputs providing relevant emotional and conceptual components. Dysfunction can therefore result from neural lesions and related psychological or sociological problems. Consequently, adequate knowledge of the research on body image assessment and treatment involves review of literature from several disciplines.

ASSESSMENT

My review of the literature on body image disturbances has shown a wide variety of assessment methods being used with physically and psychologically challenged adults. Early methods consisted of psychiatric interviews and projective techniques. Figure drawing was a typical early tool, but the variables other than body image involved in sketching a person made its validity in clinical evaluation questionable (Van Deusen Fox, 1966).

Most of the body image assessment instruments in use at the present time fall into four categories: (1) self report tools and other paper and pencil tests, (2) computer-related instruments, (3) psychophysical methods, and (4) functional tests. Tools from each of these categories have been discussed and referenced in one or more of the chapters on body image in Part II. Each category is briefly described here.

Self Report Tools and Other Paper and Pencil Tests

Many different self report instruments used to assess body image have been reported in the literature. They are of three types: (1) the semantic differential scale, (2) picture selection and, (3) responses to statements. Use of the semantic differential scale involves subjects scaling their body or body parts between bipolar adjectives such as attractive-repulsive or graceful-awkward. Picture selection instruments are used to determine whether or not selections of body shape images by patients to represent their own body are within normal limits. Many self report instruments consist of statements to which patients respond. Most statements are directly relevant, such as "I feel good about my body" (Kemeny et al, 1988).

Paper and pencil tests, other than self report tools, have been used to assess body image disturbances that are neurally based. These tests include drawing or copying figures, cancellation, and line bisection tasks. These instruments are discussed in Chapter 5.

Computer-Related Instruments

There is growing reference to computer-assisted measurement in the literature on body image. This method of evaluation is more appropriate for disturbances of the neural schema than for the psychologically based disturbances that require subjective input. Several computer-related tools are discussed in Chapter 5.

Psychophysical Methods

Psychophysical methods include size-estimation and image-distortion techniques. These procedures allow comparison of the patient's perceived body image with the patient's actual body. Size-estimation and image-distortion techniques have been thoroughly described in the literature on anorexia. They are included in Chapter 6.

Functional Tools

It is of particular interest to rehabilitation specialists to be able to determine whether or not body image problems are interfering with the occupational performance of their patients. Functional tools are now being developed, particularly for those patients having neural-based disturbances. These tools relate practical everyday performance to the body schema disturbance.

CLASSIFICATION

Lacey and Birtchnell (1986) classified four types of body image disturbances, which I have adopted in Part II of this book. Their first two categories involved primary disturbances of the neural body schema; their second two categories focused on the psychosocial aspects of body image disorders. Consequently, classification is relevant to treatment goals.

Neurological Disorders

The first grouping discussed by Lacey and Birtchnell (1986) included disturbances due to neurological disorders. Dysfunction can result from cerebral lesions or from effects of drugs. The unilateral neglect of post-stroke patients illustrates body image dysfunction in this category. Because stroke patients are frequent recipients of rehabilitation services, this type of body image disturbance was chosen from the first category for detailed discussion in a subsequent chapter.

Phantom Phenomena

The second body schema category described by Lacey and Birtchnell (1986) was that of disorders from acute dismemberment, the phantom phenomena. This phenomenon is defined by the lingering sensation of the missing part following amputation. Chapter 7 deals with this type of body image disturbance. The phantom phenomena also are discussed in the chapters describing body image disturbances related to mastectomy and spinal cord injury, although psychosocial aspects of body image are of greater importance for these problems.

Disturbances with Physical Disability

The third category included potential body image problems for those persons with actual physical disability. Patients may acquire negative aspects of body image from societal attitudes. From this category, I have included discussions on body image disturbances associated with burns, spinal cord injury, and arthritis.

Disturbances Without Physical Disability

Lacey and Birtchnell's (1986) last category was one in which body image disturbance is present without an actual predisposing physical disability. Many psychiatric patients show this kind of problem. Anorexia nervosa patients present body image distortion of this type. I discuss the considerable body of research about their problem in a subsequent chapter.

References

Kemeny MM, Wellisch DK, Schain WS: Psychosocial outcome in a randomized surgical trial for treatment of primary breast cancer. Cancer 62:1231–1237, 1988.

Lacey JH, Birtchnell SA: Review article—body image and its disturbances. J Psychosom Res 30:623–631, 1986.

Siev E, Freishtat B, Zoltan B: Perceptual and cognitive dysfunction in the adult stroke patient (rev ed). Thorofare, NJ, Slack, 1986.

Van Deusen Fox J: Body Schema Defects in the Neurologically Impaired: Current Approaches to Evaluation and Treatment. *In* Allard I (Chair): Body Image. Proceedings of the Ohio Occupational Therapy Association, Cleveland, Ohio, 1966.

5

JULIA VAN DEUSEN

UNILATERAL NEGLECT FROM BRAIN LESION

Unilateral neglect (UN) is the body schema disorder of the neurologically impaired individual that presents the greatest problem for favorable occupational performance and rehabilitation outcome. In this chapter, I review the current thinking on the relation of the nervous system to UN with emphasis on the attentional deficit perspective. Many options for the assessment of UN have been discussed in the literature. Measurement tools range from simple paper and pencil line bisection to sophisticated computer tests. Occupational performance tests are also available for UN. Treatment procedures for UN have evolved both from neural and from learning theory. However, there are few reports showing the efficacy of these procedures. Although much research has been conducted that is pertinent to rehabilitation of persons with UN, there is need for studies directed to results of intervention procedures.

The term unilateral neglect typically denotes a deficit affecting the awareness of the body half and extrapersonal space contralateral to the site of a brain lesion. Body schema often is the term used to connote the neural part of body image. In the introduction to Part II, I discussed Lacey and Birtchnell's (1986) categories of body image disturbances. Their category disturbances due to neurological disorders is the appropriate one for UN.

From the writing of Cumming (1988), I can further clarify the relationship of UN to other body schema disorders. Cumming defined body schema as the awareness of spatial characteristics of one's own body, an awareness formed by current and previous sensory input. He stated that it is impossible to lose complete awareness of the body from neurological disease. Disturbances take different forms depending on lesion sites.

From the clinical perspective, there are two forms of body schema: conscious and nonconscious. Because the conscious form is typically transient and uncommon (Cumming, 1988), it is not a major problem in a rehabilitation department. Nonconscious body schema problems are of three types: (1) anosognosia, (2) Gerstmann's syndrome, and (3) the neglect syndrome. In anosognosia, hemiplegics deny the existence of their affected extremities. Because anosognosia is a transient state of the acute stage post-stroke patient (Cumming, 1988), it is unlikely to be encountered in a rehabilitation setting.

The second type of nonconscious body schema disturbance is Gerstmann's syndrome, which includes the inability to identify digits when sensation is intact and the inability to identify right and left body parts. Component parts of this syndrome occur independently. The major basis of this syndrome is considered to be a language disconnection within the dominant hemisphere (Cumming, 1988). Simple tests for adults with body schema disturbances of this type were developed by Benton and colleagues (1983) and include tests of right-left orientation and finger localization. In support of their validity, Benton and colleagues (1983) cited several studies indicating that these tests discriminate between normal subjects and those with brain disease. Also, performances of normal children consistently improved with age. From my clinical experience, it appears that problems with right-left orientation and finger localization are more of a verbal or manual identification problem than a functional problem and do not limit occupational performance to any great extent. Adult patients who perform poorly on tests of right-left orientation and finger localization do not necessarily have deficits in daily living skills. Although there may be a relationship in young children (Ayres, 1972; Benton et al, 1983), there is no indication of an association between reading ability and finger identification or right-left discrimination in adults.

The nonconscious body schema disturbance that *is* a major problem in rehabilitation is the neglect syndrome. As many as 90% of subjects with right hemisphere lesions have shown left visual neglect depending on the evaluation procedure used (Schenkenberg et al, 1980). Incidence of right visual neglect is decreased but, with activities of daily living items, has been reported at 37% (Wilson et al, 1987). Consequently, because of the high incidence and functional significance of these problems, I have devoted this chapter to review of the wealth of literature in this area.

Depending on the theoretical perspective, UN has been labeled hemineglect, spatial neglect, extinction, imperception, hemi-inattention, unilateral spatial agnosia, or visuospatial agnosia (Gianutsos et al, 1983). Function can be affected relative to the neglected body side or to the neglected space. In its severe functional manifestation, the patient fails to bathe or dress the neglected side. Evidence has indicated that the neglected space can be relative to the body vertical or to an environmental reference (Calvanio et al, 1987). Nearly all reports of patient UN involved neglect in the horizontal dimensions of extrapersonal space (eg, ignoring lines on the left side of a paper). However, a study of one patient showed visual and tactual "altitudinal" neglect (Rapcsak et al, 1988). This subject perceived only the tops of objects that appeared to be floating in space. Unlike the typical UN patient, she was conscious of this defect, which was verified by the researchers with a repeated trials design. A 3-month follow-up showed no change.

UN should not be confused with hemianopsia, a specific visual field defect that is often, but not necessarily, present with neglect (Weintraub and Mesulam, 1988). The presence of hemianopsia may amplify the functional deficit of UN (Gianutsos et al, 1983; Heilman et al, 1985). A visual field defect is a sensory deficit from lesions to the optic pathways or visual cortex. In a fixed, straight-ahead viewing position, the left and right visual fields coincide with those of hemispace. If the head or eyes are moved, as to the left, visual fields are displaced but not the left hemispace (Ogden, 1987). That hemianopsia is not synonymous with UN is supported by the results from a study of five subjects with left-side neglect, in whom movement of a line bisection task into the perceived right hemispace improved performance as opposed to requiring mere head movements (Heilman et al, 1983).

NEUROLOGICAL BACKGROUND

UN frequently has been observed in patients after cerebrovascular accidents, but the condition also is present in patients with other diagnoses, such as brain tumors. A wide range of lesion sites may be associated with UN, the right parietal lobe being the most frequent (Butter, 1987). Subcortical sites also have been verified (Fero et al, 1987). Vallar and Perani (1987) drew the following conclusions from the anatomical research: Lesions in the frontal and parietal lobes, thalamus, and basal ganglia have been associated with left UN, the parietal lobe (cortical) and thalamus (subcortical) being major sites; the frontal lobe may be involved in a motor component of left UN or in right neglect, but frontal lobe involvement needs further verification. Ogden (1987) found that UN was associated with posterior lesions in the right hemisphere and with anterior lesions in the left hemisphere. One explanation is that the posterior part of the left hemisphere is the verbal center.

Several neurological theories to explain unilateral neglect have been proposed (Bisiach et al, 1985; Heilman et al, 1985). These various theoretical positions involved (1) sensory deficit, (2) a central representational disorder, and (3) attentional dysfunction. At the present time, there is little evidence in support of a sensory deficit position. Bisiach and colleagues (1985) have been strong advocates of the representational deficit theory and have described neural models in support of this position. The crucial role of parietal lobe lesions in unilateral neglect has given strong support to the view that UN is associated with inadequate body schema, representational mapping, and spatial perception.

Poppelreuter and, later, Critchley (both cited by Heilman et al, 1985) first linked UN with attentional dysfunction. According to the attentional deficit adherents, clinical observations and animal research revealing UN from lesions outside the sensory and sensory association areas made the perceptual construct as the essential explanation of UN no longer feasible (Heilman and Watson, 1977). Villardita (1987) interpreted the research showing UN to be modality specific as support for the attentional position, because attention is selective. Although UN has been observed in tactile, auditory, and visual spheres, UN is not necessarily evident in all modalities together. Other authors have suggested that both representational (spatial perceptual) and attentional dysfunction may result in UN depending on the kind of problem (Calvanio et al, 1987; Ogden, 1987).

Because of the extensive body of research in support of the attentional deficit position and because of its value in guiding intervention, I have covered this area in greater depth than the other positions. Also, results of two studies that we conducted were consistent with the attentional rather than the perceptual dysfunction hypothesis regarding unilateral neglect (Van Deusen Fox and Harlowe, 1984; Van Deusen and Harlowe, 1987). In the first study, we analyzed a stroke evaluation battery. Five factors were defined. The measures of perception—body scheme, figure-ground, position in space, spatial relations, and stereognosis—all loaded on one factor. The only other perceptual measure in the rotated factor pattern was the measure of UN, and it did not load on this perceptual factor, which suggests that it is not part of a perceptual dysfunction construct. Our second study showed that scores on a line bisection test correlated significantly with the stroke battery's UN scale but not with the perceptual ratings from this battery. Edmans and Lincoln (1989) also found no significant relationship between overall perceptual scores and UN in their stroke patients.

Studies have suggested that UN is a defect in the neural attentional (orienting or arousal) mechanism. I have reviewed research relevant to rehabilitation (Van Deusen Fox, 1983) and cited a number of papers that showed associations among structures in the cortico-limbic-reticular activating loop. The researchers suggested that defects in this loop were pertinent to UN. Positing that UN can occur following disruption anywhere in the cortico-limbic-reticular loop, Mesulam (1981) suggested a function for each neural component in relation to UN. The parietal lobes, frontal cortex, limbic system, and reticular structures, respectively, function for internal sensory mapping, motor programming, motivation, and arousal.

Butter (1987) has stated that it is generally (but not universally) agreed that UN is caused by attentional deficits. He described the two types of dysfunction: reflex and voluntary. Although many neural structures are involved, Butter considers the inferior temporal cortex of major importance for voluntary attention but the inferior temporal cortex can be damaged and still leave reflex attention intact. The typical line bisection and cancellation tasks evaluate voluntary attention. The midbrain reticular formation is of particular importance for reflex attention, which can be considered intact if the patient is attracted by novel stimuli.

One early proponent of the attentional deficit point of view was Kinsbourne (1977), who proposed that UN represented an imbalance in lateral orienting tendencies. Normal subjects reflected hemispheric preference by looking to the left while solving perceptual problems and to the right while solving verbal problems. Kinsbourne suggested that the UN patient with right brain damage is experiencing an imbalance in orienting response in favor of verbal over perceptual responses. The strong verbal stimulation from human intercommunication in the clinic setting enhances this imbalance for these patients, whereas it decreases imbalance in the case of patients with left brain lesion.

A study of six stroke patients (Heilman and Watson, 1978) supported the view that verbal stimuli can aggravate left-side neglect and that perceptual stimuli can lessen it. In a task involving crossing out verbal and perceptual stimuli, neglect of the left side was significantly less with the perceptual than with the verbal activity. Diller and colleagues (Weinberg et al, 1977) found no neurological changes in their subjects with UN, who improved on a number of academic tests after training. The use of verbal stimuli in their training protocol could account for the lack of neurological changes.

On the other hand, later studies using shapes and verbal stimuli did not provide support for the Kinsbourne position (Caplan, 1985; Edmans and Lincoln, 1989; Weintraub and Mesulam, 1988). Delis and colleagues (1988) showed that subjects with UN from both right and left side lesions performed best on tasks with letters, next best on shapes that could be named, and poorest on shapes without names.

Although interpreting their 1978 study results as support for Kinsbourne's (1977) position, Heilman and associates (1985) later noted their lack of complete theoretical agreement. Heilman and Kinsbourne share the thesis that hemispheral imbalance of orientational tendencies is a major problem in the neglect syndrome. Whereas Kinsbourne emphasizes imbalance due to increased stimulation of the nonlesioned side, Heilman believes damage to the neurons involved in attention, that is, decreases in the lesioned hemisphere, are responsible for imbalance.

At the present time, Heilman's position is representative of one of the major neurology research–based positions on UN. The extensive research of Heilman and colleagues has involved the neglect syndrome in animals and in people with or without brain lesions (Heilman and Watson, 1978, 1977; Heilman et al, 1987, 1985, 1983).

Heilman and colleagues (1985) have discussed the neglect syndrome under four categories: (1) hemi-inattention, (2) extinction, (3) akinesia, and (4) hemispatial neglect (Fig. 5–1). Hemi-inattention is the neglect of sensory input to the body side contralateral to the side of the brain lesion. It can involve auditory, somesthetic, or visual input and is an attentional arousal disorder induced by dysfunction in a corticolimbic-reticular loop. Lesions in multiple sites in the cortex or in subcortical areas can cause hemi-inattention.

According to Heilman's view, the phenomenon of extinction of

Figure 5-1. Heilman's neglect syndrome. (Adapted from Heilman KM, Valenstein E, Watson RT: The neglect syndrome. *In* Fredericks JAM (ed): Handbook of Clinical Neurology, Vol 45-1. Clinical Neuropsychology. New York, Elsevier Science, 1985, pp 153–183.)

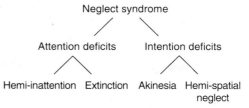

simultaneous stimulation is a limited attention situation. As the neurons involved in attention recover, minimal response to stimuli contralateral to the lesion side is possible, but this side ceases to be the focus of attention when the ipsilateral side is stimulated at the same time.

A factor analysis of an occupational therapy battery (Fraser and Turton, 1986) gave only partial support to this idea of extinction as limited attention. Loading heavily on the factor defined as attention were tests of double-tactile stimuli and bilateral motor coordination. Double-tactile stimuli were defined operationally by a test in which simultaneous pencil eraser touches to hand or face, or both, were identified by the subject with vision occluded. Bilateral motor coordination was evaluated by the subjects' imitation of the tester's hand-to-thigh movement. Double-tactile stimuli also loaded on the factor defined as "registration of sensory input," a situation that speaks to the complexity of the extinction phenomenon.

Questioning the theoretical orientation of Heilman (1985), DeRenzi and associates (1984) tested the implications drawn from Heilman's position on extinction. They suggested that if extinction is limited attention and attention is a general function, then extinction should be multimodal. The research of DeRenzi and associates showed that very few subjects with brain damage exhibited both auditory and visual extinction. If extinction is a recovery phase of hemi-inattention, then all UN subjects should eventually show extinction—an assumption not supported by the data. Furthermore, the implication that the incidence pattern of UN and extinction should be similar also was not supported; DeRenzi and associates (1984) found no significant difference in incidence of extinction between subjects with right and left brain damage.

The results of Anton and associates (1988) differed from those of DeRenzi and colleagues (1984). Anton and associates found that both clinical and computerized testing identified greater frequency of visual extinction than of neglect, and that neglect was never found without extinction. These authors (consistent with Heilman's view) concluded that neglect was a severe manifestation of extinction. Whether or not extinction is an aspect of UN remains unclear.

Heilman and colleagues (1985) described the neglect syndrome as incorporating intentional as well as attentional deficits. Akinesia is a nonmotor deficit in starting a movement and involves lesions of the frontal lobe as well as sensory association and limbic or reticular areas. Activities requiring bilateral limb motion may overcome this intentional deficit as may eliciting cognitive control.

The last category of Heilman's (1985) neglect syndrome is hemispatial neglect. Neglect of space contralateral to the side of the brain lesion is an intentional (as opposed to attentional) defect. According to the Heilman position, the intention to act in that hemispace left of midline has been lost by the patient with right brain damage. These researchers (Heilman et al, 1983) interpreted their pointing study as support for this intentional as opposed to attentional point of view. This study found that subjects with right brain damage as opposed to left brain damage or normal controls showed less ability to accurately point to space at arms' length directly in front of the sternum. Because success in this task required neither visual perception nor memory, poor performance was attributed to failure of intention to address the space.

Heilman and associates (1985) believe that the right brain controls the intention to act in both sides of space, whereas the left brain is limited to control of the right side of space. Thus, if the right brain is damaged, there may be loss of intention to act in left space. A manual exploration study by Weintraub and Mesulam (1987) is among the research providing support for this position. On a manual search task with vision occluded, right lesioned subjects differed from controls in both right and left hemispaces, with performance worse for space contralateral to the side of the lesion.

In summary, Heilman's group considers the neglect observed with brain damage to involve deficits in attention to sensory input contralateral to the side of the lesion as well as a limited attention recovery phase (extinction). UN also comprises deficits in the intention to move the limb or to address the space contralateral to the lesion side.

SEVERITY OF NEGLECT

There is general agreement that UN is manifested in severe and less severe forms. However, the definitions of severe or mild neglect have varied considerably. Chedru (1976) defined mild UN as neglect shown only in writings or drawings rather than in activities of daily living. Weinberg and associates (1977) referred to the definition of mild left UN as more omissions than normal on the left side of space in a testing situation, such as a letter cancellation task when obvious clinical manifestations of neglect were absent. On the other hand, for Blanton and Gouvier (1987), poor performance on a cancellation task was evidence of a more severe form of neglect. These researchers, using highly discriminating tests of reaction time, oral reading, and search for embedded figures, identified neglect in right cerebrovascular accident patients who had not been identified by a letter cancellation task. Heilman and associates (1985) considered the mild or improved stage of UN to be manifested by the patient responding only to the unimpaired side during double simultaneous stimulation (extinction). Johnston and Diller (1986) derived a scoring method using two discriminating tests of UN so that a score could denote the severity of neglect.

At least subcortically, lesions similar in location, size, and age produced different degrees of severity of neglect (Ferro et al, 1987); yet, much evidence has been produced indicating that neglect by patients with right hemisphere lesions was of the more severe form (Colombo et al, 1976; Gainotti et al, 1972; Ogden, 1987; Vilkki, 1989). Ogden (1987) concluded from his work that the incidence of mild UN was the same for right and left hemisphere lesions in the acute stage. The incidence of severe neglect is greater with right side lesions. This severe neglect clears less readily than does less severe neglect. Consequently, studies of patients several months after onset of UN typically show only the severe neglect from right side lesions evidenced in the left side neglect.

Weintraub and Mesulam (1987) were interested in visual and in manual exploration. Visual search was of a random shape cancellation task. On the left side of the page, performance of right-lesioned subjects differed significantly from left-lesioned and control subjects, whose performance did not differ from each other. Thus, the right-lesioned subjects were able to cancel fewer targeted shapes on the left side of the page than were the other subjects. On the right side of the page, right-lesioned subjects again differed significantly from the others. These indications of neglect were found even in those patients showing no motor or sensory deficits. On the manual search task (vision occluded), in which average time to target on each side of a board was scored, right-lesioned patients differed from controls in both right and left hemispace, whereas no significant differences were observed for the left-lesioned subjects. Performance for the right-lesioned subjects was worse for left than for right hemispace. Follow-up studies of UN indicated that it was not a transitory problem, although UN would seem to decrease with time. At 6 months postadmission, one study found UN still present in 9 of 13 patients (Denes et al, 1982). Fullerton and colleagues (1986) cited the following percentages of neglect 6 months after stroke: present in 35% of the patients, uncertain in 30%, and not present in 35%. In subcortical neglect, two of eight patients showed complete recovery in 3 months, but there was still evidence of neglect in three patients followed into the chronic stage (Ferro and colleagues, 1987). Although Colombo and colleagues (1983), in their 10-month follow-up study, found that only a few subjects had failed to improve at all, most did retain some minor signs of UN. Evaluation of 12 UN patients four years after stroke (Kotila et al, 1986) showed visual neglect in all but one patient, whose visual neglect had been of the mild type.

VARIABLES ASSOCIATED WITH NEGLECT

A number of studies have dealt with variables associated with right or left side neglect. Edmans and Lincoln (1989) found no significant relation between the perceptual scores and the UN scores on the Rivermead Perceptual Assessment Battery, whereas Vilkki (1989) did find a relation in left side neglect (right lesion) to judgment of line orientation and speed of verbal response. Differences in results can be explained by differences in test items. Neither left nor right neglect was related to general mental deterioration.

Johnston and Diller (1986) evaluated the relation of visual neglect to eye movements during a visual searching task. A non-invasive photo-electric technique was used to evaluate oculomotor behavior. Oculomotor behavior did discriminate subjects with severe neglect from those with mild neglect and from control subjects, but no significant difference between subjects with mild neglect and controls was observed. The authors concluded that factors other than eye movement must contribute to UN.

A study comparing function in large and small spaces showed that 41% of right-lesioned subjects and 37% of left-lesioned subjects exhibited UN on a large space task. However, on the small space task, right- and left-lesioned subjects did differ significantly, because the percentage of left-lesioned subjects showing neglect declined to 11%. The only condition not differing from control subjects was the left-lesioned subjects' performance on the small space task (Gainotti et al, 1986).

Weintraub and Mesulam (1988) studied the relation to UN of search strategies and structured versus random stimuli formats. Letters or shapes were irregularly positioned (random) or in regular rows and columns (structured). Different-colored pencils were used at sequential times throughout the tasks so that strategies could be analyzed. Consistent with results of others, these researchers found that right- and left-lesioned subjects showed evidence of contralateral UN, with less severe neglect for the left-lesioned subjects. Right-lesioned subjects differed significantly from control subjects for format and strategy. Right-lesioned subjects showed less evidence of UN with a structured format that was associated with a more systematic search strategy. Left-lesioned subjects did not differ from controls on strategy or with type of format, only on number of omissions in right hemispace.

Deles and associates (1988) compared perceptions of a holistic type with those involving detail in relation to site of lesion and UN. Right-lesioned subjects showed problems with holistic and left-lesioned subjects with detailed stimuli. Performance also differed from controls in terms of contralateral hemispace, with right-lesioned subjects also differing in ipsilateral space in a copying task.

I have discussed the research on cuing and the use of shapes versus verbal stimuli in the section on treatment, because it is of particular importance to intervention strategies. The literature clearly indicates that many variables must be addressed if therapy for UN is to be effective.

ASSESSMENT

Clinical procedures for the evaluation of UN have long been reported in the literature. Lawson (1962) described postcard-size test cards for use with UN patients. The easier card contained coherent material for reading; the other, jumbled words. Neglect was evident in omissions of the left side of the reading material. Pigott (1966) reported five clinical tests with standardized administration and scoring, from which patient neglect profiles could be obtained by nurses. Tasks requiring reading, writing, line bisection, circling of initials, and naming of objects were presented midline to patients. Measurements were taken from the left, at points where a patient began, and these points connected to form an individual profile of the area of neglect for each patient.

I (Van Deusen Fox, 1983) have reviewed other clinical procedures that included having the patient copy or draw figures, carry out pegboard and puzzle activities, perform cancellation tasks, and identify or move body parts on command. Diagnosis of UN was made if the patient consistently failed to fully complete activities or tasks contralateral to lesion site. Based on these clinical procedures, more rigorous tests of unilateral neglect were developed. My later review on UN (Van Deusen, 1988) also included discussion of evaluation methods. Parts of both of these reviews, with permission, have been directly reproduced in this chapter.

Colombo and colleagues (1976) reported a set of "space exploration" tests with more precision than was typical of tests of that period. At a time when test data from control subjects usually were not collected, these authors reported cut-off scores based on the data of 50 control subjects. Among their instruments was a ball and hole test, for which a box 105 cm long and 45 cm high was used. Fifteen holes were placed on the left and 15 on the right. Subjects inserted balls in these holes with and without the use of vision. Although formal validity and reliability studies were not conducted, parts of Colombo and associates' battery did discriminate between subjects with brain damage and the control subjects.

At this time, reports of computer-assisted evaluation of UN began to appear in the literature. An early example of this type of instrumentation is the teletype keyboard used by Chedru (1976). Twenty-six keys were positioned to each side of the subject's axis of vision. When, as instructed, the subject had tapped 200 keys at random as quickly as possible, the number of right and of left keys tapped was recorded by the computer connected to the keyboard. This method discriminated UN subjects with right hemisphere damage who did not have field defects from other subjects when vision of all subjects was occluded. Unlike those subjects with UN, the subjects with left hemisphere damage and the control subjects produced symmetrically balanced keyboard taps.

Line bisection tests have been used clinically for decades to evaluate patients for UN. In this procedure, patients are asked to draw a line through the midpoint of each of several lines presented midposition. Lines crossed markedly to the right of midpoint are considered evidence of left side neglect.

Recently, several studies have documented the validity of this tool. Schenkenberg and associates (1980) designed a paper and pencil line bisection test having two practice lines and six horizontal lines, 100 to 200 mm in length (Fig. 5–2). Six lines each were placed to the left, right, and center on the page. Rotation of the paper created a comparable alternate form, as tested with 38 normal subjects. This line bisection test was evaluated with 20 subjects who had diffuse cerebral damage, 20 subjects who had left and 20 who had right cerebral hemisphere damage, and 20 control subjects. The line bisection test clearly differentiated from the other groups the subjects with right brain lesions, 90% of whom had UN. Harlowe and I (Van Deusen and Harlowe, 1987) also supported the construct validity of the Schenkenberg test by establishing an association between it and the St. Mary's clinical ratings of bilateral awareness,

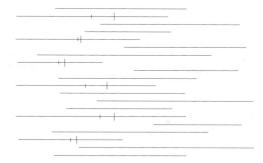

Figure 5–2. Sample Data from the Line Bisection Test. (The Line Bisection Test was used for research by J. Van Deusen by permission of Schenkenberg T, Bradford DC, Ajax ET: Line bisection and unilateral visual neglect in patients with neurologic impairment. Neurology 30:509–517, 1980.)

Key   Patient's Line |
True Mid-point |

their subtest of UN. However, Downing (1986) found no significant relationship between a computerized line bisection test and the Schenkenberg test. Apparently, the computerized version was not measuring the same construct as the Schenkenberg test.

The reliability of the Schenkenberg tool also has been examined. The test's authors reported test-retest coefficients from r = 0.84 to 0.93 (Schenkenberg et al, 1980), indicating excellent consistency of results when the test was readministered. Because UN frequently is observed in elderly rehabilitation patients and the mean age of the control subjects in the Schenkenberg study was 49 years, I (Van Deusen, 1983) provided normative data from 93 elderly subjects with a mean age of 70.5 years (Table 5–1). Measurements of skewness and kurtosis showed data to be symmetrical but more peaked than for a normal distribution. The test-retest reliability coefficient for left-placed lines was only moderate, at r = 0.68. Downing (1986) also obtained a moderate (r = 0.60) test-retest coefficient with her 40 elderly well subjects.

Dissatisfied with the tools available for UN evaluation, Gianutsos and associates (1983) developed more sensitive tests. Their Search-A-Word (SAW) and Speeded Reading of Word Lists (SRWL)

Table 5–1. LINE BISECTION TEST DATA FOR LEFT-SIDE LINES

Mean	− 0.48
Standard deviation	5.55
Skewness	0.32
Kurtosis	3.36
Test-retest reliability	0.68

From Normative Data for Ninety-Three Elderly Persons on the Schenkenberg Line Bisection Test. By Van Deusen J: Phys Occup Ther Geriatr 3:51, 1983. Copyright © 1983 by Haworth Press. Reprinted by permission.

are speeded, verbal instruments suitable for literate, English-speaking patients having no verbal language dysfunction. The SAW compares search times for left versus right side identification of word targets on standard size paper containing a number of letter arrays. SRWL involves computerized speeded word reading in three parts.

Four scores can be obtained from SRWL: (1) anchoring errors, (2) scanning effectiveness, (3) proportion of success with side-placed versus center-placed words, and (4) a periphery monitoring score. Data were obtained for control subjects and subjects with brain damage. Construct validity was supported both by test scores distinguishing subjects with right side brain injury from other subjects and by means of a factor analysis. Two factors were clearly identified: left spatial hemi-imperception and lateral eye movement efficiency, that is, efficient eye function in scanning stimuli. Two foveal imperception factors were less clear. These authors emphasized that research was needed to relate these test results to functional activities.

In order to have a test more directly relevant to rehabilitation needs, Wilson and associates (1987) developed a behavioral skills test of visuospatial neglect, the Rivermead Behavioral Inattention Test. Items involved simulated meal eating, use of a telephone, reading a menu, sorting coins, telling time, copying an address, and map reading. Errors on this skills test were significantly related to errors on conventional clinical tests such as copying drawings and letter cancellation. There was 82% agreement between medical diagnoses of UN from hospital records and those made by means of the skills tests. Test-retest (alternate form) reliability was good, with r = 0.83, and interrater agreement was 100%.

The Arnadottir OT-ADL Neurobehavioral Evaluation (A-ONE) (Arnadottir, 1990) is another instrument using activities of daily living items. UN as well as other problems, can be assessed while observing dressing, hygiene, mobility, and feeding activity. Statistical data are being obtained for this tool, with some data currently available.

Caplan (1987) also used an occupational performance activity to evaluate UN—a reading test. He suggested that use of this 3-minute test be incorporated in UN screening procedures. This test consists of 30 lines on the topic trees. The left margin is variable with zero to 15 space indentations, whereas the right margin is essentially straight. The test can be reversed to evaluate for right side neglect. A trial with 66 brain-lesioned subjects showed it identified UN as well as the two tools selected to define UN in these patients.

Computers have continued to be appropriate aids in assessment of UN in brain-lesioned patients. Dick and associates (1987) described a device that they considered to have potential for rehabilitation of UN patients. The authors have described the necessary hardware and available software in great detail. The device involves a horizontal line with a light at each end and a third sliding light that can be used to simulate a line bisection task. Six conditions are possible with the end lights continuously illuminated, simultaneously or alternately flashing. This programmable visual display can be used for assessing UN. From their work with 12 control subjects and 7 UN patients, the authors also found that a flashing alternate light can get the left UN patient to attend to the left side; therefore, the device also has potential for treatment.

Others (Anton et al, 1988) also have advocated the use of a computerized test for UN in the rehabilitation setting. Their test allows analysis of responses to lights in right and left hemispace and to simultaneous lights for evaluation of extinction. Results of this computerized test were compared for 25 right cerebral vascular accident patients with their results on traditional occupational therapy and physician-administered clinical tests. The computerized test identified more patients with UN and extinction than either of the other procedures.

Considering the array of instruments available to rehabilitation personnel, there is little doubt that a tool for UN assessment can be found that is appropriate for any need and setting. I would prefer to see work toward increased reliability and validity data on existing instruments or on their revisions rather than the development of new tools.

TREATMENT

Therapy aimed at increasing the function of UN patients can be viewed from two perspectives: changing the environment or changing the subject. I (Van Deusen, 1983, 1988) previously discussed these approaches to treatment, and parts of my presentation here have been reproduced by permission from the original articles.

Environmental Adaptation

Environmental adaptation has long been suggested as a therapeutic possibility for UN patients (Burt, 1970; Heilman et al, 1985). Burt recommended placing food, a call button, and a telephone on the UN patient's less involved side as well as addressing the patient from the side of nonneglect. Heilman and colleagues

(1987) have recommended that UN patients have their hospital beds placed in such a way that their less involved side faces the area of personal interactions. On discharge, these patients' home environments also should be adapted.

A retrospective study (Kelly and Ostreicher, 1985) gave little support to the notion that environmental manipulation is associated with outcome for UN patients. This study involved 39 UN patients whose beds were positioned in such a way that they could enjoy views or access functional equipment. Bed position was not related to length of hospitalization, recorded depression, discharge disposition, or occurrence of accidents.

There is an obvious need for further research in this area. As well as investigating functional effects of environmental adaptation to the less involved side, it would be of interest to study environmental adaptations designed to stimulate the neglected side. Such an approach would suggest a goal of patient change and could be included in restorative programming.

Patient Change

Feasible approaches to therapy for change in patients exhibiting UN are those aimed at compensating for central nervous system deficits and restoring central nervous system functions through a neurological approach.

Compensatory Approach

The rationale for this approach to therapy stems from research in learning theory. Training procedures relate to Skinnerian operant conditioning, with behavior being shaped through feedback and positive reinforcement, as well as principles from other approaches to learning. As I pointed out in an earlier paper (Van Deusen Fox, 1983), clinical studies involving application of learning theory to the UN patient have long been reported.

Lawson (1962) reported two extensive case studies involving UN. Evaluations were conducted by means of drawing and reading printed words. The training programs consisted of telling patients about missed things on the left, continued urging to look to the left, and directing of attention to the left side of print by the examiner's flashlight or pencil or by the patients' use of their own hands. Gradually each patient's reading was graded farther and farther to the left. Both patients improved in their ability to scan print but retained neglect of picture drawing.

Pigott (1966) reported training procedures for use by nurses with UN patients. Her carefully planned program included demonstrating evidence of UN to the patient, practice in scanning, use of a visual guide, and very specific application of operant conditioning principles. The visual guide was a bright tape or paper on a 6-inch metal strip with a clip so that it could be attached to the patient's food tray, book, or other object. The patient was requested to turn his or her head until the bright guide was viewed. The author emphasized that there was little transfer of training so that, for adequate function, the patient needed to practice scanning a variety of tasks.

Burt (1970) recommended a self-care training procedure for patients with UN. Cue cards with specific concrete steps of dressing were given to the patients, who talked themselves through dressing, saying, "I put the left hand in the sleeve; I pull the sleeve up my arm," and continuing until the left side was fully clothed.

Anderson and Choy (1970) also described treatment for UN of space and body. Techniques included therapist stimulation of the patient's involved side with texture or cold as the patient watched, followed by patient multimodal self-stimulation of the involved side. Finally, the patient would move the involved limb to midline and then across the midline. This program was designed to compensate for neural damage, but the authors failed to provide convincing data for its efficacy.

Formal investigations of UN patients receiving compensatory training were first emphasized during the 1970s. Diller and colleagues reported a series of studies from the learning theory point of view (Diller and Weinberg, 1977; Gordon et al, 1985; Weinberg et al, 1977; 1979). They studied the effects of three training programs with subjects whose test results indicated presence of left visual inattention. Diller and colleagues (Gordon et al, 1985) viewed their programming as treatment for a hierarchy of dysfunctions in the neglect syndrome. Principles basic to their training protocols were as follows (Diller and Weinberg, 1977):

1. Presentation to the left of a task sufficiently compelling to cause head turning (eg, reading material).
2. Provision of a left side anchoring point (eg, vertical line).
3. Provision of verbal cues gradually reduced.
4. Guidance for even-paced environmental search (eg, reading out loud).
5. Decrease of density of stimuli (eg, letters, words).
6. Provision of feedback on correct performance.

Improvements observed in the Diller studies can be attributed to compensation for deficits because pre- and postexaminations in their initial study revealed no changes in neurological status (Weinberg et al, 1977).

In their initial study (Weinberg et al, 1977), training with a scanning machine significantly differentiated between test battery scores of experimental subjects and those of control subjects. Major improvements were made by subjects having the severest neglect on tasks of academic character closest to the training procedures.

The test battery included three levels of tests from primary (closest to the areas trained in the subjects) to tertiary (least related). The primary and secondary tests measured reading, arithmetic, and letter cancellation skills; the tertiary tests included tasks such as object assembly. Few significant differences between groups were observed in the performance of the tertiary tasks.

The second experiment of Weinberg and associates (1979) was designed to also incorporate procedures for spatial organization and sensory awareness with the purpose of improving test scores previously not changed. The researchers' premise was that problems in sensory awareness and spatial organization are secondary to the visual neglect of space, so that training procedures involved localization of touch to the trunk and practice estimating the length of rods. This type of training resulted in the subjects with mild UN improving on six more tasks than in the first study. Those with severe UN improved on five more tasks.

A third training method was developed by these researchers (Gordon et al, 1985) that incorporated complex spatial perceptual tasks within the visual scanning procedure. The intent of this training was to improve performance on the more cognitively demanding tasks in which a subtle left-side inattention might hinder performance. Their 4-month follow-up study used all three training modules sequentially. At rehabilitation discharge, the experimental UN subjects differed from the control subjects on several measures commonly considered to evaluate UN. Significant differences were observed on cancellation, line bisection, and matching tasks. By 4 months after discharge, the control subjects also had improved so that group differences had essentially disappeared. The long-term value of this type of treatment can, therefore, be questioned. However, control subjects did undergo the routine rehabilitation procedures, and the authors attributed the improvement of control subjects to improved routine rehabilitation intervention based on the experimenters' procedures. For example, therapists had begun to provide left side visual anchors for all UN patients.

The pattern of daily activities, assessed by structured interview, also showed no significant differences at 4-month follow-up. Only one minor difference was observed at discharge (ie, amount of leisure reading). Thus, congruent with Pigott's report (1966), evidence of functional generalization from use of this approach was lacking. It might appear that the studies based on learning principles for compensation have been fruitless. However, if a body of research stimulates others to do their own research in an area, the original research has served an important function. The upsurge of research literature on the treatment of cognitive-perceptual dysfunction following the Diller groups' publications speaks to the influence of their pioneer work in stimulating research in this area. Although UN treatment was not the major thrust, some of this research did focus on scanning or basic attention. Carter and associates (1983) showed a difference on a visual scanning cancellation task between trained and control acute stroke patients. One elaborate long-term project (Scherzer, 1986) used a modified Ben-Yishay model, a seven-component rehabilitation program for adults with severe head trauma. One module used throughout the entire training program included exercises to improve basic attention and visual scanning and tracking. One of the positive results of this study was in the area of attention.

Of more relevance to rehabilitation for UN is the application of the compensatory approach to studies involving functional activities. Webster and associates (1984), using a single-subject design, investigated the wheelchair mobility of three UN subjects. Their scanning task involved a large, suspended board with colored light anchors, and their training incorporated movements in wheelchairs while scanning. All three subjects improved in left-side obstacle avoidance on their wheelchair evaluation course. This study is illustrative of research directly pertinent to rehabilitation of UN patients. The integration of activities of daily living training with the principles from the Diller research series can provide many avenues for future studies.

The work of Dick and associates (1987) has added to our knowledge on the use of the anchoring point in compensatory training for UN patients. These researchers found that use of a left side, alternately flashing light attracted the attention of their left UN patients to the left side of hemispace. They recommended their computer device for training in UN.

Riddoch and Humphreys (1983, 1987) also investigated effects of anchoring points. They evaluated left UN patients with anchor cues to the right, to the left, at both right and left, and a no cue condition. Results from analysis of variance showed that performance improved only when the left-side anchor point was used.

Results of other studies also have given us clues to aid compensatory training. Structuring paper and pencil tasks should improve performance of UN patients, according to the Weintraub and Mesulam study (1988) described above. There is evidence that use of the left hand by patients with left UN enhances performance in left hemispace (Joanette et al, 1986; Vilkki, 1989). With certain tasks, use of the left hand could be feasible. Villardita (1987) showed that right-lesioned subjects with left visual neglect preferred tactile scanning of the left. He suggested that tactile scanning could be used in left hemispace to compensate for the visual neglect of that space.

Heilman and associates (1987) demonstrated that repeated trials (fatigue) increased neglect but that feedback on results may reverse this fatigue effect. Because of their attentional stance on UN, they attributed the feedback effect to increased arousal.

Restorative Approach

In general, the clinical literature emphasized use of learning principles to compensate for UN. However, Zoltan and associates (1986) did include a neurodevelopmental restorative approach in their review of treatment for neglect. They suggested participation in bilateral tasks for total body awareness. Tactile and proprioceptive facilitation through "handling" and movement also were recommended. This therapeutic touching of the patient provides the normal sensations of movement necessary for improved body schema. I found no formal research evaluating the effects of restorative therapy for UN reported in the literature.

Because of theories regarding adult brain plasticity with their implications that rehabilitation can be effective (Moore, 1986), it is realistic to study therapy aimed at re-establishing lost nervous system functions. The neurological research regarding UN cited above suggests many avenues for rehabilitation research.

An attentional-deficit point of view of UN can lead to research evaluating the effect of input directed toward the reticular activating system. The reticular neurons are multimodal, responding to cutaneous, proprioceptive, vestibular, visual, and auditory inputs. According to Butter (1987), the distraction of novel stimuli is of particular relevance to subcortical (reflex) attention. Subcortical attention mechanisms can still be intact when cortical lesions interfere with voluntary attention. It would seem theoretically pertinent for health care professionals to investigate the effects on unilateral neglect of activities providing novel somatic and visual inputs to the subjects to facilitate reflex attention.

Two approaches might be tried for the experimental treatment directed toward intentional dysfunction. The effects of bilateral activities on the increased ability to initiate movement with the involved limb could be studied. Teaching the subject with left neglect to cognitively cue the start of a motion or to address left hemispace is another approach that readily lends itself to research. There is an obvious need for clinical studies of the efficacy of interventions for patients dysfunctional from UN.

OCCUPATIONAL PERFORMANCE

Unilateral neglect is a serious rehabilitation problem because of its association with deficits in reading, writing, and various basic self-care skills (Caplan, 1987; Denes et al, 1982; Fullerton et al, 1986; Gordon et al, 1985; Jesshope et al, 1990; Kinsella and Ford, 1980; Kotila et al, 1986; Lawson, 1962). Gorden and associates (1985) found that their UN patients reported more recreational reading after treatment than did their control group. Caplan (1987) cited the two types of reading errors found in UN patients, omitting the first part of a word ("unbroken" as "broken") or omitting the first word in its entirety. Jesshope and associates (1990) reported an association between UN and self-washing and dressing at the time of patient discharge from their rehabilitation unit.

Although Edmans and Lincoln (1990) found little relationship between UN and activities of daily living, four studies indicated that having unilateral neglect was a major predictor of poor recovery in terms of activities of daily living (Denes et al, 1982; Fullerton et al, 1986; Kinsella and Ford, 1980; Kotila et al, 1986). Denes and associates (1982) found that UN was the important variable related to the difference in activities of daily living improvement between right- and left-lesioned subjects. In a second study (Fullerton et al, 1986), UN, evaluated by means of Albert's test of crossing out lines at various angles, was found through regression analyses to be the significant predictor of functional activity 6 months after stroke. Kinsella and Ford (1980) demonstrated that poor activities of daily living outcome was not associated with right side lesions unless UN was a part of the patient's deficit.

In a long-term follow-up study (Kotila et al, 1986) in which 66 patients were re-examined 4 years after onset, 12 patients had UN, 5 having the milder type. With motor problems controlled, these patients with UN showed poorer results with activities of daily living than did the other 54 patients who also were re-examined. The milder UN patients were better in activities of daily living than were the ones with severe UN.

Thus, there is increasing evidence that UN is a major problem (if not the major problem) interfering with the long-term recovery of occupational performance in stroke patients. The search for effective treatment for UN is a major task for all of us concerned with the rehabilitation of the vast number of our population challenged by the residuals of cerebrovascular accident or other brain lesion.

CASE REPORT

TC was admitted to the acute rehabilitation unit at a large, nonprofit hospital in the greater Los Angeles area. She was referred to occupational therapy where evaluation showed that she was deficient in most activities of daily living skills. The following case report is partially, but not completely, based on this real stroke patient's rehabilitation.

Information shared by the rehabilitation team at its first conference addressing TC's problems revealed that she was a 58-year-old married woman, 1 month post cerebrovascular accident, who was from an upper middle-class environment. TC's major interest was golf. She had essentially no use of her left limbs with severe motor system impairment from the stroke. Speech was unimpaired, and she was a highly verbal, well-educated person. The team recommended a complete rehabilitation evaluation and interventions as necessary.

TC was discussed a record number of times at team conferences. Evaluations showed a severe left-side neglect, and even with moderate motor return, TC was unable to benefit from activities of daily living training. Her therapists used a learning theory approach with simple sequences and much cuing. Although TC occasionally could perform the various steps, when she was left unsupervised she dressed the right half of her body perfectly, but her left side was completely unclothed.

Eventually, TC was discharged from the acute rehabilitation unit having had a stay of several months beyond the typical patient stay. She could walk with assistance, but she remained far from independent in self-care activities. Although an excessive amount of time had been spent with TC in rehabilitation attempts, the outcome was not good, and the rehabilitation staff expressed major frustration.

Two years later (in regard to a research project), I had the opportunity to meet again with TC. At this time, she had resumed playing golf and was undergoing acupuncture as treatment for her cerebrovascular accident residuals. The UN apparently had lessened considerably, and her current concern was for the remaining motor-based impairment of her left arm. Because she did not become involved in the research, I saw TC only briefly at this time. One wonders how much the rehabilitation process may have been responsible for the eventual lessening of the UN? Could the rehabilitation have resulted in long-term effects? Or was TC's lessened UN merely a matter of waiting for time to heal? Certainly, TC's story is typical of those patients who have led to the emphasis on researching UN during the past decade. This area continues to be one in need of major study.

References

Anderson EK, Choy E: Parietal lobe syndromes in hemiplegia. Am J Occup Ther 24:13–18, 1970.

Anton HA, Hershler C, Lloyd P, Murray D: Visual neglect and extinction: a new test. Arch Phys Med Rehabil 69:1013–1016, 1988.

Arnadottir G: The Brain and Behavior—Assessing Cortical Dysfunction Through Activities of Daily Living. St Louis, CV Mosby Co, 1990.

Ayres AJ: Types of sensory integrative dysfunction among disabled learners. Am J Occup Ther 26:13–18, 1972.

Benton AL, Hamsher K, Varney NR, Spreen O: Contributions to Neuropsychological Assessment. New York, Oxford University Press, 1983.

Blanton PD, Gouvier WD: Sex differences in visual information processing following right cerebrovascular accidents. Neuropsychologia 25:713–717, 1987.

Bisiach E, Capitani E, Porta E: Two basic properties of space representation in the brain: evidence from unilateral neglect. J Neurol Neurosurg Psychiatry 48:141–144, 1985.

Burt M: Perceptual deficits in hemiplegia. Am J Nurs 70:1026–1029, 1970.

Butter CM: Varieties of Attention and Disturbances of Attention: A Neuropsychological Analysis. *In* Jeannerod M (ed): Neurophysiological and Neuropsychological Aspects of Spatial Neglect. Amsterdam, North-Holland, 1987, pp 1–23.

Calvanio R, Petrone PN, Levine DN: Left visual spatial neglect is both environment-centered and body-centered. Neurology 37:1179–1183, 1987.

Caplan B: Assessment of unilateral neglect: a new reading test. J Clin Exper Neuropsychol 9:359–364, 1987.

Caplan B: Stimulus effects in unilateral neglect. Cortex 21:69–80, 1985.

Carter LT, Howard B, O'Neil W: Effectiveness of cognitive skill remediation in acute stroke patients. Am J Occup Ther 37:320–326, 1983.

Chedru F: Space representation in unilateral spatial neglect. J Neurol Neurosurg Psychiatry 39:1057–1061, 1976.

Colombo A, deRenzi E, Faglioni P: The occurrence of visual neglect in patients with unilateral cerebral disease. Cortex 12:221–231, 1976.

Colombo A, deRenzi E, Gentilini M: The time course of visual hemi-inattention. Archiv für Psychiatrie und Nervenkrankheiten 231:539–546, 1982–83. From Psychological Abstracts 69:13015, 1983.

Cumming WJK: The neurobiology of the body schema. Br J Psychiatry 153(suppl 2):7–11, 1988.

Deles DC, Kiefner MG, Fridlund AJ: Visuospatial dysfunction following unilateral brain damage: dissociation in hierarchical and hemispatial analysis. J Clin Exp Neuropsychol 10:421–431, 1988.

Denes G, Semenza C, Stoppa E, Lis A: Unilateral spatial neglect and recovery from hemiplegia, a follow-up study. Brain 105:543–552, 1982.

DeRenzi E, Gentilini M, Pattacini F: Auditory extinction following hemisphere damage. Neuropsychologia 22:733–744, 1984.

Dick RJ, Wood RG, Bradshaw JL, Bradshaw JA: Programmable visual display for diagnosing, assessing and rehabilitating unilateral neglect. Med Biol Eng Comput 25:109–111, 1987.

Diller L, Weinberg J: Hemi-inattention in Rehabilitation: The Evolution of a

Rational Remediation Program. *In* Weinstein EA, Friedland RP (eds): Advances in Neurology. New York, Raven Press, 1977.

Downing D: Line bisection: a criterion related validity study. (unpublished master's project). Department of Occupational Therapy, University of Florida, Gainesville, FL, 1986.

Edmans JA, Lincoln NB: The frequency of perceptual deficits after stroke. Br J Occup Ther 52:266–270, 1989.

Edmans JA, Lincoln NB: The relation between perceptual deficits after stroke and independence in activities of daily living. Br J Occup Ther 53:139–142, 1990.

Ferro JM, Kertesz A, Black SE: Subcortical neglect: quantitation, anatomy, and recovery. Neurology 37:1487–1492, 1987.

Fraser C, Turton A: The development of the Cambridge Apraxia Battery. Br J Occup Ther 49:248–252, 1986.

Fullerton KJ, McSherry D, Stout RW: Albert's test: a neglected test of perceptual neglect. Lancet 1(8478):430–432, 1986.

Gainotti G, D'Erme P, Monteleone D, Silveri MC: Mechanisms of unilateral spatial neglect in relation to laterality of cerebral lesions. Brain 109:599–612, 1986.

Gainotti G, Messerli P, Tissot R: Qualitative analysis of unilateral spatial neglect in relation to laterality of cerebral lesions. J Neurol Neurosurg Psychiatry 35:545–550, 1972.

Gianutsos R, Glosser D, Elbaum J, Vroman GM: Visual imperception in brain-injured adults: multifaceted measures. Arch Phys Med Rehabil 64:456–461, 1983.

Gordon W, Hibbard MR, Egelko S, et al: Perceptual remediation in patients with right brain damage: a comprehensive program. Arch Phys Med Rehabil 66:353–359, 1985.

Heilman KM, Bowers D, Valenstein E, Watson RT: Hemispace and Hemispatial Neglect. *In* Jeannerod M (ed): Neurophysiological and Neuropsychological Aspects of Spatial Neglect. Amsterdam, North-Holland, 1987, pp 115–150.

Heilman KM, Bowers D, Watson RT: Performances on hemispatial pointing task by patients with neglect syndrome. Neurology 33:661–664, 1983.

Heilman KM, Valenstein E, Watson RT: The neglect syndrome. *In* Fredericks JAM (ed): Handbook of Clinical Neurology (Vol 45-1). Clinical Neuropsychology. New York, Elsevier Science Pub, 1985, pp 153–183.

Heilman KM, Watson RT: Changes in the symptoms of neglect induced by changing task strategy. Arch Neurol 35:47–49, 1978.

Heilman KM, Watson R: The Neglect Syndrome—A Unilateral Defect of the Orienting Response. *In* Harnard S (ed): Lateralization in the Nervous System. New York, Academic Press, 1977, pp 285–302.

Jesshope H, Clark M, Smith DS: The Rivermead Perceptual Assessment Battery: its application to stroke patients and relation with function. Paper presented at the 10th International Congress of the World Federation of Occupational Therapists, Melbourne (abstract), April 1990.

Joanette Y, Brouchon M, Gauthier L, Samson M: Pointing with left vs right hand in left visual field neglect. Neuropsychologia 24:391–396, 1986.

Johnston CW, Diller L: Exploratory eye movements and visual hemi-neglect. J Clin Exp Neuropsychol 8:93–101, 1986.

Kelly M, Ostreicher H: Environmental factors and outcomes in hemineglect syndrome. Rehabil Psychol 30:35–37, 1985.

Kinsbourne M: Hemineglect and Hemisphere Rivalry. *In* Weinstein EA, Friedland RP (eds): Advances in Neurology. New York, Raven Press, 1977, pp 41–49.

Kinsella G, Ford B: Acute recovery patterns in stroke patients: Neuropsychological factors. T Med J Aust 2(12):663–666, 1980.

Kotila M, Niemi ML, Laaksonen R: Four-year prognosis of stroke patients with visuospatial inattention. Scand J Rehabil Med 18:177–179, 1986. Abstract.

Lacey JH, Birtchnell SA: Review article—body image and its disturbances. J Psychosom Res 30:623–631, 1986.

Lawson IR: Visual-spatial neglect in lesions of the right cerebral hemisphere. Neurology 12:23–33, 1962.

Mesulam MM: A cortical network for directed attention and unilateral neglect. Ann Neurol 10:309–325, 1981.

Ogden JA: The "Neglected" Left Hemisphere and Its Contribution to Visuospatial Neglect. *In* Jeannerod M (ed): Neurophysiological and Neuropsychological Aspects of Spatial Neglect. Amsterdam, North-Holland, 1987, pp 215–233, 1987.

Pigott R, Brickett F: Visual neglect. Am J Nurs 66:101–105, 1966.

Rapcsak SZ, Cimino CR, Heilman KM: Altitudinal neglect. Neurol 38:277–281, 1988.

Riddoch MJ, Humphreys GW: The effect of cuing in unilateral neglect. Neuropsychologia 21:589–599, 1983.

Riddoch MJ, Humphreys GW: Perceptual and Action Systems in Unilateral Visual Neglect. *In* Jeannerod M (ed): Neurophysiological and Neuropsychological Aspects of Spatial Neglect. Amsterdam, North-Holland, 1987, pp 151–181.

Schenkenberg T, Bradford DC, Ajax ET: Line bisection and unilateral visual neglect in patients with neurologic impairment. Neurology 30:509–517, 1980.

Scherzer BP: Rehabilitation following severe head trauma: results of a three-year program. Arch Phys Med Rehabil 67:366–374, 1986.

Vallar G, Perani D: The Anatomy of Spatial Neglect in Humans. *In* Jeannerod M (ed): Neurophysiological and Neuropsychological Aspects of Spatial Neglect. Amsterdam, North-Holland, 1987, pp 235–258.

Van Deusen Fox J: Unilateral neglect: evaluation and treatment. Phys Occup Ther Geriatr 2:5–15, 1983.

Van Deusen Fox J, Harlowe D: Construct validation of occupational therapy measures used in CVA evaluation: a beginning. Am J Occup Ther 38:101–106, 1984.

Van Deusen J: Normative data for ninety-three elderly persons on the Schenkenberg Line Bisection Test. Phys Occup Ther Geriatr 3:49–54, 1983.

Van Deusen J: Unilateral neglect: suggestions for research by occupational therapists. Am J Occup Ther 42:441–448, 1988.

Van Deusen J, Harlowe D: Continued construct validation of the St Mary's CVA Evaluation: Bilateral Awareness Scale. Am J Occup Ther 41:242–245, 1987.

Vilkki J: Hemi-inattention in visual search for parallel lines after focal cerebral lesions. J Clin Exp Neuropsychol 11:319–331, 1989.

Villardita C: Tactile exploration of space and visual neglect in brain-damaged patients. J Neurol 234:292–297, 1987.

Webster J, Jones S, Blanton P, Gross R, Beissel G, Wofford J: Visual scanning training with stroke patients. Behav Ther 15:129–143, 1984.

Weinberg J, Diller L, Gordon W, et al: Training sensory awareness and spatial organization in people with right brain damage. Arch Phys Med Rehabil 60:491–496, 1979.

Weinberg J, Diller L, Gorden W, et al: Visual scanning training effect on reading-related tasks in acquired right brain damage. Arch Phys Med Rehabil 58:479–486, 1977.

Weintraub S, Mesulam M: Right cerebral dominance in spatial attention: further evidence based on ipsilateral neglect. Arch Neurol 44:621–625, 1987.

Weintraub S, Mesulam M: Visual hemispatial inattention: stimulus parameters and exploratory strategies. J Neurol Neurosurg Psychiatry 51:1481–1488, 1988.

Wilson B, Cockburn J, Halligan P: Development of a behavioral test of visuospatial neglect. Arch Phys Med Rehabil 68:98–102, 1987.

Zoltan B, Siev E, Freishtat B: Perceptual and Cognitive Dysfunction in the Adult Stroke Patient (2nd ed). Thorofare, NJ, Slack, 1986.

JULIA VAN DEUSEN

ANOREXIA NERVOSA

In this chapter, I review the extensive literature related to body image disturbances of persons with anorexia nervosa. Described are the many methods that investigators have developed to assess body image in research with subjects experiencing eating disorders. Included are semantic differential scales, instruments using silhouettes, various questionnaires, and size estimation and image distortion techniques. Studies are summarized that compare the body image of subjects diagnosed as anorexic with that of control subjects. Although research on the efficacy of treatment of body image disturbances of people with anorexia nervosa is scarce, the clinical literature provided valuable ideas on treatment that I

149

describe. Occupational performance problems of persons with anorexia nervosa typically involve excessive activity rather than performance deficits. I point out the need for research in this area.

Anorexia nervosa is an eating disorder found predominantly in the female adolescent (American Psychiatric Association, 1987; Waltos, 1986). The incidence in males is about 5%. Age of onset is from prepuberty to the early 30s, with high-risk ages between 12 and 18. It is a disorder characterized by an intense drive for thinness and is typically accompanied by psychological, neuroendocrinological, and sociocultural abnormalities. It is defined by four criteria (American Psychiatric Association, 1987):

1. Refusal to maintain weight within reasonably normal limits.

2. Although underweight, an intense fear of becoming fat.

3. Disturbance in body image in terms of the way weight, size, or shape is *experienced*.

4. Amenorrhea (disturbed menstrual cycles—female). Incidence has been reported in from 1 in 100 to 1 in 800 female adolescents.

Prevalence of this disorder has been associated with weight-oriented professionals such as models, ballet dancers, and jockeys (Waltos, 1986). In a study of 252 referrals, Sykes (1988) found an association with religion and race. A lower incidence of anorexia nervosa was reported for African Americans and those of Protestant faiths, although these data could be the result of weaknesses in the study. Because anorexia nervosa is a disorder of adolescents, it is hardly surprising that Sykes found a 99% incidence of single people in the referral group.

Although the work of Bruch (1962) stimulated the rash of research on anorexia in the past decades, this disorder was described in the medical literature as early as the 17th century (Beumont et al, 1987). It had emerged as a distinct clinical entity by the 19th century. By the 1980s, it was clearly apparent that anorexia nervosa was a multidimensional problem (Garfinkel and Garner, 1982).

There is evidence to support a hereditary basis (Holland et al, 1988; Waltos, 1986). Others have interpreted research in support of central nervous system dysfunction (Hamsher et al, 1981; Mills, 1985). Because hypothalamic dysfunction is highly associated with anorexia nervosa, it could be responsible for the emotional and eating disturbances observed in this syndrome. This notion is supported by reports of several patients with hypothalamic tumors showing characteristic symptoms of anorexia nervosa (Garfinkel and Garner, 1982). Whether or not etiology is essentially biological, physical treatment typically is necessary for survival, but such treatment is beyond the scope of this chapter.

Since the 1960s, there has been considerable concentration on the psychological aspects of anorexia nervosa (Beumont et al, 1987; Bruch, 1982; Garfinkel and Garner, 1982). Because of this emphasis on psychological etiology, I have placed the body image disturbance of anorexia nervosa in the Lacey-Birtchnell category (1986), in which body image distortion occurs without predisposing physical factors.

The literature revealed four approaches to treatment of patients with anorexia, methods that assumed a primary psychological etiology (Beumont et al, 1987; Giles, 1985). These approaches are (1) behavioral, (2) family therapy, (3) psychoanalytical and, (4) cognitive. Although all these treatment methods are not used to treat the body image distortion aspect of anorexia nervosa, I briefly review them here for background.

Proponents of the behavioral approach treat anorexia nervosa as a phobia. Attempts are made to decondition the associated anxiety, and eating is paired with powerful reinforcers. Although this approach demonstrates some immediate gains, it is unable to maintain weight gain.

The family therapy approach focuses on the family as the unit of treatment. Appropriate interpersonal behavior and restructure of the family system are goals of this approach.

The psychoanalytical approach explains both physical and psychological symptoms in terms of "oral ambivalence." The psychoanalyst tends to interpret the refusal of food as the patient's defense against "magical" impregnation. In isolation from other approaches, psychoanalysis rarely has been found to be effective. However, psychodynamic approaches that emphasize underlying psychological variables but deviate from traditional psychoanalysis have been viewed favorably by clinicians (Bruch, 1982; Wooley and Wooley, 1985).

The cognitive (or perceptual) approach considers body image distortion to be of major importance. Adherents of this approach use cognitive therapy to restructure attitudes in this and other dysfunctional areas.

RESEARCH ON BODY IMAGE DISTURBANCE

Having observed 12 anorexic patients over a 10-year period, Bruch (1962) reported the patients' body image disturbances as well as their inability to perceive internal sensations of hunger or fullness. Bruch's comments led to a number of increasingly rigorous investigations of body image dysfunction of anorexic subjects.

Collaborating with Allen for clinical relevance, I reviewed these studies (Van Deusen and Allen, 1986). With the permission of Haworth Press, parts of this review have been reproduced in this chapter. These early studies primarily were concerned with determining whether or not anorexics suffered from a disorder of body image in which the subject's perception is that the body is abnormally large. Among the questions typically addressed were: Do anorexic patients overestimate their body width? Do they overestimate the size of their various body parts? More recently, attention has been directed specifically toward body shape as opposed to body size (Whitehouse et al, 1988). In order to address such questions, an emphasis was given to the problem of precise measurement methods.

Assessment of Body Image

So many types of tools for assessing body image are available that categorization is necessary. My categories have been derived from those of Meermann (1983), Slade (1985), and Touyz and Beumont (1987). Body image studies of anorexia nervosa have involved four kinds of evaluation tools: (1) the psychiatric interview, (2) the projective technique, (3) self-report questionnaires, and (4) psychophysical methods. The last two categories are of greatest relevance to a variety of rehabilitation personnel for patient intervention or for research.

Self-Report Tools

Three types of self-report instruments were discussed in research reports on anorexia. One approach was that of the semantic differential scale using evaluative bipolar adjectives for the concept "my body right now." Subjects rated this concept along a scale of 10 adjectives, such as beautiful to ugly, desirable to undesirable, and attractive to repulsive (Leon et al, 1985).

The second method involved a subject's selection of pictures like one's perceived self and one's ideal self from figures of varying widths. Because the same stimuli were used, valid comparisons could be made across subjects. Channon and associates (1990) used stimulus material derived from photographs of an anorexic patient at various weights, clothed and unclothed. This tool discriminated between anorexic and control subjects and between stable-weight and increased-weight anorexics. Manley and associates (1988) used the Perceived Body Image Scale, which consisted of 11 cards with profile and front views of the female figure ranging from emaciated to obese. Their work showed evidence of body image disturbance in anorexia only under test directions calling for affective as opposed to perceptual or cognitive responses.

Other researchers have tried to simplify this type of approach. Williamson and associates (1989) constructed a simple test from nine silhouettes of thin to obese body frames. Statistical data were obtained for this tool using 234 persons with eating disorders (133 with anorexia or bulimia nervosa) and 425 control subjects. This assessment allowed comparison of current and ideal body image with normative data. Preliminary test-retest and concurrent validity data were acceptable.

A third type of self-report tool consisted of subject responses to statements about body size, shape, or both. The Fisher Body Distortion Questionnaire (Strober et al, 1979), the Body Shape Questionnaire (Cooper et al, 1987), and the Body Dissatisfaction Subscale of the Eating Disorder Inventory (Garner et al, 1983) are examples of this type of instrument used in anorexia research.

As used by Strober and associates (1979) to discriminate anorexics from control subjects, the Fisher Body Distortion Questionnaire consisted of 82 items, such as "My body feels unusually heavy," "My stomach feels blocked up," and "I feel distant from my own body." This tool had previously shown stability. Scores were not related to such attributes as intelligence and social desirability. The Fisher Body Distortion Questionnaire discriminated between 18 anorexic subjects and 24 patients with other diagnoses on the same psychiatric unit, not at admission but after 5 months of treatment.

When the literature began to place greater emphasis on the distinction between body size and body shape, a questionnaire specific to body shape distortion was developed (Cooper et al, 1987). This tool was refined to 34 items, making completion time approximately 10 minutes. Examples of items were "Have you felt so bad about your shape that you have cried?" and "Has being naked, such as when taking a bath, made you feel fat?" Validity data were reported. The test discriminated between normal subjects and those with eating disorders and also between normal subjects rated "concerned about slimness" and those rated "unconcerned." Moderate criterion-related validity coefficients were reported (in the r = 0.60s range).

Garner and colleagues (1983) developed an instrument to assess a variety of psychological characteristics related to anorexia nervosa. After preliminary analysis, 8 of 11 constructs were retained. The one directly pertinent to body image (Body Dissatisfaction

Subscale) reflected the belief by anorexics that their body parts are too large and other similar feelings. The Body Dissatisfaction Subscale has nine items pertaining to hips, thighs, buttocks, and stomach as too large or just right and a general item on satisfaction of body shape. Six choices for response are offered, ranging from always to never satisfied. The estimate of internal consistency of this subscale was 0.90 for anorexic patients and 0.91 for control subjects. Good criterion-related validity also was shown. For example, there was a high level of association between anorexic scores and psychiatrist and psychologist ratings.

Continuing study has strengthened the body of data on the Eating Disorder Inventory. Wear and Pratz (1987) demonstrated stability of scores over 3 weeks with a 0.96 test-retest reliability coefficient for the Body Dissatisfaction Subscale. The factor structure, both for eating-disorder and nonpatient subjects, has been reported (Welch et al, 1990, 1988). In the patient population, the Body Dissatisfaction Subscale was defined independently as one of the eight factors predicted by Garner and associates' original work with the inventory. Nonpatient subjects evidently interpreted items from a different perspective because analysis showed a three-factor solution. However, the items from the Body Dissatisfaction Subscale loaded on a factor concerned with shape, weight, and eating, all of which would seem to relate to body image.

Psychophysical Methods

There are many highly technical research studies evaluating anorexics in which measurement has been sophisticated. This type of measurement has been called the psychophysical or experimental method (Meermann, 1983). Several researchers have reviewed the various assessments in this category (Garfinkel and Garner, 1982, 1977; Meermann, 1983; Slade, 1985; Touyz and Beumont, 1987).

Two basic procedures have been used: the size estimation and the image distortion methods. In the size estimation method, image of body parts was evaluated by the movable caliper or by the image-marking technique. In the image distortion method, the distorting process involved photography or television, and general body image was evaluated.

Size Estimation

In the anorexia studies, the earliest method of size estimation was by a movable caliper device. Subjects adjusted beams of light to estimate the width or depth of body regions such as the face, waist, or hips. From the resulting measures, a body perception index could be calculated in which the subject's perceived width was divided by her actual width and multiplied by 100. The reviews of four studies for intercorrelations of measures of various body parts such as hips, face, and waist have shown internal consistency coefficients ranging from r = 0.25 to 0.93 for this procedure with an average of 0.72 for anorexic subjects and 0.63 for control subjects (Garfinkel and Garner, 1982; Slade, 1985). Fichter and associates (1986) reported a coefficient of 0.98 (Cronbach's Alpha). Test-retest reliability coefficients over a 1-day interval were reported from r = 0.75 to 0.79 (Bowden et al, 1989). Thus, on the whole, reliability coefficients have indicated moderate to excellent consistency for this procedure.

A second method of size estimation was image marking, a less complex and more economical procedure. The undressed subject imagined that she was facing a mirror and marked widths of shoulders, waist, and hips on a paper placed on the wall in front of her. Garfinkel and Garner (1982) cited internal consistency coefficients for this method of r = 0.30 to 0.75, with an average of 0.60. The results of Strober and associates (1979) showed stability of this measure over a 6-month period despite the intervening variable of hospital treatment. Bowden and associates (1989) reported 1-day test-retest reliability coefficients of 0.71 to 0.85. Other body parts have been added since the original Askevold description, such as cheeks and calf (Meermann, 1983). An adaptation of this image-marking method in which subjects imagine their photograph on a smaller paper was also reported (Fichter et al, 1986).

Image Distortion

Garfinkel and associates (Garfinkel and Garner, 1982; Garfinkel et al, 1979, 1977) employed the distorting whole body photograph technique for their series of anorexic studies. Subjects estimated their real and ideal sizes using a projected photograph that could be decreased or increased in width by 20 per cent. A control object also was estimated. One-year test-retest reliability coefficients for anorexic subjects were r = 0.56, and were r = 0.70 for control subjects, showing moderate stability over a long span of time.

A second method of estimating the whole body (as opposed to parts) was used by Meermann (1983). Subjects were required to adjust their distorted video images on a television screen. Three trials each were given of distortion toward fatness and thinness. Reliability coefficients ranged from r = 0.62 to r = 0.79 (item intercorrelations).

Touyz and associates (Touyz and Beumont, 1987) also used the distorting television image procedure in their anorexic research. The patient's own body, ideal shape, and least desired shapes were evaluated with images varied horizontally without distorting height. Test-retest reliability coefficients for the patient's own body were r = 0.82 (10-min interval), 0.63 (24-h interval) and 0.61 (8-week interval).

Bowden and associates (1989) reported a 1-day test-retest coefficient of 0.92 for their television distortion data. Fichter and associates (1986) reported an internal consistency coefficient of 0.91 for this type of assessment. From both the patient service and the research perspectives, I concluded that reliable tools are now available for assessment of body image in anorexia nervosa. However, because of the complexity of this construct, the validity of these instruments still might be questioned.

Validity

Garfinkel and Garner (1982) discussed the validity of body image measures for anorexia nervosa, concluding that on the whole, evidence for criterion-related validity was weak, although they had reported a strong relationship between scores from the Body Dissatisfaction Subscale and the photograph procedure. They also cited a moderate correlation between the size estimation (caliper) and image distortion (photograph). However, Strober and associates (1979) found essentially no relationship between the results of the image-marking technique, the Fisher self-report measure, and a body concept scale involving drawing a person. Coefficients ranged from 0.11 to 0.41, but the number of subjects was very small (18 anorexic and 24 control subjects). Pierloot and Houben (1978) also found no significant relationship between results of the caliper procedure and indices in the Rorschach test, usually considered body image estimates.

Evidence of predictive validity was provided by the association in anorexic studies of body image evaluations with prognosis and pathology. Some of these studies are reviewed below. Because construct validity of a measure also is supported when relevant hypotheses using that instrument are supported, the body of research on anorexia nervosa cited below also provided considerable evidence of the construct validity of the various body image tools.

Results of Body Image Studies

Results of studies evaluating body image of patients with anorexia nervosa have been inconsistent. However, certain patterns have emerged from the research reviews reported during the past decade (Garfinkel and Garner, 1982; Hsu, 1982; Slade, 1985; Touyz and Beumont, 1987; Van Deusen and Allen, 1986). Research into the 1990s is not inconsistent with these patterns.

1. Size estimation and image distortion measures produced different results.

2. Failure to correctly estimate width of one's body or its parts was not unique to anorexics.

3. Perception of body size was qualitatively different for anorexic than for control subjects in terms of meaning for the patient.

4. Overestimation of body size was associated with a poor prognosis and greater pathology in anorexia nervosa. The summaries of research that follow illustrate these patterns.

Fries (1977) found that body perception indices significantly differentiated his anorexic subjects from control subjects, a finding that Fries considered to be congruent with previous results of the classic Slade and Russell (1973) study. Because several controls overestimated their size by 21% to 33%, Fries was not convinced that overestimation was specific to anorexia nervosa. He stressed the point, however, that "the body perception index represents a bodily experience, which is essential and of great importance . . ." for such patients.

Garfinkel and associates (1977a, 1977b) investigated by the image distortion method the clinical outcome of anorexics in terms of their self-perception of body size. Those patients with poor outcomes were overestimators. Those with excellent outcomes were underestimators. Garfinkel and associates suggested treatment directed toward better self-perception if patients have benefited only marginally from conventional therapy.

Button and associates (1977), using the size estimation method, found no significant differences between anorexic and control subjects, both of whom overestimated body size. Marked overestimation by anorexics was associated with an early relapse. In contrast to the Button study, Wingate and Christie (1978) showed significant differences between control subjects and anorexic patients in the perception of body width when the mean age of subjects and controls was identical. This finding was contrary to the notion that age differences may explain observed body image difference between anorexic and control subjects (Hsu, 1982).

Using neurotic patients as controls, Pierloot and Houben (1978) also found significant differences between anorexic subjects' estimations of body size and those of control subjects, although the latter also overestimated. Size estimation technique was used. In direct contrast to these findings were those of Strober and associates

(1979), who found no significant differences (either at hospital admission or 6 months later) between controls and anorexic subjects in size perception. Both groups overestimated their body dimensions. However, the authors concluded that greater pathology of anorexics was linked to greater body size exaggeration.

The results of another study (Casper et al, 1979) agreed with those of Strober and associates (1979), adding increasing evidence to the notion that overestimation of size of body parts was not unique to patients with anorexia nervosa. Again, degree of overestimation was associated with characteristics indicative of poor outcome for the anorexic patient.

Ben-Tovim and associates (1979), also using size estimation technique, showed that as the body narrows, it is misperceived to a greater degree. When this finding was taken into account, no body image differences were evident between anorexic and control subject. To further confuse the issue, a study by Meermann (1983), using two measures in two planes, showed significant differences in size estimation for lower extremities but not for upper trunk and face between anorexic subjects and gymnastics and ballet pupils.

The research of Touyz and colleagues (Touyz and Beumont, 1987; Touyz et al, 1984) used the image distortion method. There were no significant differences between anorexic and control subjects on judgments of their own bodies. The anorexic subjects relative to the control subjects tended to either overestimate or underestimate their body size. Ideal body shapes were smaller than their real ones for both anorexic patients and control subjects. However, when one is emaciated, such an ideal is qualitatively different from that of a person whose weight is well within normal limits. Also, anorexic subjects relative to control subjects underestimated the size of a neutral figure of normal weight. The authors interpreted this result as showing the marked distortion by anorexics of what is normal body size.

The differences in results from different measurement methods were shown by Fichter and associates (1986) in a small but rigorous study. Through discriminant analysis, they found that the caliper and image-marking procedures correctly classified acute and chronic anorexic and control subjects, whereas image distortion and a "spin-off" of the image-marking method were not satisfactory. No difference in size estimates were observed before or after meals. Hsu (1983) described a number of variables that influenced overestimation, including perceived carbohydrate content of a meal and various personality traits.

Several studies in the 1986 and 1987 literature contributed further to the idea that there was a qualitative difference in body image between anorexic and control subjects and that overestimation of body size by the former was predictive of poor outcome. In a follow up study, Toner and associates (1987) found that on the Body Dissatisfaction Scale assessing degree of dissatisfaction of 18 body parts, symptomatic anorexic subjects were rated significantly higher than asymptomatic anorexic or control subjects. Button (1986) verified that anorexic subjects' overestimation of body size was related to poor treatment outcome if admission assessments of size estimation were used. Huron and Brown (1986) compared anorexic and control subjects and, although no significant differences in body-size estimation were found, there was a difference in how subjects felt about their bodies. Anorexic subjects' impressions of body size also did not differ from those of controls regardless of information provided by tight- or loose-fitting clothing (Collins et al, 1987). However, anorexics were less consistent in their body image impressions.

A study by Bell and associates (1986) again showed that results of body image comparisons vary with the measuring tool. These researchers used a simple silhouette chart (Fig. 6–1) for responses to questions such as ideal body image, present self-image, and self plus or minus 10 lbs. Although there were no differences in ideal image, significant differences were observed between obese, normal weight, and anorexic subjects on all three present-self responses. Unlike the logical responses of obese or normal-weight subjects, 10

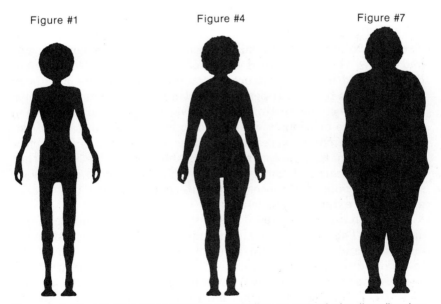

Figure #1   Figure #4   Figure #7

Figure 6–1. Sample silhouette test items used in the assessment of eating disorders. (From Bell C, Kirkpatrick S, Rinn R: Body Image of Anorexic, Obese, and Normal Females. J Clin Psych 42:433, ©1986. Reprinted by permission of Dr Sue Kirkpatrick, University of Alabama in Huntsville.)

lbs added or subtracted represented a huge amount of weight to anorexics.

Gardner and Moncrieff (1988) used the image distortion method (television) in a very thorough study to compare anorexic and control subjects' judgments of actual and ideal body size. Data were collected for 100 trials for eight anorexic and eight control subjects, both for how their bodies actually felt and for their ideal bodies. Both groups underestimated actual body size. There was a significant difference between ideal and actual judgments across groups, with lower weight being desired. Again, there is a qualitative difference in desire for lower weight between an anorexic and a person of "normal" weight.

In the same article, these authors (Gardner and Moncrieff, 1988) reported a second study, an analysis from signal detection theory that allowed separation of sensory discrimination aspects from bias (motivation, values) in a discrete discrimination task. There was no significant difference between anorexic and control subjects in sensory sensitivity when detecting the distorted image of self. The anorexic subjects' biases were in the direction of distortion, whereas the control subjects' biases were toward the normal image. From this study, the researchers concluded that anorexics do not show deficits in the actual perception of their bodies, the deficit being in inappropriate responses while viewing their body image. Treatment must then be directed toward appropriate responses.

Finally, several studies have addressed the influence that test directions might have on results of body image assessment. Proctor and Morley (1986) examined effects of ambiguous, confrontational, external, and internal instructions on anorexic subjects' own body size estimates by the caliper method. Under ambiguous directions, anorexic subjects overestimated relative to control subjects. When told they were previously wrong and to be more accurate (confrontational), estimates were significantly reduced in both subject groups. When told to estimate from the perspective of another person (external) and "how you feel you are" (internal), there were significant group differences, with internal producing larger estimates than external instructions.

Bowden and associates (1989) also studied the influence of test directions. They used size estimation procedures (caliper and image marking) and image distortion (television) under affective and cognitive directions, for example, "Stop the moving lights where you *feel* the part is" (affective) versus "where you *know* the part is" (cognitive). On the size estimation measures, 12 anorexic and 12 bulimic subjects significantly overestimated relative to 24 control subjects under both affective and cognitive directions. No significant differences were observed between bulimic and anorexic subjects. On the image distortion measure, the eating-disorder subjects overestimated under affective directions but were more accurate than control subjects under cognitive directions. On the control stimulus, a box, there was no overestimation of size. Again, the research demonstrated different results from different body image measures. Despite the differences observed in overestimation under affective directions, the authors pointed out that, because *all* anorexics did not overestimate, these results should not be interpreted to support body image distortion as a necessary requirement for a diagnosis of anorexia nervosa.

Four types of directions were compared by Manley and colleagues (1988). Directions addressed a subject's own body image from perceptual, cognitive, and affective perspectives. Perceptual directions requested response in terms of how subjects saw themselves in mirrors: affective, in terms of how subjects felt in their bodies, and cognitive, in terms of how subjects thought they looked. The fourth direction addressed the ideal body image or the image desired by subjects. Anorexic, bulimic, and control subjects completed the Perceived Body Image Scale under each set of directions. The principal investigator also rated the subjects, and the difference between subject responses and these ratings was used as the measure of body image disturbance. There was a significant difference between both groups of eating-disorder patients and the control subjects only under affective directions. Eating-disorder patients overestimated relative to control subjects.

In summary, there would seem to be consistent evidence that although anorexic patients do, under certain measurement conditions, overestimate width of their body and its parts, they do not all respond in this manner, and they are in no way unique in such overestimation. Evidence supports a considerable qualitative difference, probably in the affective domain, between judgments of body size by anorexic and control subjects. Results of a number of studies have associated pathological symptoms and poor clinical outcome with overestimation of body size by patients with anorexia nervosa. Because of this evidence, the literature contains a small body of information dealing with the treatment of body image disturbance in anorexia. Although some research has been conducted, much of this literature consists of clinical reports.

TREATMENT

The literature contained many suggestions for treatment of body image disturbance of anorexia nervosa patients. A few reports contained objective evaluative data, but most gave clinician impressions as the major criterion for efficacy. I believe that Fairburn and Cooper's (1987) statement is still applicable—reports of completed, systematic research on treatment of body image problems in anorexia are not to be found.

From a theoretical perspective, most reported body image treatment procedures stem from behaviorism, cognitive restructuring, and psychodynamic approaches to treatment. Wooley and Wooley (1985) presented a different perspective. From their review of the literature on the phantom phenomenon, these authors suggested that part of the anorexic's body image problem might be the continued sensory experience of lost fat as a phantom. Although phantom fat is an intriguing idea, at present it lacks support. Because of the complex nature of body image disturbances, techniques frequently were derived from several of the theoretical positions (Fig. 6–2). Depending on the setting, a variety of disciplines have been concerned with body image treatment, including nursing, psychology, medicine, social work, and occupational therapy.

Mirror and Video Feedback

Several authors have discussed the use of video equipment and mirrors in the treatment of body image disturbances (Barabasz, 1987; Biggs et al, 1980; Giles, 1985; Vandereycken, 1987; Wooley

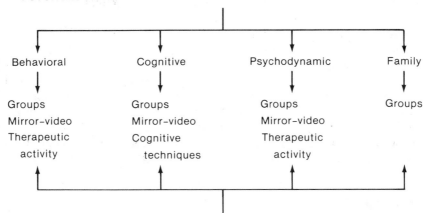

Figure 6–2. Treatments for body image disturbances in anorexia.

and Wooley, 1985). The purpose was to decrease body image distortion and related psychological problems through confrontation of the actual body.

In a study involving six anorexic and six control subjects, Biggs and colleagues (1980) found that only one viewing of their bodies on videotape was followed by an increase in positive feelings by "normals" and a decline in positive personal evaluations by the anorexic subjects. These authors concluded that video feedback could be a useful tool in the treatment of body image distortion in anorexia nervosa. Giles (1985), in his discussion of occupational therapy for anorexia, agreed with this position and also considered reading material on anorexia nervosa a useful adjunct.

Wooley and Wooley (1985) described their use of video feedback with initial, less-threatening tapes made of patients seated at a table in group therapy. Discussions were a vital component of treatment and could involve comparison of one anorexic subject's picture with that of another. Those patients comfortable with whole body movement experienced more complex video feedback sessions.

Vandereycken (1987) emphasized sensory awareness of the body through massage, breathing-relaxation exercises, and mirror or video feedback training. Later, mirror and video feedback, along with peer group feedback, was directed toward acceptance of the body. A videotape of each patient in a swimsuit in standardized position was shown at the first group session. A similar tape was made just before discharge. Each group session also was videotaped and discussed. Relative to body image, exit questions on the effect of therapy revealed that video confrontation increased anorexic subjects' sensitivity to their own bodies but also could initially produce increased anxiety and decreased self-esteem. Gradually, the patients reported, they came to enjoy the therapy.

Use of actual or pretend mirrors also has been discussed by Barabasz (1987) and Wooley and Wooley (1985). Barabasz illustrated with case studies the success of a program of 35 to 40 minute mirror sessions extending over several weeks to several months. Behaviorism was the approach used. The patients described their body parts being viewed in the mirror and were verbally reinforced for all accurate comments.

An exercise described by Wooley and Wooley (1985) involved anorexic subjects pretending a large piece of vertical paper was a mirror and drawing their imagined figure. This image was compared with the therapist's actual tracing of the patient's shape on the same paper. The distortion was discussed. Past body images were explored by imagining these images in a mirror and talking about them. When the stage of considering control of feelings about their bodies was reached, mirror viewing by patients in partial dress was used to the limit of their tolerable anxiety levels.

Cognitive Therapy Techniques

Several authors who have been extensively involved with anorexia nervosa recommended cognitive therapy as the appropriate method of dealing with body image distortion (Fairburn and Cooper, 1987; Garner and Bemis, 1985; Giles, 1985). Their basic premise was that the anorexic subjects' faulty attitudes about their shape and weight were primary to their irrational behavior and the maintenance of their disorder. For successful therapy, it is essential that a relationship of mutual trust be developed between the therapist and the patient.

The anorexics must be helped to attribute their misperceptions regarding body shape to their disorder, that is, to know that their feelings in this specific area are unrealistic. Patients need to trust the therapist's opinion or objective results of weighing as being a superior indicator of body size to that of their own feelings. Anorexic patients are taught to repeat statements regarding the unrealistic nature of their body shape judgments in an effort to completely convince themselves of the veracity of these statements. Eventually, they internalize what they have been saying. During periods of high anxiety (such as following a meal), distractions should be planned to prevent declines in new attitudes about their bodies. Meeting or phoning a friend might be appropriate. Good results have been reported from cognitive programming. However, no research report was found on its efficacy.

Therapeutic Activities

Activities dealing with food and clothing often have been used in the treatment of anorexia nervosa because of their relevance to body image. Art also has been incorporated (Giles, 1985; Martin, 1985; Wooley and Wooley, 1985). Creative activities such as drawing, painting, and making collages, pottery, and sculpture have been used for self-expression and assessment of past and present feelings about the body.

Art media have been used early in therapy to express current patient feelings, such as fat feelings after eating, or past feelings, such as perception of the body image as a child. Wooley and Wooley (1985) used the making of clay figures by anorexic subjects as a means to interpret predisorder, onset, present, and future body image perceptions.

Clothing-related activities have been found appropriate for middle-stage intervention. Through cooperation of local stores, persons with anorexia tried on clothes suggested by clerks, an activity thought to make the body image more flexible. A more realistic body image can be developed through both shopping for and making new clothes, a necessity with weight gain. The therapist should work closely with patients in these situations in order to deal with various problems such as anxiety.

By definition, the problems of anorexic subjects are food related; therefore, grocery shopping, meal planning and preparation, and social dining activities should be reserved for the late stages of treatment. In discussing these later activities, Martin (1985) pointed out that grocery shopping could be especially threatening because of the fear of losing control around such large quantities of food. Giles (1985) mentioned the problem that anorexics may have in planning balanced meals because of their preoccupation with low calorie content. Therapists should foster relaxed dinner groups and grade group meals, from those in an occupational therapy clinic to a hospital cafeteria to public restaurants.

Use of the Group

Although all of the above-mentioned treatment procedures have been used in group as well as individual format, Inbody and Ellis (1985) and Yellowlees (1988) specifically addressed group treatment of body image disturbance in anorexia. Yellowlees evaluated the results of group therapy for nine anorexic patients. The group examined central issues of common relevance such as body image. After 28 weekly meetings, three patients were greatly improved, three were slightly improved, and three were not improved. Yellowlees considered that there was evidence to suggest that patients with anorexia could form supportive groups for mutual sharing on topics such as body image. Thus, he discussed the need for controlled research on the efficacy of group therapy for anorexia. Yellowlees suggested two therapists for each group, one man and one woman, one of whom should have expertise in group process, the other in treatment of patients with eating disorders. Research groups should be evaluated throughout their course with long-term follow up study of subjects. Evaluations should include weight and body perception change and social functioning.

Inbody and Ellis (1985) evaluated seven patients, aged 13 to 21, with either anorexia or bulimia. They met for 1 hour and a half weekly for 8 months. Subjects began to be aware of their body image distortion in 2 to 3 months by identification with others in the group. Each individual could perceive the emaciation of their peers and gradually began to realize that they too might appear the same. The therapists did not comment on a patient's physical appearance but facilitated comments by the other anorexic patients. Because of the complexity of group interactions, the authors stated that two therapists were needed. Inbody and Ellis also agreed with the position, often reported in the literature, that any weight gained by anorexic patients in treatment would be temporary *unless body image distortion* was corrected. At the end of group therapy, all the patients in the Inbody and Ellis group reported recognition of body image distortion and expressed feelings of improved self-image.

Other Procedures

Several other valuable therapeutic procedures addressing body image disturbances have been reported in the literature. I considered hypnosis and various procedures from neopsychoanalysis of minimal relevance to the health-related professional in rehabilitation and have eliminated them from my discussions.

One other goal addressed in the treatment process of body image of patients with anorexia must be considered, an awareness of sociocultural issues surrounding the "virtue" of thinness (Garner and Bemis, 1985; Wooley and Wooley, 1985). Care must be exercised to provide, at the appropriate time in each patient's treatment, education on the difference between the healthy lack of obesity and the unhealthy concept of extreme thinness prevalent in the western culture. In the past decades, extreme thinness as a necessity for the "goodness" and "beauty" of women has been promoted by special interest groups such as the fashion and diet food industries. It is my impression that current clothing catalogues and other sources are beginning to provide a healthier image of the female body, perhaps as a result of the popularization of the anorexia nervosa disorder. In any case, anorexic patients need to develop a healthy, rather than a culturally biased, concept of desirable body image.

Research on Intervention

I was not able to find any systematic, controlled research on intervention directed toward body image disturbance in anorexia nervosa. Quite appropriately, rehabilitation of patients with this disorder is complex, addressing many goals other than the body image problem. Although my discussions are limited to body image, I in no way intend to diminish the importance of other aspects of rehabilitation for anorexia. Because rehabilitation is a total approach, the research studies I located incorporated body image as a part of broader study. I have cited only those parts related to body image.

The St. George's study (Gowers et al, 1989) was still in progress at this report, and no analysis of present data is given. Because this study was long-term, a number of weaknesses in method were unavoidable and have been detailed by the authors. The purpose is to compare an inpatient program for anorexia with two outpatient protocols and controls. Outpatient therapy includes individual, group, and family sessions. Inpatients undergo therapy of a psychodynamic nature followed by the outpatient program. All patients have had an initial assessment and a nutritional component. Assessments evidently are conducted by the interview method.

The inpatient program of the St. George's study was described in detail by Crisp and associates (1985). There are three elements: (1) general management, (2) psychotherapy, and (3) specific medical programming provided by various members of the five-discipline treatment team. There are pretarget and posttarget weight protocols. Projective art therapy is included early, and movement groups later, in the first protocol. After reaching target weight, patients wear street clothes and begin preparation of their own meals. Progressive amounts of leave time are permitted. During later stages, patients attend occupational therapy cooking groups and dine in restaurants.

Steinhausen (1985) described research on a program that included psychotherapy and behavior modification procedures. Admission and discharge data on this comprehensive program were compared. Those assessments relevant to body image showed that scores for "fear of fatness" and on "drive for thinness" declined while self-attributions on body image increased. The average stay in this inpatient program was 11 weeks.

Leon and colleagues (1985) partially supported the value of their intervention program by showing positive change after treatment on one of their measures, the Body Evaluation Scale. Their programming included supportive encouragement to eat, individual psychotherapy, and work with the family.

In summary, the literature review provided many ideas for intervention for body image disturbances of anorexia nervosa patients. Although clinical observations would indicate the availability of effective techniques, extensive research addressing efficacy of treatment related to body image has not been completed.

OCCUPATIONAL PERFORMANCE

There is no literature indicating that body image disturbances of persons with anorexia nervosa interfere with occupational performance or even that there is a relationship between body image problems and poor occupational performance. Those who have worked clinically with anorexics (Barris, 1986; Bruch, 1982; Van Deusen and Allen, 1986) have reported that anorexics are typically high achievers in scholastic, work, and recreational activities. However, their performance is not within normal limits but apparently involves excessive energy discharge and an exaggerated need for occupation. Yates (1990), in his discussion of the poor prognosis for anorexia, reported that even when starved, these persons showed continued occupational and educational functioning. In other words, the anorexic person's main problem with occupational performance is not one of deficit but one of excess. How this excess relates to body image disturbance has not been investigated. Only one study has even approached this question.

Yager and associates (1987) obtained from a mass survey 628 subjects meeting the criteria for a "simulated" diagnosis of anorexia nervosa or bulimia. One of their criteria for the diagnosis was body image disturbance. These eating disorder subjects indicated in their responses that their work and nonwork activities were influenced by their problem. Comparison of those subjects who had had treatment with those who had not showed no difference in statements as to influence on work or nonwork.

The only area related to occupational performance in which anorexics have shown deficits is that of social skills and relationships. Several authors have pointed out this problem (Barris, 1986; Leon et al, 1985; Yates, 1990). Relationship problems can interfere with interpersonal aspects of work, school, and leisure activities. Using the semantic differential approach, Leon and associates (1985) not only showed a significant difference in body evaluation between anorexics and controls but also a difference in social skills. Again, there is no evidence to link the two problems. There is an obvious need for research to determine if the body image disturbances observed in anorexia nervosa are related to their occupational performance problems.

CASE REPORT

This description of an anorexic patient, CB and her rehabilitation program as it relates to her body image problem has been adapted from case reports presented by Bailey (1986) and Goodsitt (1985). Although her total programming was complex, with a number of health professionals involved, I have discussed only interventions by CB's psychologist and activity therapist because they were directly related to her body image distortion.

At age 19, CB was 31% underweight, exhibited eating patterns typical of anorexia, and was admitted to an eating disorders unit. The social worker's report concluded that she came from a "destructive home environment." At the initial psychological evaluation, CB sat and pressed her hands against her stomach. She stated that she felt as if her abdomen would "hang out" if she stood. For the therapist to point out that her stomach was flat only would aggravate the problem and make CB believe that she was crazy. The psychologist approached the body image distortion problem by agreeing that food and water do expand the abdomen, which would be especially observable when a person's stomach was flat. The therapist continued by wondering why CB could not tolerate this slightest of bodily imperfections and, gradually, throughout the course of therapy, progressed into CB's major life problems.

CB's perfectionist standards also were revealed in her activity therapy evaluation. Although skilled in both art and dance, she showed acute discomfort throughout evaluations in both media. CB agreed with the evaluator's assessment of her perfectionist drive, probably as an act of compliance rather than insight. Although initially distressed by the slightest imperfection in her ceramic art project, by 6 weeks she could work independently with less attention to precise details. In dance therapy, CB was able to integrate bodily sensations with her emotions.

At CB's discharge from the eating disorders unit, evaluators considered her body image disturbance to have lessened, with all physical manifestations gone. Because psychological progress was being made, CB was referred for individual outpatient therapy to continue in-depth work on her emotional problems. She also joined a therapy group of four other young women recovering from anorexia nervosa. One focus of this group was social skills training. Another focus was family problems. Because all of the young women in this group showed weights within normal limits, group entry photographs were taken and retaken at monthly intervals. This procedure enabled the group members to reinforce acceptable body shapes and to discuss any indications of a member's potential relapse.

References

American Psychiatric Association: Diagnostic and Statistical Manual of Mental Disorders (3rd ed). Washington, DC, Author, 1987, pp 65–67.

Bailey MK: The evaluation and treatment of eating disorders. Occup Ther Mental Health 6:89–116, 1986.

Barabasz M: Case report—body self perception technique and behavioral counseling in the treatment of anorexia nervosa: a new approach. Int J Psychosom 34:12–14, 1987.

Barris R: Occupational dysfunction and eating disorders: theory and approach to treatment. Occup Ther Mental Health 6:27–45, 1986.

Bell C, Kirkpatrick SW, Rinn RC: Body image of anorexic, obese, and normal females. J Clin Psychol 42:431–439, 1986.

Ben-Tovim DI, Whitehead J, Crisp AH: A controlled study of the perception of body width in anorexia nervosa. J Psychosom Res 23:267–272, 1979.

Beumont PJV, Al-Alami MS, Touyz SW: The Evolution of the Concept of Anorexia Nervosa. In Beumont PJV, Burrows GD, Casper RC (eds): Handbook of Eating Disorders, Part 1: Anorexia and Bulimia Nervosa. New York, Elsevier, 1987, pp 105–116.

Biggs SJ, Rosen B, Summerfield AB: Video-feedback and personal attribution in anorexic, depressed and normal viewers. Br J Med Psychol 53:249–254, 1980.

Bowden PK, Touyz SW, Rodriquez PJ, Hensley R, Beumont PJV: Distorting patient or distorting instrument? Body shape disturbance in patients with anorexia nervosa and bulimia. Br J Psychiatry 155:196–201, 1989.

Bruch H: Perceptual and conceptual disturbances in anorexia nervosa. Psychosom Med 24:1987–1994, 1962.

Bruch H: Anorexia nervosa. Therapy and theory. Am J Psychiatry 139:1531–1538, 1982.

Button E: Body size perception and response to in-patient treatment in anorexia nervosa. Int J Eating Disorders 5:617–629, 1986.

Button EJ, Fransella F, Slade PD: A reappraisal of body perception disturbance in anorexia nervosa. Psychol Med 7:235–243, 1977.

Casper RC, Halmi KA, Goldberg SC, Eckert ED, Davis JM: Disturbances in body image estimation as related to other characteristics and outcomes in anorexia nervosa. Br J Psychiatry 134:60–66, 1979.

Channon S, deSilva P, Hemsley D, Mukherjee K: Body-size perception and preferences in stable-weight and improved-weight anorexic patients. Int J Eating Disorders 9:403–408, 1990.

Collins JK, Beumont PJV, Touyz SW, Krass JL, Thompson F, Philips T: Accuracy of body image with varying degrees of information about the face and body contours. Int J Eating Disorders 6:67–73, 1987.

Crisp AH, Norton KRS, Jurczak S, Bowyer C, Duncan S: A treatment approach to anorexia nervosa—25 years on. J Psychiatr Res 19:393–404, 1985.

Cooper PJ, Taylor MJ, Cooper Z, Fairburn CG: The development and validation of the body shape questionnaire. Int J Eating Disorders 6:485–494, 1987.

Fairburn CG, Cooper Z: Behavioural and Cognitive Approaches to the Treatment of Anorexia Nervosa and Bulimia Nervosa. In Beumont PJV, Burrows GD, Casper RC (eds): Handbook of Eating Disorders, Part 1: Anorexia and Bulimia Nervosa. New York, Elsevier, 1987, pp 271–298.

Fichter MM, Meister I, Koch HJ: The measurement of body image disturbances in anorexia nervosa. Experimental comparison of different methods. Br J Psychiatry 148:453–461, 1986.

Fries H: Studies on Secondary Amenorrhea, Anorectic Behaviour and Body Image Perception. In Vigersky RA (ed): Anorexia Nervosa. New York, Raven Press, 1977, pp 163–176.

Gardner RM, Moncrieff C: Body image distortion in anorexics as a non-sensory phenomenon: a signal detection approach. J Clin Psychol 44:101–107, 1988.

Garfinkel PE, Garner DM: Anorexia Nervosa: A Multidimensional Perspective. New York, Brunner/Mazel, 1982.

Garfinkel PE, Moldofsky H, Garner DM: The outcome of anorexia nervosa: Significance of Clinical Features, Body Image, and Behavior Modification. In Vigersky RA (ed): Anorexia Nervosa. New York, Raven Press, 1977a, pp 315–329.

Garfinkel PE, Moldofsky H, Garner DM: Prognosis in anorexia nervosa as influenced by clinical features, treatment and self-perception. CMA Journal 117:1041–1045, 1977b.

Garfinkel PE, Moldofsky H, Garner D: The stability of perceptual disturbances in anorexia nervosa. Psychol Med 9:703–708, 1979.

Garner DM, Bemis KM: Cognitive Therapy for Anorexia Nervosa. *In* Garner DM, Garfinkel PE (eds): Handbook of Psychotherapy for Anorexia Nervosa and Bulimia. New York, Guilford Press, 1985, pp 107–146.

Garner DM, Garfinkel PE: Measurement of Body Image in Anorexia Nervosa. *In* Vigersky RA (ed): Anorexia Nervosa. New York, Raven Press, 1977, pp 27–30.

Garner DM, Olmstead MP, Polivy J: Development and validation of a multidimensional eating disorder inventory for anorexia nervosa and bulimia. Int J Eating Disorders 2:15–34, 1983.

Giles GM: Anorexia nervosa and bulimia: An activity-oriented approach. Am J Occup Ther 39:510–517, 1985.

Goodsitt A: Self Psychology and the Treatment of Anorexia Nervosa. *In* Garner DM, Garfinkel PE (eds): Handbook of Psychotherapy for Anorexia Nervosa and Bulimia. New York, Guilford Press, 1985, pp 55–82.

Gowers S, Norton K, Yeldham D, et al: The St George's prospective treatment study of anorexia nervosa: a discussion of methodological problems. Int J Eating Disorders 8:445–454, 1989.

Hamsher K, Halmi K, Benton A: Prediction of outcome in anorexia nervosa from neuropsychological status. Psychiatry Res 4:79–88, 1981.

Holland AJ, Sicotte N, Treasure J: Anorexia nervosa: evidence for a genetic basis. J Psychosom Res 32:561–571, 1988.

Hsu LKG: Brief communication: is there a disturbance in body image in anorexia nervosa? J Nerv Ment Dis 170:305–307, 1982.

Huron GF, Brown LB: Body images in anorexia nervosa of bulimia nervosa. Int J Eating Disorders 5:421–439, 1986.

Inbody DR, Ellis JJ: Group therapy with anorexic and bulimic patients: implications for therapeutic intervention. Am J Psychother 39:411–420, 1985.

Lacey JH, Birtchnell SA: Body image and its disturbances. J Psychosom Res 30:623–631, 1986.

Leon GR, Lucas AR, Colligan RC, Ferdinande RJ, Kamp J: Sexual body-image, and personality attitudes in anorexia nervosa. J Abnorm Child Psychol 13:245–257, 1985.

Manley RS, Tonkin R, Hammond C: A method for the assessment of body image disturbance in patients with eating disorders. J Adolesc Health Care 9:384–388, 1988.

Martin JE: Occupational therapy in anorexia nervosa. J Psychiatr Res 19:459–463, 1985.

Meermann R: Experimental investigation of disturbances in body image estimation in anorexia nervosa patients and ballet and gymnastics pupils. Int J Eating Disorders 2:91–99, 1983.

Mills I: The neuronal basis of compulsive behaviour in anorexia nervosa. J Psychiatr Res 19:231–235, 1985.

Pierloot RA, Houben ME: Estimation of body dimensions in anorexia nervosa. Psychol Med 8:317–324, 1978.

Proctor L, Morley S: 'Demand characteristics' in body-size estimation in anorexia nervosa. Br J Psychiatry 149:113–118, 1986.

Slade PD: A review of body-image studies in anorexia nervosa and bulimia nervosa. J Psychiatr Res 19:255–265, 1985.

Slade PD, Russell GFM: Awareness of body dimension in anorexia nervosa: cross-sectional and longitudinal studies. Psychol Med 3:188–199, 1973.

Steinhausen H-C: Evaluation of inpatient treatment of adolescent anorexic patients. J Psychiatr Res 19:371–375, 1985.

Strober M, Goldenberg I, Green J, Saxon J: Body image disturbance in anorexia nervosa during the acute and recuperative phase. Psychol Med 9:695–701, 1979.

Sykes DK, Leuser B, Melia M, Gross M: A demographic analysis of 252 patients with anorexia nervosa and bulimia. Int J Psychosom 35:5–9, 1988.

Toner BB, Garfinkel PE, Garner DM: Measurement of psychometric features and their relationship to clinical outcome in the long term course of anorexia nervosa. Int J Eating Disorders 6:17–27, 1987.

Touyz SW, Beumont PJV: Body Image and its Disturbances. *In* Beumont PJV, Burrows GD, Casper RC (eds): Handbook of Eating Disorders, Part 1: Anorexia and Bulimia Nervosa. New York, Elsevier, 1987, pp 171–187.

Touyz SW, Beumont PJV, Collins JK, McCabe MF, Jupp JJ: Body shape perception and its disturbance in anorexia nervosa. Br J Psychiatry 144:167–171, 1984.

Vandereycken W, Depreitere L, Probst M: Body-oriented therapy for anorexia nervosa patients. Am J Psychother 41:252–259, 1987.

Van Deusen J, Allen L: Is there perceptual-motor dysfunction in anorexia nervosa? Suggestions for research by therapists. Phys Occup Ther Pediatr 5:51–58, 1986.

Waltos DL: Historical perspectives and diagnostic considerations. Occup Ther Ment Health 6:1–13, 1986.

Wear RW, Pratz O: Test-retest reliability for the Eating Disorder Inventory. Int J Eating Disorders 6:767–769, 1987.

Welch G, Hall A, Norring C: The factor structure of the eating disorder inventory in a patient setting. Int J Eating Disorders 9:79–85, 1990.

Welch G, Hall A, Walker F: The factor structure of the Eating Disorders Inventory. J Clin Psychol 44:51–56, 1988.

Whitehouse AM, Freeman CPL, Annandale A: Body size estimation in anorexia nervosa. Br J Psychiatry 153(suppl 2):23–26, 1988.

Williamson DA, Davis CJ, Bennett SM, Goreczny AJ, Gleaves DH: Development of a simple procedure for assessing body image disturbances. Behav Assess 11:433–446, 1989.

Wingate BA, Christie MJ: Ego strength and body image in anorexia nervosa. J Psychosom Res 22:201–204, 1978.

Wooley SC, Wooley OW: Intensive Outpatient and Residential Treatment for Bulimia. *In* Garner DM, Garfinkel PE (eds): Handbook of Psychotherapy for Anorexia Nervosa and Bulimia. New York, Guilford Press, 1985, pp 391–430.

Yager J, Landsverk J, Edelstein C: A 20-month follow-up study of 628 women with eating disorders, I: course and severity Am J Psychiatry 144:1172–1177, 1987.

Yates A: Current perspectives on the eating disorders: II. Treatment, outcome, and research directions. J Am Acad Child Adolesc Psychiatry 29:1–9, 1990.

Yellowlees P: Group psychotherapy in anorexia nervosa. Int J Eating Disorders 7:649–655, 1988.

JULIA VAN DEUSEN

PHANTOM LIMB PAIN

ETIOLOGY	**Reliability**
Peripheral Etiology	**Validity**
Central Etiology	**TREATMENT**
INCIDENCE	**Physical Procedures**
ASSESSMENT	**Behavioral Procedures**
Factor Structure	**CASE REPORT**

Phantom pain is a neural-based body image problem that can severely interfere with the rehabilitation of persons with amputations. Its incidence is high; its exact etiology is unclear; and documentation of successful treatment is sparse. Many different physical and behavioral treatment procedures have been tried. There are many avenues for research on phantom limb pain by health professionals in rehabilitation fields.

The phantom limb phenomenon is the feeling that an amputated body part is still there. If this sensation is painful, it is called phantom pain (Dernham, 1986; Postone, 1987). Stump pain also can be present. Jensen and associates (1983) clearly differentiated phantom pain from these other phenomena associated with limb amputation:

1. Phantom limb—any nonpainful sensation in the missing limb.

173

2. Phantom pain—painful sensations referred to the lost body part.

3. Stump pain—painful sensations localized to the stump.

In Lacey and Birtchnell's (1986) categories of disturbances of body image, phantom pain was included as a disorder following acute dismemberment. In this dismemberment category, the body is markedly altered, but the neural-based perception of the body remains unaltered.

Although amputation of body parts other than the extremities may result in the phantom phenomenon (see Chapter 8), phantom limb pain has been the most extensively documented. Clinically, phantom limb pain can be distinguished from both stump pain and phantom limb sensation (Postone, 1987; Siegfried and Zimmermann, 1981). For example, stump pain can be abolished with a local nerve block, whereas phantom pain generally is not ended by this procedure. Unlike phantom pain, phantom sensation is the "normal" sequela to limb amputation. This phantom sensation may be a tingling feeling, typically at the distal part of the original limb. An individual who has had a limb amputated can experience telescoping, a perception of the digits being attached to the short stump. The movement of the phantom limb may or may not follow the movement of the stump (Jones, 1988; Postone, 1987; Siegfried and Zimmermann, 1981). Some amputees perceive their amputated limb as whole and functional. Examples are the person with a lower extremity amputation who tries to stand on the missing limb (Postone, 1987) and the individual who reaches for a glass of water with the phantom arm (Dernham, 1986).

Fortunately, phantom pain typically does not follow limb amputation. It varies in intensity and may be continuous or intermittent. The time of onset of the pain as well as the duration also varies. The quality of phantom pain typically is described as excruciating and of a sticking, cramping, burning, or squeezing nature (Postone, 1987).

According to Siegfried and Zimmermann (1981), the idea of the phantom limb was first described in 1545, and the term was first used in 1871. Phantom pain was first described in 1649 (Lacey and Birtchnell, 1986; Postone, 1987). Thus, there is little doubt that medical personnel have been acquainted with this phenomenon for centuries. Postone (1987) quoted the 1649 phantom pain description of the French surgeon Ambroise Pare: "Verily it is a thing wondrous strange and prodigious. . . ." Probably because of this attitude, as well as its relationship to the rehabilitation process, phantom limb pain is still receiving extensive attention in the professional literature.

ETIOLOGY

Historically, phantom limb pain was attributed to psychological factors (Sherman et al, 1987). However, studies have shown that people with phantom limb pain are no different from the general population from a psychological perspective; that is, they are not more neurotic and do not show a different personality pattern (Danke, 1981; Sherman et al, 1987; Steigerwald et al, 1981).

However, there is general agreement that psychological factors can precipitate pain when phantom pain is of the intermittent variety and can contribute to the long-term maintenance of phantom pain (Postone, 1987; Sherman et al, 1987). Problems with the psychological aspects of body image, anxiety, depression, and rigidity have been suggested as those characteristics of amputees with phantom pain that influence this pain (Dernham, 1986; Postone, 1987; Sherman et al, 1987; Steigerwald et al, 1981). In particular, disturbances of psychological body image have been noted in persons with phantom pain after surgical replantation related to limb and digit traumatic amputation (Grunert et al, 1988; Schweitzer et al, 1986). There is sound evidence to support Postone's (1987) suggestion that a multifactorial approach (including both psychological and physiological variables) should be used for a genuine understanding of the phantom pain phenomenon.

Although most authors attribute the etiology of phantom pain to the nervous system, there is still disagreement as to the specific etiology. The peripheral system, the spinal cord, the brain stem, or the cortex, or various combinations, may be involved.

Peripheral Etiology

Earlier authors considered phantom pain to be essentially peripheral in nature, resulting from the continued pain response of stump nerve endings (Dernham, 1986; Postone, 1987). According to results of a study of 58 subjects by Jensen and associates (1984), the distribution of the phantom sensation did not correspond to the peripheral nerve supply or dermatome in a single case. Such sensory correspondence is necessary to the credibility of a peripheral etiology of phantom pain.

Central Etiology

There is a growing body of evidence to support the notion that phantom pain is, at least in part, a central nervous system phenomenon. Some authors have explained phantom pain as a spinal cord problem (Carlen et al, 1978; Wall, 1981); others cited higher cerebral centers as the major influence (Jones, 1988; Postone, 1987).

Wall (1981) considered phantom pain to result from spinal cord cells no longer being under inhibitory control owing to peripheral sensory loss. Studies of cord injury support this spinal cord centrality position as opposed to positions emphasizing higher centers. Recent evidence (Christensen et al, 1990) showed no significant differences in incidence of phantom pain between 114 spinal cord–injured subjects and 66 lower extremity amputees. An earlier report was of less vivid phantom pain reported by patients with spinal cord injury (Carlen et al, 1978). The adherents of the spinal cord etiology position maintain that, theoretically, if higher inhibitory influences are of major importance and are lessened by decrease of stimulation from peripheral input, spinal cord injury with greater peripheral effects than limb amputation should result in the more extensive decrease in input to the inhibitory centers. The result would be more vivid phantom pain experiences for the spinal cord–injured patient, a situation not verified by the research data.

Postone (1987) cited the evidence that the reticular activating system serves a major function in phantom pain. Because of the severed peripheral nerves, there is decreased input to the reticular tonic inhibitory influences, which, in turn, are decreased. With less inhibition, pain sensation can be interpreted at the cortical level (Fig. 7–1).

Other authors have provided evidence associating cortical function with the phantom phenomenon, although not necessarily with phantom pain (Drechsler and Schrappe, 1981; Jones, 1988; Yarnitsky et al, 1988). Jones (1988), in particular, has cited studies in support of his position that phantom limbs seem to result from

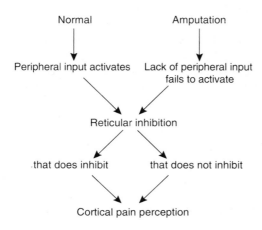

Figure 7–1. The relation between phantom pain and the central nervous system.

activity of the sensorimotor cortex. Jones stated that amputees still perceive their phantom limb even when they have lost a former ability to move their phantom limb from muscular afferent feedback. He considered this evidence for the existence of a central body schema independent of peripheral sensory input. However, because phantom sensation lessens over time, Jones believes that peripheral sensory input is necessary to originate or update this internal body image. Postone (1987) has pointed out that failure to distinguish between phantom sensation and phantom pain weakens the central etiology position.

Because of the diversity of opinion on the etiology of phantom pain, it is not surprising to find a wealth of intervention procedures being used for this problem. I will discuss these procedures after describing the incidence of the phantom pain problem as recorded in the literature.

INCIDENCE

During the past decade, many investigators have studied the incidence of phantom limb pain. These surveys have involved large numbers of American subjects (Sherman and Sherman, 1983; 1985; Sherman et al, 1984) and subjects from other cultures (Buchanan and Mandel, 1986; Carlen et al, 1978; Jensen et al, 1983). They have included subjects amputated because of trauma, vascular disease, and neoplasm (Carlen et al, 1978; Jensen et al, 1983; Sherman et al, 1984; Wall et al, 1985). Consequently, there is adequate documentation of the incidence of phantom limb pain. Incidence does not vary with location of the amputation (Buchanan and Mandel, 1986). Depending on the length of time since onset, how conservative the interpretation of reports, and other variables, reported incidence of phantom limb pain in the amputee population ranged from 46% to 88%.

The most extensive research on the incidence of phantom pain has been the Sherman studies (Sherman and Sherman, 1985, 1983; Sherman et al, 1984). A trial survey was followed by a major investigation of American males, whose amputations were related to military service and were primarily of traumatic origin. In the initial study (Sherman and Sherman, 1983), the 61% response rate to a three-page questionnaire provided 764 subjects, of whom 85% unambiguously reported phantom pain. The most conservative possible interpretation, considering all nonrespondents to be pain free, would still result in an incidence of 51%. The major investigation (Sherman et al, 1984) provided a 55% usable return, so that 2694 responses to the shorter two-page survey could be analyzed.

Seventy-eight percent of these 2694 responses included reports of phantom pain. If all of the nonrespondents are assumed to be pain free, there would still be an incidence in this population of 46%. Figures from other studies on incidence are in Table 7–1.

From a review of study results, a plausible estimate of the incidence of phantom limb pain seems to be in the 60% to 70% range, an incidence sufficiently great to merit the considerable attention being given to phantom pain in the rehabilitation literature.

Further analyses of their data by Sherman and associates (1984) showed the time course of phantom pain. Phantom pain was perceived from 1 day per month (14%) to over 20 days per month (27%). The greatest number of subjects (32%) reported 2 to 5 h of pain per day. Individual episodes varied greatly. Thirty-eight percent reported duration of only a few seconds, whereas 12% experienced continuous pain. Fifty-six percent of those experiencing phantom pain stated that it decreased or disappeared over time. Jensen and associates (1985;1983) found that 59% of their subjects still reported phantom pain at 2-year follow-up, a slightly higher incidence rate than in the Sherman and associates study.

A third study (Sherman and Sherman, 1985) of 436 amputees not having military-related amputation consisted of volunteers for a phantom pain study. Incidence data were not reported for these subjects. This group of subjects showed a time course of phantom pain similar to that of the military-related subjects.

It is difficult to find out about the incidence of intensity, severity, and quality of phantom pain because of inconsistencies of definition and measurement. Using a scale graded zero to 100, Wall and associates (1985) recorded a 36% severity rate. Nine of their 22 patients with phantom pain had thus scored above 50 on the scale, Wall and associates' definition of severe pain. However, Ashburn and Fine (1989) considered only 5% to 10% of amputees with phantom pain to have debilitating pain. The Sherman study (1984) operationalized "intensity of pain," with a pain scale of zero (no pain) to 10 (pain so intense that one would commit suicide). On this scale, the average intensity of phantom pain at its least intense was rated 2.9 and at its most intense, 7.7. Subjects with non–

Table 7–1. INCIDENCE OF PHANTOM PAIN AS REPORTED IN THE LITERATURE

Author	Date	Percentage	Number of Subjects
Carlen et al	1978	67	73
Buchanan & Mandel	1986	62.4	716
Wall et al	1985	88	25
Jensen et al	1983; 1985	72	58

military related amputations rated intensity essentially the same as the military subjects (Sherman and Sherman, 1985). Jensen and colleagues (1985, 1983) reported incidence of the different kinds of pain. Over 50% of persons with phantom pain initially described it as a knifelike sensation. Over prolonged periods, the dominant sensations reported were of a burning or squeezing quality of pain.

In summary, the literature has provided excellent data on the incidence of phantom limb pain as reported by persons with limb amputation. Because many amputees are affected by this pain phenomenon, which continues for prolonged time periods at varying degrees of intensity, it is imperative that rehabilitation professionals address the issues of assessment and treatment.

ASSESSMENT

In the literature on amputations, there is little information on assessment directly geared to phantom pain. Consequently, I have described tools being used in rehabilitation for chronic pain in general (McCormack and Johnson, 1990). McCormack and Johnson discussed behavioral assessments related to occupational performance. I briefly describe two of these instruments—the Dallas Pain Questionnaire and the Activity Pattern Indicator—from their review and elaborate on a third, the Pain Disability Index (PDI). Before reading the comments by McCormack and Johnson (1990), which also are positive, my own review of the literature on the PDI (Pollard, 1984; Tait et al, 1990, 1987) had convinced me of the particular value of this instrument for rehabilitation research and practice.

Among the areas the Dallas Pain Questionnaire seeks to assess is the relation of chronic pain to activities of daily living (ADL) and to work and leisure activities. It is a self-report scale rated from zero to 100% in six increments. Persons with chronic pain are asked to judge the degree to which pain impacts on various activities. Positive aspects of this tool are its sensitivity and good reliability data; negative aspects are the complex directions and scoring system (McCormack and Johnson, 1990).

The Activity Pattern Indicator also is a self-report tool. Subjects are requested to provide the number of times they participated in various activities in their most recent typical week. Work and leisure activities are included. McCormack and Johnson (1990) considered this a useful tool.

The PDI is a brief assessment tool that relates pain and ADL. The researchers involved with this instrument considered it feasible for clinical use as part of an assessment battery as well as for use in longitudinal research. Although the PDI has not been researched specifically with a large group of phantom pain subjects, there are data from a large number of chronic pain patients. According to Sherman and associates (1987), patients with phantom pain do not differ psychologically from other chronic pain patients. Thus, the PDI seems to be a reasonable instrument for use with phantom pain patients.

Pollard (1984) developed the PDI to measure the extent to which chronic pain interferes with seven categories of life activity. On a scale of zero (none) to 10 (total), patients rate their disability in family and home responsibilities, recreation, social activity, occupation, sexual behavior, self-care, and life support activity (Fig. 7–2). Assuming each of these activity areas to be of equal weight, Pollard described a general disability score obtained by summing the ratings of the seven categories. He began validation procedures by showing that this tool discriminated between nine persons with lower back pain who had been working full-time for a year and nine who had just received surgery.

Because the PDI showed promise both as a clinical and as a research tool, a series of studies have been conducted to examine its psychometric properties (Tait et al, 1990, 1987).

Factor Structure

Data from the PDI were factor analyzed in two separate studies ($n = 108$ and $n = 401$). Results indicated that the PDI has two factors. Loading high on one factor were data on disability related to the voluntary activities of home, recreation, social activity, occupation, and sexual behavior. Loading high on a second factor were those activities essential for living: self-care and life-support. Because of this two-factor structure, it may be of questionable meaning to sum all categories for an overall disability score, as originally proposed by Pollard (1984).

Reliability

Using data from 108 chronic pain patients, a coefficient of 0.87 (Cronbach's alpha) was derived. A second study of patient pain data ($n = 444$) showed a coefficient of 0.86. These high coefficients indicate that, overall, the PDI is an internally consistent tool. Alpha coefficients of 0.85 for the voluntary activities factor and 0.70 for the obligatory factor indicate reasonable internal consistency for each factor.

Evaluation of test-retest reliability over a 2-month time span (n = 46) resulted in a Pearson Product-Moment coefficient of r = 0.44. This moderate correlation is encouraging considering the time lapse and small number of subjects. Stability of the PDI over time should be re-evaluated using a large number of subjects.

Validity

Several studies have been reported that support the validity of the PDI (Tait et al, 1990, 1987). Assuming that pain patients who were inpatients would show greater disability than those who were outpatients, 36 former outpatients were compared on the PDI to 37 former inpatients. The initial assumption was verified by showing inpatients reporting greater distress than outpatients on such variables as depression, anxiety, area in pain, lying down time, and having to stop activities. When PDI scores were separated in terms of obligatory and discretionary activity, outpatients were significantly less disabled by pain than were inpatients on both factors.

In another validity study, variables were categorized under psychological distress, pain description, disability, and pain history. Two-hundred and four PDI low scorers (less disability) were compared with 197 high scorers. Analyses showed high scorers reporting more psychological distress, pain, and disability than did low scorers. There were no significant differences between low and high scorers on pain history. Patients who scored high on the PDI stopped activity more, were in bed more during the day, and spent more days and weeks in bed than those scoring low. Again, results showed the PDI to be a valid measure of the extent to which chronic pain interferes with ADL.

Two other studies also supported the validity of this tool. Multiple regression procedure revealed that time in bed, stopping of activity, psychological distress, and work status predicted PDI scores. Results showed that patients who were working had lower PDI scores than those who were unemployed. Tait and associates' (1990) last validity study to date showed that high PDI scorers had higher rates of pain behavior than did low scorers, with the communication aspects of pain behavior showing the best relation to the PDI scores. Communicative aspects included such behaviors as verbal complaints and grimaces. In this study, both nurses and patients rated patient pain behavior. Nurses reported lower rates of patient pain behavior than did the patients.

Although there are obvious weaknesses of the PDI as a measure of pain-related ADL dysfunction (Tait et al, 1990), I believe that

(1) Family/home responsibilities
This category refers to activities related to the home or family. It includes chores or duties performed around the house (eg, yard work) and errands or favors for other family members (eg, driving the children to school).

0	1	2	3	4	5	6	7	8	9	10

no
disability

total
disability

(2) Recreation
This category includes hobbies, sports, and other similar leisure time activities.

0	1	2	3	4	5	6	7	8	9	10

no
disability

total
disability

(3) Social activity
This category refers to activities that involve participation with friends and acquaintances other than family members. It includes parties, theater, concerts, dining out, and other social functions.

0	1	2	3	4	5	6	7	8	9	10

no
disability

total
disability

(4) Occupation
This category refers to activities that are a part of or directly related to one's job. This includes non-paying jobs as well, such as that of a housewife or volunteer worker.

0	1	2	3	4	5	6	7	8	9	10

no
disability

total
disability

(5) Sexual behavior
This category refers to the frequency and quality of one's sex life.

0	1	2	3	4	5	6	7	8	9	10

no
disability

total
disability

(6) Self-care
This category includes activities which involve personal maintenance and independent daily living (eg, taking a shower, driving, getting dressed, etc.).

0	1	2	3	4	5	6	7	8	9	10

no
disability

total
disability

(7) Life-support activity
This category refers to basic life-supporting behaviors such as eating, sleeping, and breathing.

0	1	2	3	4	5	6	7	8	9	10

no
disability

total
disability

Figure 7–2 *See legend on opposite page*

this instrument has considerable value in the assessment of phantom pain patients in a rehabilitation setting. Although other studies are needed to fully validate this instrument, there has been sufficient development of this test to merit its use to supplement clinical judgments. PDI also deserves serious consideration as a research instrument.

TREATMENT

The phantom limb sensation commonly experienced by adult amputees contributes to perception of a complete body image. According to Mensch and Ellis (1986), the lower limb amputee who is experiencing enhanced proprioceptive feedback via a phantom limb is aided in ambulation training. However, when the phantom limb is painful, the situation is reversed. A painful phantom limb interferes with gait training. A study by Helm and associates (1986) supported this position, because phantom and stump pain were associated with reduced ambulation. Carabelli and Kellerman (1985) also have described the interference of severe phantom pain with prosthetic training in lower extremity amputees. Thus, any painful component of the amputee's body schema must be addressed by rehabilitation personnel not only to enhance the quality of life of the patient but also to improve ADL. As is usual in rehabilitation, multidisciplinary participation by practitioners of physical and occupational therapy, psychology, and other disciplines best serves the patient with phantom pain (Ashburn et al, 1989).

Because my book has been designed for rehabilitation personnel, I have emphasized those conservative treatment procedures typically considered for rehabilitation, such as biofeedback, phantom exercises, transcutaneous electrical nerve stimulation (TENS), and behavior modification. Only those treatments reported in the

---

Figure 7–2. Pollard's Pain Disability Index (PDI). (Reproduced by permission from Tait RC, Pollard CA, Margolis RB, Duckro PN, Krause SJ: The pain disability index: psychometric and validity data. Arch Phys Med Rehabil 68:438–441, 1987.)

Directions: The rating scales on the opposite page are designed to measure the degree to which several aspects of your life are presently disrupted by chronic pain. In other words, we would like to know how much your pain is preventing you from doing what you would normally do or from doing it as well as you normally would. Respond to each category by indicating the *overall* impact of pain in your life, not just when the pain is at its worst.

For each of the seven categories of life activity listed, please circle the number on the scale that describes the level of disability you typically experience. A score of 0 means no disability at all, and a score of 10 signifies that all of the activities in which you would normally be involved have been totally disrupted or prevented by your pain.

research literature are addressed, because this book assumes the presence of entry level clinical knowledge by its readers.

Sherman (1980) and Dernham (1986) categorized the wealth of treatment procedures being used by rehabilitation personnel in an attempt to decrease phantom limb pain. I have considered the various treatments under a modification of the categories proposed by others, eliminating those important chemical and surgical procedures less relevant for our purposes. There are two main categories of treatment methods: physical procedures and behavioral procedures. There are two main objectives for treatment: provision of a nearly normal pattern of impulses to the brain and the alteration of the interpretation of pain stimuli. Although these two objectives also involve both chemical and surgical treatments, I have discussed only the physical and behavioral procedures, because they are typically used by rehabilitation personnel. Physical procedures have been tried with the objective of regaining normal stimulation from periphery to the brain. Behavioral procedures have been directed toward altering interpretation of pain signals.

Much of our information on phantom pain intervention is a result of the work of Sherman and colleagues (Sherman, 1980; Sherman et al, 1984, 1983, 1980). Their extensive data were compiled from literature reviews and surveys through the United States Veterans Administration, medical schools, pain clinics, and similar sources. Both amputees and personnel working with phantom pain were surveyed. Thousands of subjects contributed data. Sherman and associates (1984) reported conclusions on treatment results. Their cited success rate (including chemical and surgical as well as physical and behavioral methods) was, at maximum, 8.4% of amputees treated for phantom pain. Only 0.7% of the patients perceived a large permanent change in phantom pain status, and only 0.4% reported cure; that is, only 1.1% received important long-term benefits from any kind of intervention. Decreased pain for the other 7.3% "successes" was temporary. Such results are undeniably discouraging both for persons with phantom pain and for clinical personnel. For the rehabilitation researcher, there is a vast arena for study.

Physical Procedures

The following nonsurgical physical interventions were reported: TENS to the stump; other stump stimulation procedures including tapping, pressing, vibration, and wrapping; relaxation and biofeedback training; phantom limb and stump exercises; heat and massage; ultrasound; change of a prosthesis or of its use; and acupuncture. Of these physical procedures, Sherman and colleagues (1984) found minimal permanent success only with TENS, heat, massage, ultrasound, and prosthesis change. However, these data were from survey reports, not from the results of experiments. Previously, from empirical study of a few subjects, Sherman and colleagues (Sherman, 1976; Sherman et al, 1979) had demonstrated that biofeedback and relaxation seemed to decrease phantom limb pain. From their surveys, only one person reported permanent change from relaxation and none reported permanent change from biofeedback.

Other authors also have surveyed amputees on factors relieving pain (Nebel et al, 1981; Jensen et al, 1985;1983). Two thirds of 154 older adults surveyed preferred treatments involving heat or cold for pain relief, but permanence of results was not studied. Of the 11 subjects reporting relief of pain after 6 months, one cited pressure to stump, and three cited stump elevation. Pinzur (1988), from experience with hundreds of lower extremity amputees, was convinced that good prosthetic care and early weight-bearing minimized phantom pain. However, Jensen and associates (1985) surveyed 58 amputees, 71% of whom used protheses. At 2-year follow-up, there was no significant difference in the use of prostheses between those with and those without phantom pain.

In a small study, using 24 phantom pain patients as their own controls, Lundeberg (1985) provided some indication that vibratory stimulation may be effective in phantom pain treatment. This area might be one worthy of further exploration.

In a few studies of the use of TENS with phantom pain patients, results have been positive, indicating that of all the physical procedures, this one has the best potential for further research. Carabelli and Kellerman (1985) treated three patients with severe phantom pain with TENS units to sites contralateral but corresponding to phantom pain sites. For example, a right below-knee amputee with phantom ankle pain was treated by TENS unit to the left ankle. The three patients were able to participate in their prosthetic training and were still pain free at 6 months' follow-up. In a controlled study involving 51 subjects, Finsen and colleagues (1988) showed a faster improvement for TENS treated patients, but at 1 year, there were no significant group differences. At 1 year, both experimental and control subjects reported infrequent and mild pain. In a third study with 15 subjects, TENS was compared with a control stimulus, and positive results were reported (Gessler et al, 1981).

In summary, my literature review revealed very slim evidence that physical procedures can affect the painful phantom limb in any way pertinent to increased ADL or work or leisure activities of the amputee. Further, with the exception of TENS and, possibly, vibration and biofeedback, there is little evidence from the extant research to encourage further investigation of physical procedures. However, we must note that although extensive studies have been performed, most have used opinions of success by patients or health workers as data. There are virtually no controlled studies of most physical procedures in which direct observation of subjects is employed.

Another avenue for research is that of physical procedures combined with other types of intervention. For example, the analgesic calcitonin recently has been shown effective for phantom limb pain (Jaeger and Maier, 1990; Kessel and Worz, 1987), and it was suggested that it might need to be combined with physical procedures such as heat, ice, massage, and limb-training for long-term relief.

Behavioral Procedures

In his review of phantom pain treatments, Sherman (1980) cited a number of behavioral methods of altering interpretation of pain stimuli. He included psychotherapy, hypnosis, distraction training, and behavior modification. Although relaxation-biofeedback and phantom limb exercises were included with physical intervention, they also were considered behavioral procedures. The later surveys by Sherman and associates (1984;1983) showed not even one amputee with permanent change from psychotherapy, hypnosis, biofeedback, or exercises.

Sherman and associates (1987) thoroughly analyzed the literature on the psychological aspects of phantom pain. From my earlier discussion of etiology, it is apparent that phantom pain is unlikely to be caused by psychological factors. However, this kind of pain, like any chronic pain, is influenced by anxiety and depression. Because psychotherapy and hypnosis would seem to pertain more appropriately to conditions in which the etiology is psychopathological, distraction training and behavior modification are of greater relevance to rehabilitation and phantom pain. Distraction training and behavior modification were not included as part of the survey results, and Sherman's literature review also showed very few data on these procedures. Distraction training was defined as a technique that helps the amputee "learn to concentrate on tasks while ignoring concurrently presented pain stimuli." Behavior modification procedures help patients accept their pain and eliminate needs and problems that reinforce or aggravate pain. Nebel and associates (1981) have suggested group therapy and instruction, which would seem to be consistent with these goals. Both of these methods also would appear to be applicable to treatment goals of increased function in ADL, work, and leisure skills. Research into these areas would be of great importance in our search for meaningful interventions for the rehabilitation of amputees with phantom pain.

As previously pointed out, psychological considerations of phantom pain differ little from those for other types of chronic pain. Thus, another fruitful source for research ideas specific to treatment of phantom pain is the literature addressing the general category of chronic pain. For further information see, for example, the treatment and theoretical ideas in "Modulation of Pain," specially edited by G. McCormick (Dougherty and Radomski, 1990).

CASE REPORT

This case report is based on one described by Morse (1985). It has been modified to illustrate and emphasize rehabilitation procedures.

Joe is a 40-year-old petroleum engineer. At age 26, a war injury resulted in a right below-knee amputation. There were also other traumatic injuries to the right side. Twelve years later, Joe experienced intensified pain of a burning nature for which there was no apparent anatomical reason. The toes of his amputated foot were felt in his stump. This intensified phantom pain coincided with his marriage to a physician and with increased vocational stress. When his physician wife canceled the sedatives and tranquilizers that Joe had been using, he switched to analgesics. Finally, Joe was referred by his wife and his internist to a chronic pain unit for phantom limb pain and psychological stress.

Joe's admission to the pain unit occurred 14 years after his amputation. On admission, Joe's activity level remained unimpaired. He had continued to work long hours and hiked for recreation. His pain was relatively constant but perceived as of greatest intensity while sitting or resting. Relief was obtained only under heavy medication. Joe's response to chronic pain was one of anger and frustration. His wife's response was to assume a caretaker-rescuer role and to look for medical and surgical solutions.

Problems

The staff of the chronic pain unit developed the following problem list for Joe:

1. Residual phantom pain.
2. Residual pain from other sites of war injuries.
3. Stump pain.
4. "Operantly conditioned pain" from narcotic analgesic use.

Psychological testing showed no evidence of psychopathology, only the "normal" psychological reactions to chronic pain. The PDI confirmed the staff's impression that pain did not disrupt Joe's life activities. However, interview data suggested that Joe's hard-driving work habits were creating a too intense and stressful vocational life. The pain unit medical staff considered Joe's residual pain problems to be associated with various central nervous system excitatory influences from increased work tensions, extensive use of nicotine and caffeine, and analgesic dependence.

Intervention

A detoxification program to rid Joe of analgesic dependence was the immediate need. Although medication withdrawal was a difficult process, by the program's end, Joe exhibited a calm and constructive emotional state.

Other services involved in Joe's rehabilitation were physical therapy, occupational therapy, and clinical psychology. In physical therapy, Joe was retrained in the use of the TENS unit; he received massage and heat to his stump; and he participated in biofeedback training for pain reduction, phantom exercises, and weight-bearing to decrease pain. Clinical psychology provided group therapy and relaxation training for stress reduction. Joe was able to reduce his intake of nicotine and caffeine. His relationship with his wife improved to the extent that she was able to replace her medical role with the appropriate one of a loving spouse. The occupational therapist set up an activity program that allowed Joe to learn how to pace himself at work and reduce his perfectionist tendencies and excessive drive, characteristics related to vocational stress. It was the consensus of the pain unit staff that a less stressful lifestyle could increase Joe's potential for a body schema more often free from pain. A reasonably comfortable lifestyle both at home and at work was predicted for Joe.

References

Ashburn MA, Fine PG: Persistent pain following trauma. Milit Med 154:86–89, 1989.

Buchanan DC, Mandel AR: The prevalence of phantom limb experience in amputees. Rehabil Psychol 31:183–188, 1986.

Carabelli RA, Kellerman WC: Phantom limb pain: relief by application of TENS to contralateral extremity. Arch Phys Med Rehabil 7:466–467, 1985.

Carlen PL, Wall PD, Nadvorna H, Steinbach T: Phantom limbs and related phenomena in recent traumatic amputations. Neurology 28:211–217, 1978.

Christensen FL, Rosenborg D, Lind T, Jensen TS: Phantom pain and sensations in spinal cord injured patients and in lower extremity amputee patients. Paper presented at the Sixth World Congress on Pain of the International Association for the Study of Pain, Australia, April, 1990. Pain, Supplement 5, 1990. (Abstract 909.)

Danke F: The Phenomenology of Post-Amputation Pain. In Siegfried J, Zimmermann M (eds): Phantom and Stump Pain. New York, Springer-Verlag, 1981, pp 51–55.

Dernham P: Phantom limb pain. Geriatric Nursing 7:34–37, 1986.

Dougherty PM, Radomski MV (eds): Occupational Therapy Practice, 1:1–90, 1990.

Drechsler F, Schrappe O: Somatosensory Evoked Potentials in Above-Knee Amputees with Phantom and Stump Pain. In Siegfried J, Zimmermann M (eds): Phantom and Stump Pain. New York, Springer-Verlag, 1981, pp 32–41.

Finsen V, Persen L, Lovlien M, et al: Transcutaneous electrical nerve stimulation after major amputation. J Joint Surg 70:109–112, 1988.

Gessler M, Struppler A, Oettinger B: Treatment of Phantom Pain by Transcutaneous Stimulation (TNS) of the Stump, the Limb Contralateral to the Stump, and the Other Extremities. In Siegfried J, Zimmermann M (eds): Phantom and Stump Pain. New York, Springer-Verlag, 1981, pp 93–98.

Grunert BK, Smith CJ, Devine CA, et al: Early psychological aspects of severe hand injury. J Hand Surg 13B:177–180, 1988.

Helm P, Engel T, Holm A, Kristiansen VB, Rosendahl S: Function after lower limb amputation. Acta Orthop Scand 57:154–157, 1986.

Jaeger H, Maier C: Double-blind study on calcitonin IV treatment in early phantom limb pain. Paper presented at the Sixth World Congress on Pain of the International Association for the Study of Pain, Australia, April, 1990. Pain, Supplement 5, 1990. (Abstract 100.)

Jensen TS, Krebs B, Nielsen J, Rasmussen P: Immediate and long-term phantom limb pain in amputees: incidence, clinical characteristics and relationships to pre-amputation limb pain. Pain 21:267–278, 1985.

Jensen TS, Krebs B, Nielsen J, Rasmussen P: Non-painful phantom limb phenomena in amputees: incidence, clinical characteristics and temporal course. Acta Neurol Scand 70:407–414, 1984.

Jensen TS, Krebs B, Nielsen J, Rasmussen P: Phantom limb, phantom pain and stump pain in amputees during the first 6 months following limb amputation. Pain 17:243–256, 1983.

Jones LA: Motor illusions: what do they reveal about proprioception? Psychol Bull 103:72–86, 1988.

Kessel C, Worz R: Immediate response of phantom limb pain to calcitonin. Pain 30:79–87, 1987.

Lacey JH, Birtchnell SA: Body image and its disturbances. J Psychosom Res 30:623–631, 1986.

Lundeberg T: Relief of pain from a phantom limb by peripheral stimulation. J Neurol 232:79–82, 1985.

McCormack GL, Johnson C: Systems for objectifying clinical pain. Occup Ther Practice 1:21–29, 1990.

Mensch G, Ellis PM: Physical Therapy Management of Lower Extremity Amputations. Rockville, MD, Aspen, 1986.

Morse RH: The belated Viet Nam phantom. J La State Med Soc 137(5):24–27, 1985.

Nebel FW, Kuhr H, Runge G, Imschweiler A, Meyer G, Lingg P: Rehabilitation of Elderly Amputees: Stump and Phantom Pain. In Siegfried J, Zimmermann M (eds): Phantom and Stump Pain. New York, Springer-Verlag, 1981, pp 110–116.

Pinzur MS: Phantom pain: a lesson in the necessity for careful clinical research on chronic pain problems (letter). J Rehabil Res Dev 25:83, 1988.

Pollard CA: Preliminary validity study of pain disability index. Percept Mot Skills 59:974, 1984.

Postone N: Phantom limb pain: a review. Int J Psychiatry Med 17:57–70, 1987.

Schweitzer I, Rosenbaum MB, Sharzer LA, Strauch B: Liaison consultation psychiatry with patients who have replantation surgery to the upper limb. Aust N Z J Psychiatry 20:38–43, 1986.

Sherman RA: Special review, published treatments of phantom limb pain. Am J Phys Med 59:232–244, 1980.

Sherman RA: Case reports of treatment of phantom limb pain with a combination of electromyographic biofeedback and verbal relaxation techniques. Biofeedback Self Regul 1:353, 1976. (Abstract.)

Sherman RA, Sherman CJ: A comparison of phantom sensations among amputees whose amputations were of civilian and military origins. Pain 21:91–97, 1985.

Sherman RA, Sherman CJ: Prevalence and characteristics of chronic phantom limb pain among American veterans. J Phys Med 62:227–238, 1983.

Sherman RA, Sherman CJ, Bruno G: Psychological factors influencing chronic phantom limb pain: an analysis of the literature. Pain 28:285–295, 1987.

Sherman RA, Sherman CJ, Gall NG: A survey of current phantom limb pain treatment in the United States. Pain 8:85–99, 1980.

Sherman RA, Sherman CJ, Parker L: Chronic phantom and stump pain among American veterans: results of a survey. Pain 18:83–95, 1984.

Siegfried J, Zimmermann M: Preface. In Siegfried J, Zimmermann M (eds): Phantom and Stump Pain. New York, Springer-Verlag, 1981, pp v-vii.

Steigerwald F, Brass J, Krainick JV: The Analysis of Personality Factors in the Prediction of Phantom Limb Pain. In Siegfried J, Zimmermann M (eds): Phantom and Stump Pain. New York, Springer-Verlag, 1981, pp 84–88.

Tait RC, Chibnall JT, Krause SJ: The pain disability index: psychometric properties. Pain 40:171–182, 1990.

Tait RC, Pollard CA, Margolis RB, Duckro PN, Krause SJ: The pain disability index: psychometric and validity data. Arch Phys Med Rehabil 68:438–441, 1987.

Wall PD: On the Origin of Pain Associated with Amputation. In Siegfried J, Zimmermann M (eds): Phantom and Stump Pain. New York, Springer-Verlag, 1981, pp 2–14.

Wall R, Novotny-Joseph P, MacNamara TE: Does preamputation pain influence phantom limb pain in cancer patients? South Med J 78:34–36, 1985.

Yarnitsky D, Barron SA, Bental E: Disappearance of phantom pain after focal brain infarction. Pain 32:285–287, 1988.

8

JULIA VAN DEUSEN

MASTECTOMY AND BODY IMAGE

Two potential body image problems may be associated with operative procedures of the breast. The neural schema may be disturbed with occurrence of phantom breast. Much more prevalent in the research literature is concern for the psychological aspects of body image related to sexuality and femininity. After discussing operative procedures, this chapter describes the assessment and treatment procedures related to body image of postmastectomy patients. Premastectomy counseling, cognitive therapy, and support groups have shown promise as modes of intervention. The literature also has information relating postmastectomy and activities of daily living (ADL).

The most common site of cancer in women is the breast. Operative treatment is of four types (Rozin and Skornick, 1984):

1. Radical mastectomy, in which the entire breast, pectoral muscles, and axilla contents are removed.
2. Modified radical mastectomy, in which preservation of the pectoral muscles prevents dysfunction in shoulder mobility.
3. Simple mastectomy, in which only breast tissue is removed, followed by irradiation.
4. Breast-conserving procedures (partial mastectomy, segmentectomy, lumpectomy), in which the tumor is removed accompanied by irradiation.

The highest incidence of breast cancer is found in Northern European and North American countries (Case, 1984; Valanis and Rumpler, 1985). In the United States, at the present time, there is probably an inflated emphasis on the female breast as an expression of sexuality. Unlike the situation in some parts of Europe, the real breasts of average women in America seldom are displayed, so that the unreal media version becomes the standard. Furthermore, television and cinema emphasize the erotic rather than the nutrient role of female breasts. The typical woman integrates this cultural influence with her own past and present experiences for her personal breast image (Case, 1984; Valanis and Rumpler, 1985). It has long been assumed that loss of a breast will negatively affect the female body image. Consequently, there has been considerable research in this area. According to Bartelink and colleagues (1985), the cancer site most studied by psychologists and psychiatrists is the breast.

Using the classification of Lacey and Birtchnell (1986), body image disorders from breast loss are among those disorders resulting from acute dismemberment. Unlike the phantom limb, the phantom breast has not received extensive attention in the literature. Perhaps this lack of attention is because the incidence of phantom breast pain is not as great or does not interfere with functional activity such as ambulation. Perhaps the neural aspect of body image, phantom breast sensation, is overshadowed by the sexuality-femininity aspect of body image associated with breast loss. This latter aspect of body image fits the Lacey-Birtchnell category of disturbances from actual physical disability, rather than the dismemberment classification, and has been extensively addressed in the research literature. Before discussing this research, a brief description of phantom breast pain is relevant.

THE PHANTOM BREAST

Subjects experiencing breast loss have been interviewed regarding presence of a phantom part. Some subjects were questioned several weeks after loss and others more than a year after operation. Subjects represented several cultures (United States, Scandinavia, the Netherlands). An early study recorded phantom pain at a 42.9% rate as opposed to presence of a nonpainful phantom at 10.8% (Jamison et al, 1978). A second study found only 5% of subjects experiencing pain, although 35.5% reported a phantom breast (Christensen et al, 1982). Both these studies involved a small number of subjects (n = 41; n = 45). Two more recent and comprehensive records of phantom pain incidence revealed 12% to 14% of the over 100 subjects contacted (Kroner et al, 1989; Staps et al, 1985). Reasons that these researchers gave to explain the low incidence of breast pain (as compared with limb pain) were differences in peripheral sensory input and size of the relevant somatosensory cortical areas. The breast does not have the kinesthetic input of the moving limbs or as large a cortical representation.

Frequency of phantom breast pain has been recorded from many times daily to less than 10 times yearly. Character of the pain was described as erotic, tingling sensations turning painful and as knifelike, shooting, and itching (Jamison et al, 1978; Kroner et al, 1989; Staps et al, 1985). Although lacking sufficient data to support their opinion, Christensen and colleagues (1982) indicated that their subjects experiencing the phantom breast phenomenon had severe body image defects relative to those women having mastectomy but no phantom sensation. This topic is one in need of further research.

BODY IMAGE PERCEPTION ASSOCIATED WITH OPERATIVE PROCEDURES

Numerous studies have been conducted examining the relationship of body image disturbances and various operative procedures for breast cancer. The incidence of breast cancer in men is low, 0.2%, as reported by Case (1984). Consequently, studies universally deal with female subjects. Because of continual innovations in surgery related to breast cancer, the body image studies fall into three categories. The earlier studies (Jamison et al, 1978; Polivy, 1977; Ray, 1977; Worden and Weisman, 1977) were concerned with whether or not the mastectomy patient showed negative body image. Because the results were not conclusive, further studies were conducted in this area. However, the bulk of studies during the 1980s compared the body image of mastectomy patients with that of patients undergoing various breast-saving procedures or examined the relation of breast reconstruction and body image. Because our interest is in rehabilitation rather than surgery, a detailed presentation of this literature is not relevant to our purpose. I have discussed a few studies to give the reader the flavor of this body image research area.

Mastectomy

According to Polivy (1977), his study was the first to examine the relation of mastectomy and body image. Polivy collected data by interview and a 49-item scale on body image, self-concept, and intimate relationships. These data were collected before the operation, the week following, and 6 to 11 months postoperation. The subjects were 15 mastectomy patients, 18 women with negative breast biopsies, and 11 surgery patients with no cancer symptoms. Polivy concluded that, although patient denial probably interfered with the immediate body image data, mastectomy resulted in a less positive body image several months postsurgery.

A study by Andersen and Jochimsen (1985) is illustrative of those studies reporting no significant difference in body image between radical mastectomy subjects and controls. Their 16 experimental subjects were compared with 16 people seeking routine gynecological care. The body image measure consisted of 15 statements about bodily appearance or parts, each with a five-point scale.

Breast-Conserving Procedures

Research has shown little difference in survival rate for those breast cancer patients undergoing the radical versus the less radical operative procedures (Ashcroft et al, 1985; Lasry et al, 1987; Wellisch et al, 1989). When there is no medical evidence indicating need for a more radical procedure, the results of psychological research clearly suggest the value of breast-saving procedures from a body image perspective.

Review of research comparing the body image after mastectomy with the body image after breast-conserving procedures showed no result in which body image was more positive with mastectomy. One problem in drawing conclusions from the research literature is that those studies not showing a significant difference may not be reported. Another problem with this category of research studies is that, with the increasing prevalence of breast reconstruction postmastectomy, studies of mastectomy subjects without breast reconstruction become less important.

One example in the literature in which breast-saving procedures were compared with radical mastectomy is a study by Bartelink and associates (1985). Questionnaire responses of 114 subjects with breast-conserving therapy were compared with those of 58 radical mastectomy subjects 1 to 2 years postsurgery. Six items pertained to body image, as demonstrated by factor analysis of the questionnaire data. Sample items were "I feel ashamed of my body" and "I feel self-conscious about being seen nude by my husband." Significant differences were found for each of the body image items. When a total score from all six items defining the construct body image were compared between subject groups, the difference was significant, at $P < .001$.

Wellisch and associates (1989) compared the emotional aspects of body image of 22 subjects with lumpectomy, 15 subjects with mastectomy who had had breast reconstruction, and 13 subjects who had not had breast reconstruction. Groups showed significant differences on five of seven body image items. A sample item showing differences was "I think that my body looks as good as it did before breast cancer treatment." These researchers concluded that lumpectomy subjects seemed to have the best body image of the three groups studied. Although not always statistically significant, the mean scores of mastectomy patients with reconstruction were between those of the other two groups.

Breast Reconstruction

After breast removal for cancer, breast reconstruction may be performed immediately or delayed for months or even years. The procedure for reconstruction may use a myocutaneous flap from abdominal muscle or latissimus dorsi. Implants also may be used. There are advantages and disadvantages associated with the various procedures. For example, one advantage to the abdominal flap is that the patient gets a simultaneous "tummy tuck." A major disadvantage is the risk of extended time in surgery (Dinner and Coleman, 1985; Mansel et al, 1986; Scheflan, 1984).

Women differ in their reasons for having or not having breast reconstruction. Assuming appropriate information on breast reconstruction, medical or economic factors may prohibit a woman's choice for this procedure. Assuming a positive medical and financial situation, psychological factors may be the deciding influences. Fear is a primary reason for not seeking breast reconstruction—

fear of additional surgery and its risks, fear of additional pain, fear of return of cancer to the reconstruction. A second reason is guilt over the idea of spending money frivolously—"I don't deserve an operation just to look better." If reconstruction is delayed, a third reason for not choosing this procedure is that women may adjust to the mastectomy, be functioning optimally in all spheres of life, and realistically have no desire for breast reconstruction (Schain et al, 1984).

Reasons why women select breast reconstruction center on body image issues. Reasons given include the desire to feel whole again, to be comfortable without clothes and in all types of clothing designs, and to enhance feelings of femininity with associated sexual benefits (Schain et al, 1984).

From the literature, I have found consistent results regarding the positive effect on body image of breast reconstruction (Wellisch, 1989). Schain and colleagues (1985) have commented that the modern day concern is not whether to reconstruct, but when—that is, whether the procedure should be immediate or delayed. Unfortunately, definitions of these times are inconsistent in the various studies; therefore, it is not possible to evaluate the time factor's relationship to body image. For example, results by Schain and colleagues (1985), who defined immediate reconstruction as occurrence less than 1 year after mastectomy, could not be compared with those of Noone and colleagues (1982), who defined immediate reconstruction as occurrence at the time of mastectomy.

Two strategies appear in the literature for comparing body image from immediate versus delayed breast reconstruction for cancer. One design compares body image of a group of women selecting delayed reconstruction with a second group selecting immediate reconstruction (Stevens et al, 1984). The other strategy uses subjects as their own controls. Body image attitudes are compared for the immediate reconstruction of one breast with those for the delayed reconstruction of the other breast (Goin and Goin, 1982).

Some of the study results relating body image and breast reconstruction follow:

In a study by Stevens and associates (1984) 75% of subjects with delayed reconstruction reported feeling deformed, but all considered the reconstruction to have repaired these feelings; none of the subjects with immediate reconstruction felt deformed.

In a study by Noone and associates (1982), all subjects reported that they would recommend reconstruction to others, and 92% said that they had reached their desired goals through this procedure (goals such as wearing a swimsuit).

In a study by Goin and Goin (1982) all subjects, serving as their own controls, were as pleased with immediate reconstruction as with delayed reconstruction.

In a study by Mansel and associates (1986) patients' ratings of cosmetic results of reconstruction were in close agreement with those of the surgeons.

In a study by Wellisch and associates (1985) there were no differences between subjects with delayed reconstruction and those with immediate reconstruction in satisfaction with their nude or clothed appearance or with their sense of the balance of their breasts.

In general, the literature indicates that breast reconstruction has a positive effect on body image. In these situations, body image therapy probably can be limited to psychological support, pre- and postsurgery. When, for medical or psychological reasons, reconstruction is not an option, intervention for body image may be of greater significance.

ASSESSMENT

The assessment procedures that I found in the research literature were of three types: (1) questionnaires, (2) interviews, and (3) projective tests. Typically, data were from scaled questionnaire items or from psychiatrists' interviews (Goin and Goin, 1982). Farash (1979) used projective techniques, as did part of Sanger and Reznikoff's (1981) project. Although more rigorous tools are available for assessing body image, I have discussed here only those that I found used with postoperative breast cancer patients. The most promising tools to meet the needs of rehabilitation personnel consisted of body image items that could be evaluated by a Likert-type scale (strongly agree to strongly disagree). One such tool has been described earlier. (See section on Breast-Conserving Procedures.)

Kemeny and colleagues (1988) also reported use of a tool with body image items that worked well in research and should be suitable for clinical use. They used items with the following content to compare the emotional reaction to body image of patients postmastectomy and postsegmentectomy:

Like my looks just the way they are.

Feel good about my body.

Like to change some parts of body.

Feel less physically attractive.

Feel less sexually desirable now.

Feel ashamed of my body.

Body looks as good as it did before.

Kemeny and colleagues (1988) found significant differences on all items, with probabilities ranging from $P < .03$ to .007.

Sanger and Reznikoff (1981) used a five-point scale to obtain a body satisfaction score. Subjects rated 46 body parts and functions in terms of present satisfaction and satisfaction before surgery. Importance of each body part also was rated. The importance score multiplied by the satisfaction score produced a weighted body satisfaction score. This scale and a projective measure of body boundary discriminated between mastectomy subjects and those with breast-saving procedures. A word-association measure of body anxiety did not discriminate.

Kriss and Kraemer (1986) described a scale constructed so that subjects rated 17 body areas, including the amputated and remaining breast. Ratings were on a one to five scale of "like intensely" to "dislike intensely." Three different perceptions of body parts were evaluated—feelings, self-touch, and partner's touch. Kris and Kraemer (1986) obtained some significant group differences using this instrument.

Other than the limited evidence of construct validity illustrated above, very little work of a psychometric nature seems to have been done with body image scales for mastectomy patients. This area is one in need of research.

TREATMENT

The rehabilitation team often is involved in the physical programming of postmastectomy patients (Case, 1984; Dinner and Coleman, 1984; Gaskin et al, 1989). Therapists administer postoperative exercises and other procedures to prevent thrombosis, decrease edema, and maintain and improve upper extremity range of motion as indicated. Because my purpose is limited to body image treatment for self-care, work, and leisure function, I have discussed only this aspect of the total rehabilitation program. There is not necessarily a clear-cut separation of procedures for meeting physical and psychological objectives. Gaskin and associates (1989) have maintained that their physical exercise program provides the same psychological advantages as a support group.

When assessment indicates a body image or a potential body image problem for a breast cancer patient, there are two types of solutions. The physical body can be restored so that the neurological schema can be maintained or regained, or treatment may rely on adjustment of the psychological component of the body image.

Physical Restoration

I already have discussed the operative procedures for breast reconstruction. Such procedures should be accompanied by adequate psychological support. Another aspect of physical restoration is the provision of a realistic wig when adjunct therapy causes hair loss (Case, 1984). A breast prosthesis is recommended if the breast has not been replaced in a more natural manner (Case, 1984). However, it seems unlikely that the prosthesis will solve a body image problem, because evidence indicates that a prosthesis usually is not incorporated into the body image (Noone et al, 1982; Schain et al, 1985, 1984).

Psychological Treatment

From the professional literature, I have found two approaches to intervention for body image problems of mastectomy patients: individual counseling and group therapy. I have termed the first approach the educational-guidance approach.

Educational-Guidance

Valanis and Rumpler (1985) have described two models of health care decision-making: paternalism and consumerism. Rather than making a "fatherly" decision for the patient, the consumerism model involves the early sharing of information with the patient and guidance so that the patient can decide among options. Such a model allows the patient to mesh realistic information with her values and those of significant others.

Much of the literature on the educational-guidance approach addresses goals to minimize body image disturbances of patients with breast cancer through presurgical counseling. Goin (1984) emphasized this aspect of treatment. She stated that breast cancer patients need to be well educated in advance about their various alternatives, such as lumpectomy and delayed versus immediate reconstruction. It is necessary to be sure that patients have grasped the actual concepts of the various alternatives, because anxiety can interfere with their comprehension.

Dierkhising (1987) received positive evaluations from professionals, patients, and their spouses on programming toward speci-fied goals. Goals were ones such as "the patient will understand herself and her body after diagnosis" and "the patient will receive information on altered body image and its effects on sexuality and emotions."

Members of the rehabilitation team or local organizations of the National Cancer Society can provide information to patients, who need to be aware of surgical options and potential outcomes. For example, patients should be shown pictures of both excellent and poor breast reconstruction results (Schain et al, 1984).

Appropriate dissemination of information, with guidance by a health professional, would seem to go far toward prevention of body image problems for mastectomy patients. Hopwood and Maguire (1988) reported a controlled study investigating counseling for prevention by nursing specialists. Although counseling did not prevent body image disturbance, it did identify such problems early, allowing effective intervention. The type of intervention recom-mended by these authors was cognitive behavior therapy. By adjusting cognitive distortions, the mastectomy patient learns to develop a more positive attitude toward her body image. A pilot study showed favorable results from this kind of therapy when depressed mood was first addressed through medication.

Group Approach

The group approach is a second approach to intervention. A few researchers have investigated groups designed to help mastec-tomy patients with body image problems.

Farash (1979) evaluated the effectiveness of self-help groups versus individual crisis intervention on body image changes follow-ing mastectomy. Sixty subjects following radical mastectomy and 20 subjects following benign tumor removal were randomly as-signed to a self-help group, an individual therapy group, or a no treatment control group. The individual therapy emphasized feel-ings of loss and body image changes. All subjects were 2 months postsurgery, and treatments lasted for 12 weeks. Body image was assessed by projective technique. Farash's results showed untreated mastectomy subjects more likely to have body image disturbances than subjects with tumor removal or those mastectomy subjects having psychological intervention. Body image assessments were no different for subjects having individual therapy than for those in self-help groups.

This self-help or peer support group is the type of approach mentioned most often in the literature. Case (1984) stated that information on such support groups can be obtained from the

American Cancer Society. Self-help groups provide group exercise sessions. In these groups, the sharing of feelings about breast cancer and mastectomy is encouraged.

A descriptive study was reported of a self-help group in India for women postsurgery for breast cancer (David et al, 1988). The group involved counseling, prayer and scripture reading, recreational and social activities, advice on prostheses, and breast self-examinations. Interview and questionnaire data were obtained from 32 subjects, 50% of whom had body image concerns. Ninety-four per cent reported a positive outcome of the self-help group.

Kris and Kraemer (1986) chose to investigate a more in-depth type of therapy group than the support group. Sixty-two experimental subjects participated in therapy, eight to 12 per group. There were thirty-five, ninety-min sessions that included activities such as psychodrama, role-playing, and guided imagery. The aspect of their study dealing with negative body image failed to show significant differences for mastectomy subjects after therapy compared with mastectomy or nonmastectomy controls.

Although there is too little evidence for a definite opinion, the evidence to date suggests that guidance with accurate information (premastectomy) and cognitive therapy and participation in support groups (postmastectomy) may be feasible types of intervention to minimize body image dysfunction of mastectomy patients. Further research is needed.

OCCUPATIONAL PERFORMANCE

The ADL of mastectomy patients is initially limited by their physical condition (Case, 1984) so that therapists are first concerned about functional adaptations and movement precautions for these patients. My discussion does not involve the physical problems but rather addresses whether or not body image problems are related to limitations in ADL or work or leisure activities.

Lasry and associates (1987) suggested that body image problems were related to reduced activity, difficulties with sleep, and sexual behavior. Other authors also have associated sexual behavior and body image. Case (1984) stated that counseling for women who have had a mastectomy should include information on positioning for sexual relations. Although other positions may be desirable for maximum comfort, if body image is a concern, the woman on bottom position is optimal from a cosmetic point of view. Morris (1980) cited an 8 to 35% incidence of impaired sex life following primary treatment for breast cancer. Reasons given for vulnerability were psychological but not specifically body image problems. It is interesting to note that Kemeny and associates (1988) and Wellisch and associates (1989) found no significant differences in sexual behavior between patients having breast-saving procedures and mastectomy despite observing body image differences.

The only other daily activities that appeared in the literature in relation to body image of mastectomy patients were dressing and bathing. In a comparison of subjects with lumpectomy and mastectomy, Steinberg and associates (1985) found a significant difference in clothing style, the wearing of night clothes, and undressing in front of one's spouse. Wellisch and associates (1989) found that there were no differences in the wearing of night clothes to bed, a finding that was inconsistent with that of Steinberg and associates (1985). Hopwood and Maguire (1988) reported postmastectomy avoidance of bath-taking and that some women dressed and undressed in the dark.

Women reported feeling restricted in choice of clothing (Hopwood and Maguire, 1988). Women also cited the desire to be comfortable in all kinds of clothes as one of the reasons for seeking breast reconstruction (Schain et al, 1984). Even with the increase in breast reconstruction, the number of women who have had a mastectomy still not having this procedure and, thus, needing adaptive clothing was made clear by a recent advertisement in a local newspaper. A very attractive swimsuit with special built-in pockets for breast prostheses was advertised by a prominent pharmacy. Rehabilitation of mastectomy patients needs to include advice on appropriate clothing styles and sources for adapted clothes. Hints on how to dress or undress with one's partner, to maximize sexuality and minimize the body loss, also could be of value.

There are reports that adjustment in work activities (including household chores) declines after mastectomy (Morris, 1980, 1977; Stevens et al, 1984). This decline has not been linked to body image dysfunction. Morris (1977) studied 69 postoperative breast cancer patients and 91 controls. Significant differences in work adjustment were observed 3 months postoperation, but differences had disappeared within 2 years. Kemeny and associates (1988) found no significant differences between segmentectomy and mastectomy subjects in their follow-up at least 6 months after surgery. They evaluated sports activities as well as work activities. Wellisch and associates (1989) also found no significant differences in work, household chores, or sports among their subject groups. Although it has not been studied extensively, there is little reason to believe that work or recreational activity is affected by body image dysfunction of mastectomy patients except, perhaps, in the early recovery stages.

CASE REPORT

Bette is a hypothetical patient based, in part, on cases reported by Faulkner (1985) and Goin and Goin (1988).

The Problem

Bette, a childless, 42-year-old woman married for 10 years, was referred to Psychiatry 11 months following right, modified radical mastectomy. She had received no chemotherapy, and her physical condition was stable. Bette said that she was depressed because, since her mastectomy, her husband regarded her as damaged and undesirable. She believed that she looked like a freak and was not surprised that her husband would not want to touch her. Her husband had agreed with her suggestion to have separate bedrooms.

The Solution

Bette was referred to a social worker by her psychiatrist. Aware of the lack of real communication between Bette and her spouse, the social worker spent several sessions with Bette's husband. It was discovered that the husband had agreed to separate bedrooms, not because he found Bette undesirable, but because he was afraid of hurting her. Furthermore, the husband found that his insurance would finance a large proportion of a breast reconstruction procedure for his wife.

Because of her body image problems, Bette was referred post-surgery for rehabilitation services not only for physical reasons but also for major psychological support. The couple also received sexual counseling. At 6 months' follow-up, the rehabilitation team rated Bette's outcome as good.

References

Ashcroft JJ, Leinster SJ, Slade PD: Breast cancer-patient choice of treatment: preliminary communication. J Royal Soc Med 78:43–46, 1985.

Andersen BL, Jochimsen PR: Sexual functioning among breast cancer, gynecologic cancer, and healthy women. J Consult Clin Psychol 53:25–32, 1985.

Bartelink H, Van Dam F, Van Dongen J: Psychological effects of breast conserving therapy in comparison with radical mastectomy. Int J Radiat Oncol Biol Phys 11:381–385, 1985.

Case C: The Breast Cancer Digest. Bethesda, MD, US Department of Health and Rehabilitative Services, National Cancer Institute, NIH, 1984.

Christensen K, Blichert-Toft M, Giersing U, Richardt C, Beckmann J: Phantom breast syndrome in young women after mastectomy for breast cancer. Acta Chir Scand 148:351–354, 1982.

David AJ, Roul RK, Kuruvilla J: Lessons of self-help for Indian women with breast cancer. Cancer Nurs 11:283–287, 1988.

Dierkhising JT: Formulating an educational model: consideration of the impact of cancer on self-image and sexuality. J Psychol Oncol 5:89–102, 1987.

Dinner MI, Coleman C: Breast reconstruction, use of autogenous tissue. AORN J 42:490–496, 1985.

Farash JL: Effects of counseling on resolution of loss and body image disturbance following a mastectomy. Dissertation Abstracts International 39:4027-B, 1979. (Abstract.)

Faulkner A: Mastectomy: reclaiming a body image. Community Outlook, 11–13, May, 1985.

Gaskin TA, LoBuglio A, Kelly P, Doss M, Pizitz N: STRETCH: a rehabilitative program for patients with breast cancer. South Med J 82:467–469, 1989.

Goin MK: Discussion—the psychological impact of immediate breast reconstruction for women with early breast cancer. Plast Reconstr Surg 73:627–628, 1984.

Goin MK, Goin JM: Growing pains: the psychological experience of breast reconstruction with tissue expansion. Ann Plast Surg 21:217–222, 1988.

Goin MK, Goin JM: Psychological reactions to prophylactic mastectomy synchronous with contralateral breast reconstruction. Plast Reconstr Surg 70:355–359, 1982.

Hopwood P, Maguire GP: Body image problems in cancer patients. Br J Psychiatry 153. (Suppl 2):47–50, 1988.

Jamison KR, Wellisch DK, Pasnau RO: Psychological aspects of mastectomy: I. The woman's perspective. Am J Psychiatry 135:432–436, 1978.

Kemeny MM, Wellisch DK, Schain WS: Psychosocial outcome in a randomized surgical trial for treatment of primary breast cancer. Cancer 62:1231–1237, 1988.

Kriss RT, Kraemer HC: Efficacy of group therapy for problems with postmastectomy self-perception, body image, and sexuality. J Sex Res 22:438–451, 1986.

Kroner K, Krebs B, Skov J, Jorgensen HS: Immediate and long-term phantom breast syndrome after mastectomy: incidence, clinical characteristics and relationships to pre-mastectomy breast pain. Pain 36:327–334, 1989.

Lacey JH, Birtchnell SA: Body image and its disturbances. J Psychosom Res 30:623–631, 1986.

Lasry JCM, Margolese RG, Poisson R, et al: Depression and body image following mastectomy and lumpectomy. J Chron Dis 40:529–534, 1987.

Mansel RE, Horgan K, Webster DJT, Shrotria S, Hughes LE: Cosmetic results of immediate breast reconstruction post-mastectomy: a follow-up study. Br J Surg 73:813–816, 1986.

Morris T: Postoperative adjustment of patients with breast cancer. J Royal Soc Med 73:215–217, 1980.

Morris T, Greer S, White P: Psychological and social adjustment to mastectomy: a two-year follow-up study. Cancer 40:2381–2387, 1977.

Noone RB, Frazier TG, Hayward CZ, Skiles MS: Patient acceptance of immediate reconstruction following mastectomy. Plast Reconstr Surg 69:632–638, 1982.

Polivy J: Psychological effects of mastectomy on a woman's feminine self-concept. J Nerv Ment Dis 164:77–87, 1977.

Ray C: Psychological implications of mastectomy. Br J Soc Clin Psychol 16:373–377, 1977.

Rozin RR, Skornick YG: Contemporary Options in the Operative Treatment of Breast Cancer. *In* Scheflan E (ed): Symposium on Advances in Breast Reconstruction. Philadelphia, WB Saunders, 1984, pp 231–236.

Sanger CK, Reznikoff M: A comparison of the psychological effects of breast-saving procedures with the modified radical mastectomy. Cancer 48:2341–2346, 1981.

Schain WS, Jacobs E, Wellisch DK: Psychological Issues in Breast Reconstruction. *In* Scheflan E (ed): Symposium of Advances in Breast Reconstruction. Philadelphia, WB Saunders, 1984, pp 237–251.

Schain WS, Wellisch DK, Pasnau RO, Landsverk J: The sooner the better: a study of psychological factors in women undergoing immediate versus delayed breast reconstruction. Am J Psychiatry 142:44–46, 1985.

Staps T, Hoogenhout J, Wobbes T: Phantom breast sensations following mastectomy. Cancer 56:2898–2901, 1985.

Steinberg MD, Juliano MA, Wise L: Psychological outcome of lumpectomy versus mastectomy in the treatment of breast cancer. Am J Psychiatry 142:34–39, 1985.

Stevens LA, McGrath MH, Druss RG, Kister ST, Gump FE, Forde KA: The psychological impact of immediate breast reconstruction for women with early breast cancer. Plast Reconstr Surg 73:619–626, 1984.

Valanis BG, Rumpler CH: Helping women to choose breast cancer treatment alternatives. Cancer Nurs 8:167–175, 1985.

Wellisch DK, Schain WS, Noone RB, Little JW: Psychosocial correlates of immediate versus delayed reconstruction of the breast. Plast Reconstr Surg 76:713–718, 1985.

Wellisch DK, DiMatteo R, Silverstein M, et al: Psychosocial outcomes of breast cancer therapies: lumpectomy versus mastectomy. Psychosom 30:365–372, 1989.

Worden JW, Weisman AD: The fallacy in postmastectomy depression. Am J Med Sci 273:169–175, 1977.

JULIA VAN DEUSEN

DIANE HARLOWE

THE PHYSICALLY CHALLENGED ADULT

Patients who are physically disabled, or those who have conditions that involve disfigurement, have body image disturbances falling in the Lacey-Birtchnell category (1986) of negative body image from real physical disabilities. We have discussed body image disturbances of this type relative to three kinds of patients frequently treated by rehabilitation professionals; (1) patients with severe burns, (2) patients with permanent dysfunction from spinal cord injuries, and (3) patients with rheumatoid arthritis. The

207

literature concerning the body image of patients disfigured by severe burns showed that rehabilitation specialists provide both physical and psychological treatments to help these patients cope with body image problems. A major variable related to optimal body image adjustment is patients' perceptions of their social support. The literature revealed that the body image of people with burns is related to all occupational performance areas.

Adults with spinal cord injury and rheumatoid arthritis also must readjust their body image. Our review of the literature indicated that, typically, these patients require minimal support from the rehabilitation staff to cope with body image adjustment.

BURNS

The incidence of burn accidents per year has been cited at 2 million (Goodstein, 1985; Shenkman and Stechmiller, 1987). One-hundred thousand burn patients are hospitalized. Many burn patients have predisposing disabilities, such as alcoholism, epilepsy, or psychiatric disorders (Vanderplate, 1984). With the decrease of mortality rates, a major (if not *the* major) problem is the adjustment to disfigurement and scarring (Vanderplate, 1984). The body image disturbance of the burn patient is probably the most devastating in the category of body image problems from physical disability (Vanderplate, 1983). For the adolescent or young adult burn patient, women, and those people who highly value physical appearance or whose subculture places exceptional value on attractiveness relative to other personal assets, disfigurement from burns becomes a particularly acute problem (Bernstein and Robson, 1983; Johnson, 1977; Orr et al, 1989).

Johnson (1977) found that adults, ages 18 to 65, who had been hospitalized for 2 weeks showed more negative body images when greater than 50% of the body was burned than when less than 50% was affected. Also, he found that those with face and hand burns versus those with trunk and limb burns had less positive body images. Orr and associates (1989) did not find a relationship between burn sites and body image; but their study involved a posthospitalization group of younger subjects (ages 14 to 27).

From the body image perspective, the face is an especially vulnerable burn site. Shenkman and Stechmiller (1987) studied perceptions of 18 burn patients following hospital discharge. They found that those with face burns, as opposed to hand and foot burns, showed greater body image and social concerns.

Konigova and Pondelicek (1987) compared 36 persons with facial burns with 36 nonburn control subjects with psychosocial problems. The burn patients showed greater denial. The authors explained this result by noting the potential disintegration of the body schema from burns to a highly visible body part. Some rehabilitation professionals consider it advisable not to interfere with the initial denial of burn patients because of the catastrophic nature of their disability. Vanderplate (1984) stated that this denial should be supported as a positive way for the burn patient to cope.

The stages of recovery for the burn patient defined by Steiner and Clark (1977) seem pertinent to our discussion. These stages are:

Stage One—the Physiological Emergency Stage, in which life-saving and physical procedures are dominant.

Stage Two—the Psychological Emergency Stage, in which the burn patient must come to terms with the fact of a changed body, that is, the body image adjustment stage.

Stage Three—the Social Emergency Stage, in which the patient begins to cope with responses from others, a stage that lasts through the first year following hospital discharge.

Because dealing with the responses from his or her social groups never ends for the person disfigured from burns, body image adjustment is an ongoing process.

Assessment

Methods of assessment mentioned in the literature on burns and body image are similiar to those used for body image evaluation with other diagnoses. Included were use of the semantic differential (Orr et al, 1989), interviews, and various scales (Andreasen et al, 1971; Tudahl et al, 1987). A burn-specific health scale developed at Johns Hopkins University received some research attention (Blades et al, 1982). Three hundred and sixty-nine items were rated by 35 judges on an 11-point scale for relevance to post-burn performance. After analysis, the final instrument consisted of 114 items, falling into six domains, and a general health category. The body image component consisted of seven items. Sample body image items to be rated were "your general body appearance" and "the way people react to you." The scale is self-administered. Alpha coefficients were obtained for the body image domain of 0.83, and there is some evidence of construct validity (Blades et al, 1982; Shenkman and Stechmiller, 1987; Tudahl et al, 1987).

The most interesting instrument reported in the literature on burns was a measure of cosmetic disfigurement (Smith et al, 1988). This tool was developed to provide an objective measure of the degree of cosmetic disfigurement of burn patients. Using photos of burns, a brief form was constructed for rating of texture, color, and overall disfigurement. A sample item was "thickness of scarring," which was to be rated as slight, moderate, or severe. Results of a study reported by Smith and colleagues (1988) showed that with eight raters, the interrater reliability for all items would be 0.84 or better and test-retest reliability would be at least as high as 0.92. Texture was of greater importance to disfigurement evaluation than was color. Although its use in body image research or rehabilitation was not discussed by Smith and associates (1988), this tool can provide a standard for comparison of burn patients' perceived disfigurement with objective evaluation so that presence of body image distortion can be better estimated.

Treatment

The treatment of body image disturbances in burn patients is from two perspectives: physical-preventative and psychosocial. Every effort is made by medical and rehabilitation personnel to prevent permanent deformities and disfigurement. Generally, restoration to preburn appearance is not possible. Consequently, psychosocial adjustments must be made if the burned person is to return to a satisfying and productive lifestyle.

Physical

Despite the fact that many burn patients undergo multiple surgical procedures, they never regain their preburn appearance. It is important that they be appropriately confronted with this reality during rehabilitation. Rehabilitation health professionals, such as occupational and physical therapists, work closely with the surgeons from the beginning of treatment for burns. Parent (1989) has summarized their role in prevention. The major rehabilitation phase begins in the second week following admission. Two major goals—prevention of joint deformities and prevention of scarring— concern improving the patient's diminishing need for body image adjustment.

Positioning is of the utmost importance in order to prevent deformities. The general rule is to position the body segment opposite the anticipated deformity. If the patient can maintain the proper positions without use of devices, splints are not used; if the patient cannot, they are used. Parent (1989) recommended the following positions:

1. Neck—neutral or slight extension.

2. Shoulder—100 to 110 degrees of abduction with external rotation.

3. Elbow—extension with forearm in midposition.

4. Hand—wrist in 0 to 45 degrees extension.

5. Fingers—metacarpal phalangeal joints in 70 to 90 degrees of flexion with proximal and distal joints in extension.

6. Thumb—abducted and extended at all joints.

7. Hip—abducted and extended.

8. Knee—extended.

9. Ankle—neutral.

Prevention of unsightly scarring is the other major physical goal relevant to body image. Parent (1989) described interventions designed to persuade the collagen fibers to line up in rows rather than making their natural ropelike tangles. Elastic or tubular compression bandages are applied when each body area has skin cover. A wound taking longer than 21 days to heal also *must* be treated with pressure garments. Pressure garments also may be used with lesser wounds. Careful measurements must be made and these skin-tight, custom-knit garments ordered for continuous use by the patient for up to 1 year (Parent, 1989).

Transparent face masks are replacing the knit masks, which resemble those worn by robbers. We have heard of one woman who, while wearing the knit body garments, refused to wear the transparent mask. It was unclear whether a psychological problem existed or whether comfort was the problem. Indications from the literature are that refusal to wear pressure garments is comparatively rare. Historical pictures of burn patients untreated with pressure garments, compared with those of treated patients, would clearly show patients the benefits of garment use.

Psychosocial

Observations have indicated that two variables are associated with burn patients' ability to positively integrate a new body image: perceived social support and the development of, and value for, inner strengths versus external appearance.

Vanderplate's writings (1983, 1984) highlighted the need for burn patients to attribute greater importance to internal traits, such as intelligence, sense of humor, and pleasant disposition, rather than physical appearance. Finding some kind of meaning, that is, a positive aspect to being burned, is desirable. For example, patients who can believe that being burned has helped them gain greater insight into their spirituality are aided in their adjustment. Men and women who attribute their career choices in nursing to the direct influence of hospitalization for burn injuries also are aided (Sutherland, 1988).

Vanderplate (1983) described an inpatient psychotherapeutic group designed to assist burn patients in coping with various problems, a very critical one of which is body image. These groups of three to eight patients met for 1½ h per week. Participation was voluntary and confidential; 389 burn patients participated. Within the safety of the group, patients expressed their own negative reactions to their bodies as well as the negative reactions by others. The author believed that most burn patients could cope with their disfigurement by focusing on nonburned body areas or minimizing the importance of physical appearance, or both. Body image issues assumed major importance just before a patient's discharge from the burn unit. Through practice within the group, patients were able to test coping strategies before returning to social and vocational roles as disfigured people.

Although Vanderplate was the major writer whom we were able to locate dealing with intervention for strengthening inner resources of burn patients, Goodstein (1985) shared a similar position. These authors also mentioned the need to foster support of the patient's family and friends.

In a sophisticated study to find out what variables best related to body image for adolescents and young adults with burns, Orr and associates (1989) found perceived social support to be the most potent variable. Body image was evaluated by means of the Osgood Semantic Differential, modified for burn subjects. Social support was defined by a 20-item perceived social support inventory on families and friends. Perceived peer support was the stronger support variable in relation to body image adjustment.

Following their study of social support, Orr and associates (1989) suggested a three-phase approach to ensure that burn patients perceived family and peer support for optimal body image adjustment. During hospitalization, occupational, physical, and recreational therapy groups could function as peer support groups. As a transition group between hospital and permanent community memberships, volunteers could be solicited to provide the necessary support for these patients. Families should, of course, already be involved, and the rehabilitation team should educate them as to their vital role in posthospital support. Families also should help to foster patient peer support. Before discharge of the burn patient, the rehabilitation team should contact the patient's school, church, club, and other peer groups to make them acutely aware of their value in helping the patient's body image adjustment on his or her return to the community.

A practical solution to the peer support problem was described by Biehler (1981). This postdischarge group, the Burn and Scar Association, was located in Toronto, Canada. It was composed of newly discharged patients and long-time burn patients who could share coping strategies. Also included were professional health care workers, such as physical therapists and social workers. Biweekly meetings were held in the community. These meetings were conducted in two parts. An educational portion allowed for guest speakers such as plastic surgeons. The social portion consisted mainly of support activities. The group ensured ongoing peer support for every burn patient.

Occupational Performance

An increasing amount of literature has studied the relation of body image and burns to work, leisure, and ADL.

Work

Vanderplate (1984) noted that, after discharge from initial hospitalization, 30% to 50% of burn patients required a job change and 20 percent did not return to work at all. Many of these vocational problems could be interpreted from a physical or psychiatric dysfunction rather than from a body image adjustment perspective. However, a small interview study by Andreasen and associates (1971) gave some insight into possible links among body image, burns, and work.

Of 20 persons with an average age of 34 and 2 years postburn, 6 had decreased in work adjustment, 2 had increased, and 12 remained unchanged. An example of decreased job adjustment associated with body image would be a job "handicap" because of self-consciousness about one's appearance. The authors believed that the typical postburn patient gradually experienced desensitization as people began to react to the burned person as a totality and not just to his or her appearance.

Leisure

Through their interviews, Andreasen and associates (1971) found that 5 of 20 postburn adults showed decreased leisure adjustment. We believed that these changes in recreation reported by burned adults fell into three categories: (1) elimination of those activities in which disfigured body parts are exposed (swimming), (2) decrease in social activities in which physical appearance is of concern (parties), and (3) elimination of those activities related to the burn trauma (e.g., camping, when burns occurred while camping).

Activities of Daily Living

Andreasen and associates (1971) also mentioned dressing activities of postburn patients. We consider their reported dressing modifications toward concealed disfigurement to be of two types: not wearing revealing clothing, such as swimsuits, and camouflage clothing, such as high necks, long sleeves, and scarves. Self-care activities early in the rehabilitation program also are important (Goodstein, 1985). Activities such as personal hygiene, hair care, and dressing can be used to improve the body image.

Sutherland (1988) interviewed four male and four female postburn patients, the majority of whom were young adults, about their dressing behaviors. These subjects' mean time since suffering their burns was 28 months. Six initially dressed to cover scars. Resumption of preburn style of dressing was gradual and slower for women than for men. By 2 years, all had accepted their new body image. However, there was a progression in their return to preburn dressing, starting with clothing that showed scars being worn first with family, then with friends, and, finally, with the general public.

The only other activity of daily living receiving attention in the literature in relation to body image and burns was sexual activity. Bernstein (1985) has studied this major area of concern. Apart from the obvious psychological factors, scarring from severe burns interferes seriously with both visual and tactile stimulation relevant to sexual activity. Postburn patients may hesitate to remove clothing in front of their spouses (Andreasen and Norris, 1972). Bernstein (1985) described seven cases that vividly illustrated the enormous impact of body image disturbances on the sexual activity of postburn patients. Studies have shown that it takes long periods of time for partners to adjust to the disfigurement. Again, family support seems to be a key to adjustment; a consistently supportive spouse has been associated with restored positive body image and sexual relations.

Apparently, postburn restoration of positive "sexual" body image and activity is a far more crucial problem in our culture for women disfigured by burns than for men. In the Sutherland interview study (1988), none of the four young men reported a feeling of loss of attractiveness, whereas all the young women had grave concerns about their potential for marriage. Tudahl and associates (1987) studied sexual satisfaction of 54 postburn patients. There was no significant relation between sexual satisfaction and amount or site of burned area. However, a significantly poorer sexual adjustment was observed for women than for men. The less satisfactory sexual functioning for women was related to both physical dysfunction and body image.

Perhaps as attitudes about the value of women become modified in Western culture, future body image research will not show marked gender discrepancies. Our culture still places higher value on the physical attractiveness of women relative to their performance, with the reverse attitude toward men. In our opinion, this cultural bias is probably the major explanation for the observed gender-related body image adjustment discrepancies of postburn patients.

CASE REPORTS

Because of the devastating effect that burns can have on body image, we have included two case reports to illustrate the rehabilitation process.

Mary

White (1982) described a woman whose occupational performance was severely impaired because of body image disturbances following burns from a house fire. Although a rather unusual case, it certainly highlights the impact that body image disturbances following severe burns can have. Our case report is based on that reported by White, with the addition of our hypothetical rehabilitation program.

Mary was a 37-year-old woman with severe body disfigurement from burns. She had been successfully and legally employed as a prostitute. Mary was still worried about her appearance 1 year after the burns. She refused to undress in front of other people and was no longer employable in her former vocation. She had lost interest in all everyday activities and was socially inactive. Mary was referred to an occupational therapy department for prevocational exploration.

Results of a semantic differential scale showed a profile of negative adjectives for body parts concepts, confirming the therapist's impression of Mary's extremely negative body image. She was referred to a psychotherapy group and, through peer support and the leadership of her psychologist, she gradually developed coping strategies. She was able to recognize that her caring attitude and native intelligence were assets that were vocationally relevant and that these traits might lead to work even preferable to her former occupation.

In occupational therapy, she not only was able to observe the results of her positive vocational skills but also developed an interest in flower arrangement as a major recreational activity. A local, church-related garden club was contacted as a potential postdischarge support group for Mary. Vocational Rehabilitation had arranged an interview for a job in animal care with the community humane society. On discharge from the center, Mary was far from having a complete reintegration of her body image. However, her functioning was much improved, and potential for continued growth was considered good.

WS

Our second case report shows the more typical body image problems with which health workers treating persons with burns must deal. This report of a hypothetical patient is based on data from two patients treated by Kim Hoffman of Shands Hospital at the University of Florida, Gainesville.

WS is a 36-year-old, single, male construction worker hospitalized for burns to his face, chest, and arms following an explosion accident. Intervention for WS illustrates the emphasis on the appropriate procedures that can diminish potential body image problems. The initial rehabilitation contact involved discussions with the patient concerning pressure garments, range of motion and strengthening exercises, and splint needs. Initial intervention consisted of splint fabrication in coordination with WS's surgical schedule. Neck and elbow extension splints and wrist supports were fabricated. Four days following WS's surgery, the occupational therapy progress note already reflected the patient's concern about his body image. He had stated specifically how important his appearance was to him. Because this importance was not job related, his social-recreational activities were probably a major concern.

Continued programming by occupational and physical therapy consisted of splint adjustments, scar management, and range of motion and strengthening exercises, including facial exercises. WS learned to massage his own scars. Pressure garments for long-term use were ordered. His first experience with the facial mask with chin strap for scar control resulted in extreme anger and a refusal to be seen in the mask. Such a reaction is expected.

Besides the ongoing support of the therapists, nursing personnel provided the continued psychological support that eventually will enable WS to cope with his changed body picture. WS currently is being followed in the hospital's Burn Clinic. Because of the preventive intervention procedures applied early in his programming, it is likely that WS will experience as little permanent disfigurement as possible and that he will be able to realistically cope with any necessary body image changes.

SPINAL CORD INJURY

Spinal cord injury (SCI) from trauma or disease affects the limb muscles and autonomic nervous system functions below the level of the lesion. There is temporary or permanent damage to sensation, motor skills, bowel, bladder, sexual functions, and all areas of occupational performance (Hopkins and Smith, 1988). Body image disturbances have been reported both from the neurological and from the psychological perspectives (Trieschmann, 1988).

The Phantom Phenomenon

In 1917, Riddoch first reported the phantom phenomenon in spinal cord injury (Conomy, 1973). By the 1950s, thorough descriptions of SCI phantoms were being reported in the literature (Bors, 1951).

Bors (1951) interviewed 50 patients with thoracic or lumbar SCI from 2 months to 8 years postinjury. For a total of 82 interviews, 11 to 24 interviews were held at the following times: within 1 year and 1 to 3, 3 to 5, 5 to 6, and 6 to 8 years postlesion. Four categories of questions were addressed: (1) description of the phantom as a unit, (2) incidence of its parts, (3) movement, and (4) phantoms of unimpaired organs. Findings revealed that all patients with SCI had initial phantom experiences. Typically, phantoms were flexed at the hip, or the knee, or both, although a visual check verified the actual position of lower limbs as extended. Unlike the amputee, the SCI patients with the phantom phenomenon showed no telescoping. Distribution of parts of the phantom followed the cortical sensorimotor representation, decreasing from toe to hip. Distribution of willed movement of phantom parts followed a similiar pattern. There were some reports of phantoms of unimpaired organs.

Evans (1962) described the phantoms of seven patients with SCI from nontraumatic lesions, six of whom were women. Although phantom sensations were perceived in terms of pain, heat, or pressure, they were not reported as distressing. Every patient was interviewed three times, with questions repeated to allow for reliability estimation. The authors believed that their data were not very reliable but did report presence of phantoms in all subjects. Again, there was no telescoping, and phantom shape and size were that of a normal limb. Only one subject reported not being able to move the phantom.

Conomy (1971) compared the phantom phenomena of patients with traumatic and nontraumatic SCI. Unlike Evans' subjects (1962), patients with nontraumatic SCI reported to Conomy essentially no presence of phantoms. In the 18 traumatic SCI patients, 9 phantoms were cervical level and 9 were thoracic. All experienced lower limb disturbances of proprioceptive body image initially, but only two of the cervical level subjects perceived upper extremity phantoms. As with the data of Bors (1951), the phantom legs were flexed, and some could be moved to the point of fatigue. Unlike Bors' findings, phantoms did not follow the cortical sensorimotor distribution with higher incidence distally. Phantoms reported to Conomy involved the entire lower extremity. Conomy believes that the term phantom should be reserved for use with amputation and that such phenomena in SCI should be called body image disturbance.

Although the early reports suggested that phantom pain was not as pertinent to SCI as to amputation (Postone, 1987), reports at a recent pain conference showed no significant difference in the incidence of painful phantoms in the two disorders (Christensen et al, 1990). Results of a mailed survey from 114 persons with complete lesion SCI and 66 lower extremity amputees showed an incidence of painful phantom of 72% in SCI and 73% in amputation. The quality of the pain differed. SCI subjects reported a stinging, burning pain, and the amputees reported a shooting-type pain. Data from a smaller study showed probable phantom pain in only half of the traumatic SCI subjects (Stensman, 1989).

Martinez and associates (1990) discussed two types of phantom pain in SCI from a multidisciplinary assessment of 19 SCI patients with painful phantoms. Rather than supporting either a peripheral or a central nervous system origin, these investigators concluded that there are two types of pain perceived by patients with painful phantoms, a peripheral nerve projection of pain and a central phantom limb. Different modes of treatment should address these different kinds of pain.

Psychological Disturbances

Although the changes in physical appearance of persons with SCI are in no way comparable to those that can be observed in the severely burned, there are physical changes that must be incorporated into body image. Relatively minor physical differences can be devastating to adolescents and young adults, the age group with the greatest incidence of SCI (Dewis, 1989; Rutledge, 1983). Of major psychological significance is evidence of dysfunctional bowel or bladder, atrophy of limb muscles, and unsightly appliances and devices.

Several studies have addressed the psychological aspects of SCI body image. Wachs and Zaks (1960) reported an early study. Using the Draw-a-Person Test, they evaluated the body image of 30 SCI men and 30 male controls from the same institution who had chronic conditions other than SCI. A thorough analysis of data including considerable quantification as well as more subjective interpretations showed no important differences between the SCI subjects and controls. Because of the number of analyses, the few differences could have been a matter of chance.

Trieschmann (1988) reviewed several other psychological studies on body image of SCI. She cited a 1971 study in which there was no relationship between body image and improvement of SCI patients in rehabilitation. Two weak studies, in which body image was defined by barrier scores of the Rorschach test, indicated a possible relationship between body image and adjustment of SCI patients. A final study cited by Trieschmann (1988) showed that paraplegics were more accurate at judging the width of their wheelchairs than their shoulders, indicative of the minor importance that actual body image has to their function.

Trieschmann (1988) concluded that the psychological aspects of body image per se probably were not a major concern for the average SCI patient. She advocated a redefinition of body image for SCI studies, one from a social perspective. The realistic body changes in SCI must be incorporated within body image and integrated with the standards and values of society. Research needs to be directed toward realistic body image adjustment as it relates to success in dealing with the larger community.

The results of Stensman's study (1989) supported Trieschmann's conclusion of minimal differences between SCI and control subjects in body image from the psychological perspective. The body images of 10 traumatic SCI subjects were compared with 12 cerebral palsy and 43 nondisabled persons. Scores between zero and 100 (extremely negative and extremely positive) were recorded for varied situations, such as taking a shower or being outdoors. No significant differences were observed. Use of a body puzzle by subjects to compare their body size estimations with their actual measurements showed little difference between disabled and nondisabled groups (Stensman, 1989). Both SCI and cerebral palsy subjects overestimated the size of head, arms, and legs, but control subjects also overestimated head and arms. Unlike Trieschmann (1988), Stensman (1989) suggested further psychological body image studies, because his research results differed from his clinical impressions.

A recent study expanded the definition of body image beyond that typically used. Marazzani (1990) included as part of the body image concept inside and outside of body and ideal body, but she also included self (as containing body), life (existential locus of body image), sexuality (important body experience), and death (end of body experience). Using the semantic differential technique, she compared the body image of 23 young SCI men with 32 male rehabilitation students. She drew the following conclusions from her data. Inside and outside of body were described by SCI persons with neutral adjectives. Controls differed, using more positive adjectives for the outside-of-body category. Both groups recorded positive adjectives for ideal body, life, and sexuality. The category life was more clearly positive for the SCI group. Although the category death was somewhat neutral for control subjects, it was clearly negative for SCI subjects. Marazzani suggested that differences in body image should be considered because they could affect the client-therapist relationship.

Assessment

Methods of evaluating body image in SCI research were similiar to those used in other kinds of body image studies. Included were the interview (Dewis, 1988; Evans, 1962), projective techniques (Trieschmann, 1988; Wachs and Zaks, 1960), scales (Stensman, 1989), and the semantic differential tool (Marazzani, 1990). Stensman (1989) used a novel approach: a body puzzle for body size estimation.

The Body Puzzle consisted of 81 body parts from which subjects chose 9 for use in constructing a representation of their own body. The estimated sizes of the puzzle parts were compared with the subject's true measurements. No statistical data were reported. Research of this tool might be of value, because it has the simplicity for routine clinical use with patients having body image problems.

Treatment

Phantom sensation in SCI rarely is a problem. If nursing or other rehabilitation personnel make sure that the patient understands the phantom as a "normal" nervous system phenomenon and assist the patient to visually verify the position of limbs (Richmond and Metcalf, 1986), the proprioceptive body image disturbance seems to disappear without interfering with rehabilitation. Trieschmann (1988) was able to cite only one instance in which the phantom was a serious rehabilitation problem. In this case, the phantom limbs were so awkwardly placed that they caused pain when the patient's position was adjusted for pressure sore prevention. The phantom limbs were realigned through hypnosis.

Our hypothesis is that subjects with SCI typically have not shown body image differences from controls in psychological evaluations, because most are able to adjust their body image without assistance. The literature supported this point of view.

Dewis (1988) described the coping strategies of SCI young adults in relation to their body image. Using a content valid, in-depth, semistructured interview guide with a content analysis method, Dewis obtained findings on 15 SCI subjects, primarily upper extremity involved males. Although there also were other areas of concern, those related to body image included bowel and bladder accidents, "fat" belly from lack of abdominal tone, atrophied leg muscles, and all types of attention-attracting devices and equipment. Their body image was affected by being able to have shampoos and showers only twice per week. Although young adults often shampoo daily, institutional regulations limited this activity when patients were unable to perform it independently.

"Normalization" was the central principle behind coping strategies. The independently derived means to maintain normalcy showed considerable ingenuity and resourcefulness. Among these strategies were wearing loose shirts and jogging outfits; decorating splints, wheelchairs, and other equipment to incorporate as part of a positive image; and spilling drinks to cover up evidence of bladder accidents.

Stensman (1989) found a similar situation through his interviews with SCI subjects. The prevalent opinion was that living a normal life fosters body image adjustment. Participation in athletic activities is an example of that normal living.

In general, the literature indicated little need for intervention by rehabilitation personnel in relation to body image adjustment of SCI patients. Because studies are based on the typical or average person, there will be exceptional cases in which treatment is important. Several suggestions for guidance have been made (Dewis, 1988; Richmond and Metcalf, 1986). If at all possible, personal hygiene and clothing of SCI patients can be given a higher priority in the institutional setting. A graded orientation to the current real body image can be provided to both patients and their families. Psychological support can be provided during the adjustment period. Community visits can provide opportunities for patients to integrate their own changing body image with reactions from others.

The literature clearly indicated that treatment for body image disturbances of the SCI patient could be a low priority for rehabilitation professionals owing to self-management by patients. Thus, it was our opinion that a case report on body image treatment for patients with SCI would be of minimal value to the reader.

RHEUMATOID ARTHRITIS

Rheumatoid arthritis (RA) is a progressive, systemic, connective tissue disorder affecting many more women than men. There are inflammatory changes with pain, swelling, and stiffness of joints that, when severe, alter body appearance and interfere with occupational performance (Ignatavicius, 1987; Lambert, 1985).

A clinical report by Ignatavicius (1987) indicated that joint deformities usually contributed to negative body image of persons with RA. Subjects were assessed by questions such as "How do you feel about the physical change in your body?" A typical comment by a patient was "I don't like to go out because people stare at me." However, a study of 169 arthritis patients (76% with RA) versus 130 controls indicated that disturbed body image was not one of the variables affecting sexual adjustment of patients more than that of controls (Blake et al, 1987).

In a British study (Skevington et al, 1987), using a 30-item adjective checklist to address self-esteem, the adjective "attractive" was checked least often by both RA and control subjects. The authors suggested that this result was a cultural artifact due to the "English modesty."

Body Image Documentation

Because we were unable to locate studies documenting the body image of persons with RA, we conducted a small study for that purpose (Van Deusen and Harlowe, 1988). Because this study has not been published elsewhere, we have discussed it here in greater detail than we have our other studies.

Subjects were 49 ambulatory persons diagnosed as having RA and 48 controls reporting no deforming disability. No significant differences in age or sex were observed between groups. Because data for both groups were obtained from volunteer subjects in the same midwestern county within the same 3-year span, it was assumed that socioeconomic status would be similiar.

Four semantic differential scales were administered to all subjects. Standard directions were followed. These scales addressed four body part concepts: trunk, arms, hands, and legs. Each scale was constructed using ten pairs of Osgood's evaluative adjectives (Isaac and Michael, 1981), with the one modification of "unimpaired-impaired" for the "clean-dirty" dyad. The body image data for the RA subjects and controls were analyzed by means of the Sign Test and the Mann-Whitney U Test. Level of significance was set at a 0.05, two-tail test. It was hypothesized that there would be a significant difference between body image data of the RA subjects and the controls. Table 9–1 records the results.

The figures (Figs. 9–1 through 9–4) show the means for the RA and control subject ratings for each pair of adjectives. The scales have been rearranged for illustrative purposes so that all positive adjectives are on the right. With the exception of the Sign Test analysis of hands data, significant differences were observed between RA and control subjects for all body parts. Because the Mann-Whitney U is the more precise test, we can assume that a hand image difference does exist.

Although persons with RA reported body image in a more negative way than did control subjects, the RA body image on the whole was neutral to positive. In a very realistic manner, the most discriminating adjective pair for the RA versus the control subjects was "impaired-unimpaired." This is particularly observable in hand image, in which perceptions were four scale positions apart. Other particularly discriminating item dyads were "painful-pleasurable" and "ugly-beautiful," also realistic differentiations. Our conclusion from the study data was that, as a whole, the body image of persons with RA was not negative, although there were significant differences in body image between RA and control subjects. These differences realistically, were, less positive for the RA subjects.

A second study comparing the body image of RA subjects with

Table 9–1. BODY IMAGE COMPARISONS FOR 49 RA AND 48 CONTROL SUBJECTS

Concept	Sign Test (Number of inconsistencies in profiles)	Probability	Mann Whitney U	Probability
Trunk	0	$<.002$	17	$<.02$
Arms	1	$<.02$	21	$<.05$
Hands	2	$<.11$	10	$<.002$
Legs	1	$<.02$	10	$<.002$

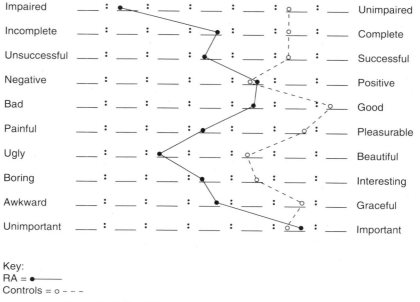

Key:
RA = •———
Controls = ○ – – –

Figure 9–1. Hands image: RA (•———) and controls (○– – –).

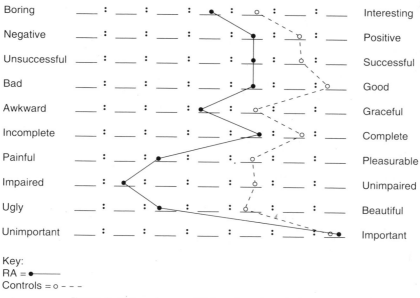

Key:
RA = •———
Controls = ○ – – –

Figure 9–2. Arms image: RA (•———) and controls (○– – –).

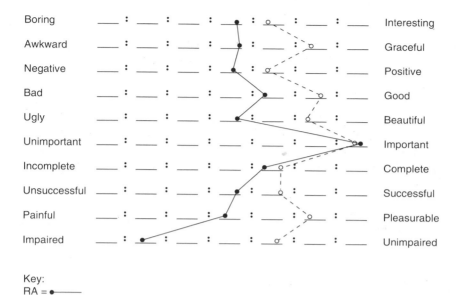

Key:
RA = •———
Controls = o - - -

Figure 9–3. Legs image: RA (•———) and controls (o– – –).

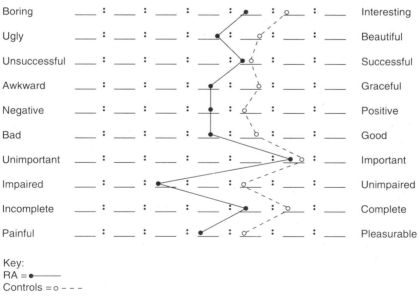

Key:
RA = •———
Controls = o - - -

Figure 9–4. Trunk image: RA (•———) and controls (o– – –).

a healthy control group recently has been reported (Cornell and Schmitt, 1990). Two hypotheses were examined—that RA subjects' body image would be more negative than that of healthy women and that, within the RA group, the better perceived health status would be associated with a more positive body image. Perceived health was evaluated by a standardized structured interview and body image by the Body Cathexis Scale. Perceived health was not related to body image. There also was no difference between body image of RA subjects and that of healthy subjects. Age and time since diagnosis of RA both were unrelated to body image. These authors documented body image problems in their subjects with systemic lupus; consequently, we cannot attribute their results with RA to inadequate procedures. We conclude (as did the authors) that persons with some types of illnesses (namely, RA) can maintain a positive body image despite their physical challenge.

Considering the limited research results available on the body image of persons with RA, it would seem necessary to complete further studies before a firm conclusion is made regarding intervention toward their improved body image. Even if, on the whole, body image is not a problem for RA patients, individuals will be found who are in need of intervention. Certainly, clinicians believe that their RA patients have concerns about body image (Ignatavicius, 1987; Rogers et al, 1982).

Assessment

Because there is a dearth of studies on body image and RA, only two instruments were discussed in the research. The Body Cathexis Scale consists of a list of 50 body parts and characteristics for which subjects indicate their satisfaction or dissatisfaction on a five-point Likert Scale (Cornwell and Schmitt, 1990). This measure of body image was developed decades ago but was just recently used to assess body image in RA. Adequate reliability coefficients— 0.83, split half; 0.72, test-retest—were reported. Validity coefficients ranged from 0.58 to 0.79. The Cornwell-Schmitt study (1990) contributed to the construct validity of this tool.

The semantic differential scale is considered a sound method of assessing the meaning of concepts (Isaac and Michael, 1981). We chose this method for our studies involving body image and RA, using it simply as an attitude scale. Our instrument involved seven undefined scale positions between 10 pairs of polar adjectives. Subjects placed a check on each scale for the particular concept under consideration—trunk, arms, hands, or legs (see Figs. 9–1 through 9–4). This instrument was used to compare body image concepts of our RA subjects with those of controls. It was used as well to compare the body image of groups of persons with RA following varying kinds of intervention.

Treatment

Health professionals have recorded suggestions for assisting the RA patient with body image adjustment on an individual basis and in groups. Loxley (1972) described an elderly RA patient who was unable to adjust her unrealistic body image to coincide with her impaired body. Her needs were displayed in a seeking of extra attention from nursing. The author suggested that nursing could help this patient rebuild her body image while she was recovering from knee surgery.

Ignatavicius (1987) recommended allowing the patient to express negative body feelings as normal while aiding in identification of personal strengths. Behaviors to improve physical appearance could be encouraged as well as independence in self-care activities.

Udelman and Udelman (1978), a husband and wife cotherapist team, conducted brief group psychotherapy for RA patients. Body image was among the group's topics. The group progressed through four stages: (1) educative, (2) social-integrative, (3) supportive-ventilative, and (4) exploratory dynamic. Although these authors provided sample case studies, none was concerned with body image.

Very little research has examined therapy designed to influence body image of physically impaired adults. Hecox and associates (1975) investigated a dance program, one goal of which was to change negative attitudes toward body image of adult physically disabled participants. These authors reported five case studies in support of the success of their programming. Arthritis was not among the diagnoses in this study. Later, arthritis patients were included, but goals at this time no longer included improved body image.

We investigated the effects of the ROM (pronounced räm) Dance Program on adults with RA (Van Deusen and Harlowe, 1988; 1987). The ROM Dance Program is a T'ai-Chi-inspired range of motion and relaxation routine developed by Harlowe and Yu to meet a number of home exercise and rest goals, including "to improve body awareness." Because the concept of body image subsumes that of body awareness, this ROM Dance Program goal partially relates to body image. With increased body awareness, a more realistic perception can change body image in either a positive or a negative direction.

Results from our studies showed that RA subjects who had

participated in the 8-week ROM Dance Program were less positive in their body image relevant to hands than were RA subjects on traditional home programs. No significant differences were observed before the treatments, but significant differences were found immediately following the ROM dance participation and 4 months later. At 1 year follow-up, this difference was still apparent. Body image was defined by scores on the semantic differential scales.

Our findings could be interpreted as indicative that traditional home programming was appropriate to foster positive image of hand deformities. However, a second interpretation was that the ROM Dance Program beneficially promoted a more realistic, although less positive, hand image of the subjects with RA. Differences noted in arm, leg, and trunk images were inconsistent across time and thus of little practical importance.

Because we have so little research on body image and RA, it is unwise to draw firm conclusions. It is an area wide open for further research.

SUMMARY

Our review relative to body image disturbances for physically challenged adults included clinical material and research from the literature on burns, SCI, and RA. There is a definite need for work with body image disturbances in burn rehabilitation. The literature is less clear regarding RA and SCI. There is little doubt that readjustment of body image is needed, but whether or not intervention by health professionals usually is required seems less clear. We do not question the need for body image assessment of any of our physically challenged patients or of intervention on an individual basis whenever it is indicated.

References

Andreasen NJC, Norris AS: Long-term adjustment and adaptation mechanisms in severely burned adults. J Nerv Ment Dis 154:352–362, 1972.

Andreasen NJC, Norris AS, Hartford CE: Incidence of long-term psychiatric complications in severely burned adults. Ann Surg 174:785–793, 1971.

Bernstein NR: Marital and sexual adjustment of severely burned patients. Med Aspects Hum Sexuality 19:217–219, 223, 229, 1985.

Bernstein NR: Trial by Fire. In Bernstein N, Robson MC (eds): Comprehensive Approaches to the Burned Person. New York, Medical Examination Publishing, 1983, pp 49–77.

Biehler MA: A self help group for burn victims. Can J Occup Ther 48:221–222, 1981.

Blades B, Mellis N, Munster AM: A burn specific health scale. J Trauma, 22:872–875, 1982.

Blake DJ, Maisiak R, Alarcon GS, Holley HL, Brown S: Sexual quality of life of patients with arthritis compared to arthritis-free controls. J Rheumatol 14:570–576, 1987.

Bors E: Phantom limbs of patients with spinal cord injury. AMA Arch Neurol Psychiatry 66:610–631, 1951.

Christensen FL, Rosenborg D, Lind T, Jensen TS: Phantom Pain and Sensations in Spinal Cord Injured Patients and in Lower Extremity Amputee Patients. *In* Abstracts of the Sixth World Congress on Pain of the International Association for the Study of Pain, Australia, April 1990. Amsterdam, Elsevier Science Pub, 1990. (Abstract No 909.)

Conomy JP: Disorders of body image after spinal cord injury. Neurology 23:842–850, 1973.

Cornwell CJ, Schmitt MH: Perceived health status, self-esteem and body image in women with rheumatoid arthritis or systemic lupus erythematosus. Res Nurs Health 13:99–107, 1990.

Dewis ME: Spinal cord injured adolescents and young adults: The meaning of body changes. J Adv Nurs 14:389–396, 1989.

Evans JH: On disturbance of the body image in paraplegia. Brain 85:687–700, 1962.

Goodstein RK: Burns: an overview of clinical consequences affecting patient, staff, and family. Compr Psychiatry 26:43–57, 1985.

Hecox B, Levine E, Scott D: A report on the use of dance in physical rehabilitation: Everybody has a right to feel good. Rehabil Lit 36:11–15, 1975.

Ignatavicius DD: Meeting the psychosocial needs of patients with rheumatoid arthritis. Orthopaedic Nurs 6:16–21, 1987.

Isaac S, Michael WB: Handbook in Research and Evaluation (2nd ed). San Diego, CA, Edits, 1981.

Johnson MA: A study of the effects of percentage and locus of burn on body image, self-concept, and social perception for an adult burn population. (Unpublished doctoral dissertation.) University of Southern California, 1977. (From Dissertation Abstracts, 1978, 38B, Abstract No 3886-B.)

Konigova R, Pondelicek I: Psychological aspects of burns. Scand J Plast Reconstr Surg Hand Surg 21:311–314, 1987.

Lacey JH, Birtchnell SA: Body image and its disturbances. J Psychosom Res 30:623–631, 1986.

Lambert V: Study of factors associated with psychological well-being in rheumatoid arthritic women. Image 17:50–53, 1985.

Loxley A: The emotional toll of crippling deformity. Am J Nurs 72:1839–1840, 1972.

Marazzani MH: Body image of paraplegics. Poster paper presented at the 10th International Congress of The World Federation of Occupational Therapy Therapists, Melbourne, April, 1990.

Martinez SN, Negro PM, Rene D, Pare M: Spinal Cord Stimulation in Painful Phantom Limb. *In* Abstracts of the Sixth World Congress on Pain of the International Association for the Study of Pain, Australia, April 1990. Amsterdam, Elsevier Science Pub, 1990. (Abstract No 159.)

Orr DA, Reznikoff M, Smith GM: Body image, self-esteem, and depression in burn-injured adolescents and young adults. J Burn Care Rehabil 10:454–461, 1989.

Parent LH: Burns. *In* Trombly CA (ed): Occupational Therapy for Physical Dysfunction (3rd ed). Baltimore, Williams & Wilkins, 1989, pp 571–580.

Postone N: Phantom limb pain. A review. Int J Psychiatry Med 17:57–70, 1987.

Richmond TS, Metcalf JA: Psychosocial responses to spinal cord injury. J Neurosci Nurs 18:183–187, 1986.

Rogers M, Liang M, Partridge A: Psychological care of adults with rheumatoid arthritis. Ann Intern Med 96:344–348, 1982.

Shenkman B, Stechmiller J: Patient and family perception of projected functioning after discharge from a burn unit. Heart and Lung 16:490–496, 1987.

Skevington SM, Blackwell F, Britton NF: Self-esteem and perception of attractiveness: an investigation of early rheumatoid arthritis. Br J Med Psychol 60:45–52, 1987.

Smith GM, Tompkins DM, Bigelow ME, Antoon AY: Burn-induced cosmetic disfigurement: can it be measured reliably? J Burn Care Rehabil 9:371–375, 1988.

Spencer EA: Functional Restoration: Neurologic, Orthopedic, and Arthritic Conditions. *In* Hopkins HL, Smith HD (eds): Willard and Spackman's Occupational Therapy (7th ed). Philadelphia, JB Lippincott, 1988, pp 461–515.

Steiner H, Clark WR: Psychiatric complications of burned adults: a classification. J Trauma 17:134–143, 1977.

Stensman R: Body image among 22 persons with acquired and congenital severe mobility impairment. Paraplegia 27:27–35, 1989.

Sutherland S: Burned adolescents' descriptions of their coping strategies. Heart and Lung 17:150–157, 1988.

Trieschmann RB: Spinal Cord Injuries: Psychological, Social, and Vocational Rehabilitation (2nd ed). New York, Demos Publications, 1988.

Tudahl LA, Blades BC, Munster AM: Sexual satisfaction in burn patients. J Burn Care Rehabil 8:292–293, 1987.

Udelman HD, Udelman DL: Group therapy with rheumatoid arthritic patients. Am J Psychother 32:288–299, 1978.

Vanderplate C: An adaptive coping model of intervention with the severely burn-injured. Int J Psychiatry Med 14:331–341, 1984.

Vanderplate C: A personal adaptation group for burn injured hospital patients. Int J Psychiatry Med 12:237–242, 1983.

Van Deusen J, Harlowe D: Body image of adults with rheumatoid arthritis. Paper presented at the 68th Annual Conference of the American Occupational Therapy Association, Phoenix, April, 1988.

Van Deusen J, Harlowe D: Brief: one-year follow-up results of ROM Dance research. Occup Ther J Res 8:52–54, 1988.

Van Deusen J, Harlowe D: A comparison of the ROM Dance home exercise rest program with traditional routines. Occup Ther J Res 7:349–361, 1987.

Wachs H, Zaks MS: Studies of body image in men with spinal cord injury. J Nerv Ment Dis 131:121–127, 1960.

White AC: Psychiatric study of patients with severe burn injuries. Br Med J 284:465–467, 1982.

JULIA VAN DEUSEN

CONCLUSIONS: ADULT BODY IMAGE, VISUAL, AND SOMESTHETIC DYSFUNCTION

VISUAL AND SOMESTHETIC PERCEPTION

For many decades, both researcher and clinician have been concerned with the perceptual dysfunction of neurology and psychiatry patients. Part I of this book has dealt with the assessment and treatment in four diagnostic classifications commonly encountered by rehabilitation professionals. It is generally accepted that perceptual dysfunction is a complex phenomenon, involving many body systems and, therefore, is difficult to discuss independently.

Although the focus of Part I has been on perception, the authors have emphasized the holistic context that is the essence of rehabilitation.

Assessment

Many tests are available for the assessment of perceptual dysfunction. A number of these have been described in the literature as being used with several different diagnostic categories. Because these instruments have been referenced when first mentioned in earlier chapters, I have not repeated references here. Like any test, tests for perceptual dysfunction cannot be considered valid for a particular patient population until research is conducted on that specific population.

Often, the same assessment tools have been used with both cerebral vascular accident (CVA) and traumatic brain injury (TBI) patients. Those tools found useful in rehabilitation for both populations and discussed in the previous chapters include:

The Motor-Free Visual Perception Test

The Hooper Visual Organization Test

The Loewenstein Occupational Therapy Cognitive Assessment Battery

Facial Recognition and 3-D Constructional Praxis from the Benton tests

Subtests from both the Southern California Sensory Integration Test and the Wechsler Adult Intelligence Scale

A number of other tools, both batteries and tests for specific kinds of perceptual dysfunction, also have been documented in the previous chapters as being of use for assessment of persons receiving rehabilitation after CVA or TBI.

Batteries for assessment of perceptual dysfunction of patients having neurological diagnoses also have been extensively used with psychiatric patients. Of particular note are the Halstead-Reitan and Luria-Nebraska Batteries, often cited in the research literature in evaluations by psychologists of TBI, alcohol-abusing, and other patient populations. Functional assessments, in which ADL items are of particular importance, have been discussed in relation to assessment in both schizophrenia and TBI. Subtests from both the Southern California Sensory Integration Test and the Wechsler Adult Intelligence Scale, as well as the Benton tests, have likewise been found suitable for psychiatric and neurological patient evaluations. Considering the extent and diversity of existing instruments for perceptual assessment, I believe that the future for those concerned with this area lies in refinement of extant tools rather than in the development of new ones. Even with the relatively new area of assessment using computers, rigorous reliability and validity studies are needed rather than new tools per se.

Treatment

Rehabilitation for patients exhibiting perceptual dysfunction has focused both on restoring perceptual adequacy and on compensating for perceptual dysfunction. For those patients referred for rehabilitation because of CVA or TBI, work with computers, self-care activities, various tasks involving forms or shapes, and special perceptual exercise workbooks have been prominent means of treatment.

Improvement of perceptual function in schizophrenia was first discussed from the perspective of sensory integration. This approach includes control of arousal and use of gross motor activities. A major focus of treatment for the schizophrenias was cognitive rehabilitation procedures.

For the recovering alcoholic patient, practice of perceptual tasks has been shown to transfer to related activities. Compensatory behavior also was discussed.

Although the clinical literature and experiences of the authors have indicated that perceptual dysfunction can be successfully treated, there is very little actual research to validate intervention procedures in any population with perceptual dysfunction. Such research should be of high priority for those in rehabilitation fields. The literature on CVA and TBI has documented the relationship of perceptual dysfunction to problems of self-care and work skills. Although there has been little research on this topic in the literature on schizophrenia or alcohol abuse, there is a clear need for studies designed to document a relationship of occupational and perceptual dysfunction.

General Research Needs

Careful review of the chapters on perceptual dysfunction will provide the reader with the research needs specific to CVA, TBI, alcohol abuse, and schizophrenia. In general, it is clear that rigorous reliability and validity studies still are needed on many of the perceptual tools in common clinical use. Studies documenting the relation of perceptual dysfunction to performance deficits in work, leisure, and ADL are required, especially in the areas of alcohol abuse and schizophrenia. Lastly, the effectiveness of intervention procedures is a topic in need of research.

BODY IMAGE

There has been a multidisciplinary concern for the relationship of body image to the rehabilitation process. Research interest in this area has shown the same cyclic upsurge and waning that is typical of research on any topic. During the late 1950s and 1960s, literature on body image was prevalent, followed by a period of decline. With the concern for the body image of persons with anorexia nervosa, the late 1970s and 1980s brought a renewed interest in body image research. The content of Part II of this book was my attempt at organizing the literature on body image in a way that could be helpful to the rehabilitation professional.

Assessment

Many instruments have been developed for assessment of body image disturbances, for both clinical and research use. Tools have been designed to evaluate problems in the neural body schema and assess psychosocial aspects of body image.

In the literature are descriptions of a number of paper and pencil tests. These tests have been used to assess all components of body image. When there is a neural-based disturbance (e.g., unilateral neglect following stroke), paper and pencil evaluation tasks for the patient include drawing or copying objects and figures, cancellation of letters or numbers, and line bisection. Body part puzzles are a common clinical method of body schema evaluation. Computer-assisted measurement for body schema problems is increasingly in use. Responses that are evaluated include key taps, line bisection, and responses to lights.

A very helpful trend from the rehabilitation worker's point of view is the use of functional tools designed to directly assess body schema as it relates to occupational performance. Tools involving reading, puzzles, balls, self-care, and other ADL skills have been reported in the literature on unilateral neglect. Tools for use with persons experiencing phantom pain have been discussed, tools that relate chronic pain to functional activity.

Traditionally, psychiatric interviews and projective tests were used to assess body image disturbances from the psychosocial point of view. At the present time, self-report tools are available and of value in body image assessment, particularly when needed in the rehabilitation setting. Easily administered paper and pencil tools include those requiring responses to pictures of the human body, statements about the body, and polar adjective pairs. Frequently, responses to these items are scaled in the Likert manner, having several choices from disagree to agree, with an average rating as the score.

Other kinds of tests described in the literature on body image have been designed specifically for a diagnostic category. The size estimation and body image distortion psychophysical procedures for anorexia nervosa (Slade, 1985; Touyz and Beumont, 1987) and the cosmetic disfigurement measure for patients with burns (Smith et al, 1988) are examples.

Unquestionably, there are many assessment tools available for both the neural body schema and the psychosocial components of body image. My impression from thorough review of the literature is that much creative effort has been expended in the development of these instruments. Some of the tests and scales have been subjected to psychometric scrutiny. Researchers in the area of anorexia nervosa have been particularly concerned with this area of instrumentation. The Body Dissatisfaction Subscale of the Eating Disorder Inventory (Garner et al, 1983) and the psychophysical procedures have considerable reliability and validity data. Thus, rehabilitation professionals have facts on these tools to help them decide on the value of each tool for any particular rehabilitation problem—clinical or research. Among the instruments used for assessing body schema with useful psychometric data are the Pain Disability Index (phantom pain) and the Line Bisection Test for unilateral neglect (Schenkenberg et al, 1980; Tait et al, 1987). Again, the more facts that are available about a specific tool, the better we can judge its merit for a specific rehabilitation use.

A wide variety of body image assessment tools are now available. Increased psychometric information will provide the clinician increased choice of evaluation methods while providing the researcher a wider selection of measurement tools.

Treatment

My review has revealed a considerable body of literature dealing with intervention for body image disturbances, for both the neural body schema and the psychosocial components. As categorized by Lacey and Birtchnell (1986), body image disturbances of neurological disorders and phantom phenomena would be treated from the perspective of neural body schema dysfunction. Psychosocial objectives may or may not be of secondary importance. Body image disturbances of patients with or without physical disability would be psychosocial in emphasis and, consequently, treated from this perspective. Examples are the disturbances associated with burns and anorexia nervosa.

When the body schema is the primary problem, treatment procedures are directed toward influencing the central nervous system or compensating for the neural abnormalities of the body schema. The restorative approach for patients with unilateral neglect is directed toward actual change in the central nervous system. Treatment focuses on control of sensory input toward lessening the neural-based neglect. The physical procedures for phantom pain and the use of modalities such as vibration, biofeedback, and TENS also are directed toward influencing the central nervous system.

Often, procedures to effect neural change are not successful, and therapy must be directed toward compensation for the neural abnormalities of the body schema. For patients with unilateral neglect, environmental adaptation or learning theory–based approaches are used by the rehabilitation professional. Such methods are used to facilitate the patient's function despite neural impairment. Behavioral procedures are used for phantom pain in an attempt to alter the patient's interpretation of the pain stimuli and, thus, improve function.

Although I found stimulating discussions of treatment pertinent to body schema disturbances, there was very little empirical research on interventions addressing such disturbances. There are reasonable explanations for this lack of research. First, designing rigorous intervention research involving human patients is difficult for ethical reasons. Second, researchers must have valid and reliable measurement tools before patient treatment research can be addressed. Thus, the initial step in the research process must be that of refining measurement methods, a step still in progress for body image research. Finally, funding is a problem because research directed toward correction of neural body schema dysfunction is seldom a current priority of the various government or private agencies. However, as rehabilitation professionals, we need the results of intervention research. Later in this chapter, I consider possible ways to encourage this kind of research.

Psychosocial issues are addressed when a patient's body image disturbances are in the Lacey-Birtchnell categories of disturbances, with or without physical disability. My discussion is not directed toward the in-depth therapies for psychiatric patients having major psychopathology related to body image disturbances. My concern is for those psychosocial methods of use to rehabilitation professionals when problems with body image could interfere with a patient's progress in a rehabilitation setting.

Potential or current body image disturbances need to be considered for the many kinds of patients frequently referred for rehabilitation including (but not limited to) the following problems: (1) anorexia nervosa, (2) mastectomy, (3) burns, (4) spinal cord injury, and (5) rheumatoid arthritis. Physical as well as psychological treatment is directed toward reducing body image disturbances. Examples of physical interventions directly related to body image are breast reconstruction for the postmastectomy patient and the use of pressure garments to reduce unsightly scarring of patients with burns.

Although a number of approaches to psychological intervention were mentioned in the literature, I have identified two that appear to be used most often for those patients typically referred for rehabilitation. These procedures for body image disturbances are group therapy or support and cognitive therapy.

Cognitive therapy involves procedures to facilitate attitude change of patients. For example, patients with anorexia nervosa are taught that their feelings regarding their own body shape are unrealistic owing to their disease; therefore, they must rely on other sources for realistic assessment in this area. Patients with severe burns learn through cognitive therapy that meaning from one's work or spiritual activity can be of higher value than a physically perfect body. Cognitive therapy is a complex intervention method requiring the therapist to have a high level of treatment expertise and appropriate personal characteristics.

The group format has been used for body image disturbance intervention for a variety of patients. Although therapy groups have been tried, clinical reports suggest that support groups also are effective. I have found descriptions in the literature of such groups being reported to benefit patients with burns, anorexia nervosa, mastectomies, and rheumatoid arthritis. Certainly, the support group is a practical method of help for patients experiencing body image disturbances of a psychosocial nature.

Although I have found an occasional dissertation or research report dealing with the psychosocial treatment of body image disturbances, there is little available research to guide our treatment efforts. Again, there are logical reasons for the dearth of this research, reasons cited above, but it is necessary to have research results if the field of rehabilitation is to mature.

Occupational Performance

My review of the literature has shown that there is a relationship between occupational performance and body image disturbances. With disruption of either the neural or the psychosocial components of body image, there is evidence of problems with various work, leisure, and self-care activities.

Several studies have shown that disturbance of the neural schema (phantom pain, unilateral neglect) is related to deficits in ADL such as dressing, bathing, or functional mobility. (See, for example, Fullerton et al, 1986.) Evidence also is available that shows reading and writing problems for patients with neglect, problems affecting both educational and recreational activities.

When the body image problem is of a psychosocial nature, occupational performance also is affected. For the postmastectomy patient, ADL problems involving dressing, bathing, and sexual activity have been documented. Several studies have shown that persons with body image disturbances from severe burns have adjustment problems in work and leisure activities. Basic self-care, such as dressing and hair styling, is affected. However, many persons with burns do *not* have these adjustment problems, and persons with spinal cord injury tend to adjust without outside help. For example, they select clothing to assist body image adjustment.

Although the literature provides little information on the relation of occupational performance to the body image disturbance of anorexia nervosa patients, there are clinical reports of excessive activity in sports and work and problems with social skills affecting recreational activities. Whether or not these occupational performance problems are related to body image dysfunction is not known. I also found no literature relating body image and occupational performance in rheumatoid arthritis.

Although the literature relating occupational performance and body image is sparse or nonexistent, I did locate enough evidence to suggest that body image disturbances need to be addressed for maximum patient performance in the rehabilitation setting. There is an obvious need for research in this area.

RESEARCH NEEDS

From my review of the literature on body image, I am suggesting certain areas where research is needed and would be of value to rehabilitation professionals. First, there is *not* a large body of research in this area. Major efforts have been directed toward measurement of body image, a necessary initial step in the research process. Continued work in measurement could focus on further reliability and validity studies. For example, it would be of interest to compare the status of burn patients on the Cosmetic Disfigurement Test (Smith et al, 1988) and the Burn Specific Health Scale (Blades et al, 1982) or to relate the performances of persons with anorexia nervosa on tests with silhouettes as items and tests requiring responses to body image statements. Continued reliability studies on the newer computerized tests for unilateral neglect would be valuable.

Because there are refined tools available, a greater need for research from the perspective of rehabilitation is in the area of treatment rather than measurement. There is very little controlled research of this type reported in the literature. Because, ethically, we are unable to choose not to treat a "needy" patient group, a control group becomes a problem for the rehabilitation researcher. I have dealt with this problem by defining the control group as the one not experiencing the treatment under investigation. Thus, to investigate the restorative approach for unilateral neglect, the control group could receive routine training in ADL. The experimental group would receive the program of sensory stimulation toward improved awareness of the neglected body side.

Other potential body image intervention studies include:

1. Training in hygiene or feeding using learning theory–based techniques such as anchoring points and feedback versus standard self-care practice for the control group.

2. Follow-up study of phantom pain patients using physical treatments (particularly TENS, vibration, and biofeedback) combined with chemical treatment (medication) compared with treatments using only medication.

3. Use of cognitive therapy techniques or therapeutic activities to improve body image of anorexic patients versus behavioral modification.

4. Use of cognitive therapy with support groups for mastectomy and burn patients experiencing body image adjustment problems versus use of verbal counseling.

Another solution to the ethical problem of control groups is the use of qualitative rather than quantitative research designs. Because body image and occupational performance are in its first stages of research, qualitative studies are appropriate. Further, the complexity of the topic might make the qualitative approach especially relevant. One source for readers wishing additional information about the application of qualitative method to health-related research is the American Journal of Occupational Therapy, volume 45, number 3.

Because agency funding priorities seldom are directed toward treatment for body image disturbances, research must either require little money or be a small portion of a research project that addresses funding priorities. My body awareness research with persons having rheumatoid arthritis (Van Deusen and Harlowe, 1987) was of the latter type. My measurement research in unilateral neglect was of the former type (Van Deusen, 1983). Regardless of agency priorities, research on body image treatment remains important.

Because client independence in ADL, work, and leisure is the major concern of rehabilitation, it is vital that we know how body image disturbances relate to such activities. There is a crucial need for studies of all activities and all types of body image disturbances. Such correlational studies necessarily precede the more complex attempts to demonstrate the effects of body image interventions on improved occupational performance of our patients in the rehabilitation setting.

TOWARD THE FUTURE

It is my hope that this book will encourage the potential and experienced researcher to conduct studies on visual or somesthetic perceptual and body image dysfunction as they relate to rehabilitation. Particularly, a research effort to relate perceptual and body image disturbances with occupational performance deficits could enhance our knowledge base toward improved rehabilitation for the many persons who are in need of these services.

References

Blades B, Mellis N, Munster AM: A burn specific health scale. J Trauma 22:872–875, 1982.

Fullerton KJ, McSherry D, Stout RW: Albert's test: a neglected test of perceptual neglect. Lancet 1(8478):430–432, 1986.

Garner DM, Olmstead MP, Polivy J: Development and validation of a multidimensional eating disorder inventory for anorexia nervosa and bulimia. Int J Eating Disorders 2:15–34, 1983.

Lacey JH, Birtchnell SA: Review article—Body image and its disturbances. J Psychosom Res 30:623–631, 1986.

Schenkenberg T, Bradford DC, Ajax ET: Line bisection and unilateral visual neglect in patients with neurologic impairment. Neurology 30:509–517, 1980.

Slade PD: A review of body-image studies in anorexia nervosa and bulimia nervosa. J Psychiatr Res 19:255–265, 1985.

Smith GM, Tompkins DM, Bigelow ME, Anton AY: Burn-induced cosmetic disfigurement: can it be measured reliably? J Burn Rehabil 9:371–375, 1988.

Tait RC, Pollard CA, Margolis RB, Duckro PN, Krause SJ: The Pain Disability Index: psychometric and validity data. Arch Phys Med Rehabil 68:438–441, 1987.

Touyz SW, Beumont PJV: Body Image and Its Disturbances. *In* Beumont PJV, Burrows GD, Csasper RC (eds): Handbook of Eating Disorders, Part 1: Anorexia and Bulimia Nervosa. New York, Elsevier, 1987, pp 171–187.

Van Deusen J: Normative data for ninety-three elderly persons on the Schenkenberg Line Bisection Test. Phys Occup Ther Geriatr 3:49–54, 1983.

Van Deusen J, Harlowe D: A comparison of the ROM Dance Home Exercise/Rest Program with traditional routines. Occup Ther J Res 7:349–361, 1987.

GLOSSARY

ACTIVITIES OF DAILY LIVING (ADL) – Procedures necessary for self-care. Independence in this area means that patients can feed and dress themselves, care for their teeth, and manage their personal grooming. ADL also include bathing and toilet hygiene as well as functional mobility (Uniform Terminology, 1989).

ALCOHOL ABUSE – A pattern of persistent and consistent alcohol use despite knowledge that it is creating occupational, psychosocial, or physical problems or risks for the individual.

ANOREXIA NERVOSA – An eating disorder characterized by unreasonable thinness, intense fear of obesity, and a qualitative disturbance of body image.

BODY IMAGE – A dynamic integration of the body schema and environmental inputs providing emotional and conceptual components.

BODY SCHEMA – A neurally derived synthesis of tactile, proprioceptive, and pressure sensory associations about the body and its parts.

BULIMIA – An eating disorder characterized by loss of control over one's eating with intermittent binge eating followed by purging.

CARETAKER ACTIVITIES – Activities involved in providing for children, elderly relatives, and other dependents. Care of pets also may be included when not considered a leisure activity (Uniform Terminology, 1989).

COGNITIVE DYSFUNCTION – A general category that includes both perceptual and conceptual dysfunction.

COGNITIVE THERAPY – Method of therapy emphasizing restructuring of attitudes in the areas of patient dysfunction.

COMPLEX VISUAL DISCRIMINATION – The ability to analyze, synthesize, and integrate the information determined by one's perception of the environment.

CONCEPTUAL DYSFUNCTION – The inability to perform tasks because of impaired memory, verbal comprehension, abstraction, or similar intellectual functions.

EDUCATIONAL ACTIVITIES – School or school-related activities such as athletics or field trips (Uniform Terminology, 1989).

EXTINCTION – Response to only one of two sets of simultaneous stimulation. The recovery phase of hemi-inattention (Heilman, 1985).

FACTOR ANALYSIS – A statistical process in which a large number of variables can be reduced to a small number of concepts through the interrelationship of these variables.

FIGURE-GROUND IDENTIFICATION – The basic perceptual process of selecting a figure from a stimulus complex; the ability to differentiate foreground from background.

FORM AND SPACE CONSTANCY – The ability to perceive variations in the form of objects and their arrangement in space.

HEMI-INATTENTION – The neglect of sensory input to the body side contralateral to the side of a brain lesion (Heilman, 1985).

HEMISPATIAL NEGLECT – Loss of the intention to act in the hemispace contralateral to brain lesion site (Heilman, 1985).

HOME MANAGEMENT ACTIVITIES – Tasks such as meal preparation, money management, shopping, cleaning, laundry, and household, auto and grounds maintenance (Uniform Terminology, 1989).

LEISURE ACTIVITIES – Exploratory or skilled activities performed for fun. Tennis, card games, folk dancing, and woodworking illustrate the gamut of leisure activities. Conversations and social occasions with friends and relatives also can be leisure activities (Uniform Terminology, 1989).

MASTECTOMY – Surgical removal of breast tissue.

METAMORPHOPSIA – Visual distortion of form of objects.

OCCUPATIONAL PERFORMANCE – Role activities as defined in the Uniform Terminology (1989), which include ADL and work and leisure activities.

PERCEPTUAL DYSFUNCTION – The inability to perform

specified activities relevant to the interpretation and use of sensory stimuli.

PHANTOM PAIN – Painful sensations referred to the lost body part.

PHANTOM PHENOMENON – The sensation that an amputated part is still present.

POSITION IN SPACE DEFICIT – The inability to identify the spatial positioning of objects in terms of in/out, up/down, and the like.

PROPRIOCEPTIVE – Pertaining to information on body position and movements.

PSYCHOANALYSIS – Method of psychotherapy based on exploration and interpretation of unconscious mental processes and childhood experiences (Freud).

SOMESTHETIC PERCEPTUAL DYSFUNCTION – Performance problems from deficient interpretation of tactile and proprioceptive input.

SPATIAL ORIENTATION – The ability to maintain spatial relations among objects, including body parts as well as objects in extrapersonal space.

TACTILE – Pertaining to stimulation of touch receptors or to the central nervous system processing of information from touch receptors.

TENS (transcutaneous electrical nerve stimulation) – Treatment by a nerve stimulator worn by the patient and designed to relieve acute or chronic pain, perhaps through the interruption of pain impulses.

TOPOGRAPHICAL DISORIENTATION – The inability to understand and remember the relationship of multiple locations to each other.

UNILATERAL NEGLECT – A neural-based deficit affecting the awareness of the body half or extrapersonal space, or both, contralateral to the site of a brain lesion.

VISUAL MEMORY – The inability to recall visual information for the location and relationships of objects and places.

VISUAL OBJECT AGNOSIAS – The inability to recognize familiar faces, spatial information, colors, forms, and shapes of objects.

VISUOCONSTRUCTIVE APRAXIA – The inability to copy or construct two- and three-dimensional designs.

VOCATIONAL ACTIVITIES – Activities involving job choice, acquisition, or performance. Also included are retirement planning and adjustment (Uniform Terminology, 1989).

WORK ACTIVITIES – Home management tasks, caretaker activities, and educational activities as well as the more commonly accepted vocational activities (Uniform Terminology, 1989).

References

Heilman KM, Valenstein E, Watson RT: The neglect syndrome. *In* Fredericks JAM (ed): Handbook of Clinical Neurology (Vol 45–1). Clinical Neuropsychology. New York, Elsevier Science Pub, 1985, pp 153–183.
Uniform terminology for occupational therapy, (2nd ed). Am J Occup Ther 43:808–815, 1989.

INDEX

Note: Page numbers in *italics* refer to illustrations;
page numbers followed by t refer to tables.